'Tamar Meisels restores social realities to the discussion of just war. This outstanding book presents a provocative, powerful, and eloquent alternative to the reigning apolitical revisionism applicable only to a far better world than this. Socially adrift abstraction here meets a formidably grounded challenger specifying principles that can be action-guiding in the world of violent groups that confronts us now.'

—*Henry Shue, University of Oxford, UK*

'Tamar Meisels' *Contemporary Just War: Theory and Practice* is a superb discussion of the major debates in contemporary just war theory and their bearing on the conflicts of today. Hers is a lucid and humane voice that speaks with precision to today's major disagreements on the morality of war and also speaks with compassion to the difficult decisions people face in war, seeking to maintain their moral bearings. Those of us who have admired Tamar Meisels' writings on these topics can now be grateful they have been developed into a single, sustained discussion that everyone concerned with these issues will want to read.'

—*Cheyney Ryan, University of Oxford, UK*

'With this accessible account of just war theory, Tamar Meisels has done us all a great service in showing us why we should still hold onto the main tenets of Michael Walzer's traditional view, and why revisionist critiques of that account fail to the degree that they cannot bridge "deep" moral theory with practical moral and legal guidance in war. Here, Meisels walks us through concrete cases to do with civil war, targeted assassinations of nuclear scientists, and pre-emptive strikes. With her feet firmly on the ground and with young soldiers often in mind, she makes it clear that just war theory – traditionalist, revisionist, or a convergence of both – can't stay in the clouds, but needs to speak directly to the realities of war.'

—*Nancy Sherman, Georgetown University, USA*

T0393873

CONTEMPORARY JUST WAR

This book offers a renewed defense of traditional just war theory and considers its application to certain contemporary cases, particularly in the Middle East.

The first part of the book addresses and responds to the central theoretical criticisms levelled at traditional just war theory. It offers a detailed defense of civilian immunity, the moral equality of soldiers and the related dichotomy between *jus ad bellum* and *jus in bello*, and argues that these principles taken together amount to a morally coherent ethics of war. In this sense this project is traditional (or "orthodox"). In another sense, however, it is highly relevant to the modern world. While the first part of the book defends the just war tradition against its revisionist critics, the second part applies it to an array of timely issues: civil war, economic warfare, excessive harm to civilians, pre-emptive military strikes, and state-sponsored assassination, which require applying just war theory in practice. This book sets out to reaffirm the basic tenets of the traditional ethics of war and to lend them further moral support, subsequently applying them to a variety of practical issues.

This book will be of great interest to students of just war theory, ethics, security studies, war and conflict studies, and IR in general.

Tamar Meisels is Professor of Political Theory in the Department of Political Science at Tel Aviv University, Israel. She is author of *Territorial Rights* (2005), *The Trouble with Terror* (2008) and co-editor of *Soft War: The Ethics of Unarmed Conflict* (2017, with Michael L. Gross).

War, conflict and ethics

Series Editors: Michael L. Gross, *University of Haifa* and James Pattison, *University of Manchester*
Founding Editor: Daniel Rothbart, *George Mason University*

This new book series focuses on the morality of decisions by military and political leaders to engage in violence and the normative underpinnings of military strategy and tactics in the prosecution of the war.

Civilians and Modern War
Armed conflict and the ideology of violence
Edited by Daniel Rothbart, Karina Korostelina and Mohammed Cherkaoui

Ethics, Norms and the Narratives of War
Creating and encountering the enemy other
Pamela Creed

Armed Drones and the Ethics of War
Military virtue in a post-heroic age
Christian Enemark

The Ethics of Nuclear Weapons Dissemination
Moral dilemmas of aspiration, avoidance, and prevention
Thomas E. Doyle, II

Chinese Just War Ethics
Origin, development, and dissent
Edited by Ping-cheung Lo and Sumner B. Twiss

Utilitarianism and the Ethics of War
William H. Shaw

Privatizing War
A moral theory
William Brand Feldman

Just War Thinkers
From Cicero to the Twenty-first Century
Edited by Daniel R. Brunstetter and Cian O'Driscoll

Contemporary Just War
Theory and Practice
Tamar Meisels

CONTEMPORARY JUST WAR

Theory and practice

Tamar Meisels

Routledge
Taylor & Francis Group

LONDON AND NEW YORK

First published 2018
by Routledge
2 Park Square, Milton Park, Abingdon, Oxon OX14 4RN

and by Routledge
711 Third Avenue, New York, NY 10017

Routledge is an imprint of the Taylor & Francis Group, an informa business

© 2018 Tamar Meisels

British Library Cataloguing-in-Publication Data
A catalogue record for this book is available from the British Library

Library of Congress Cataloging-in-Publication Data
A catalog record for this book has been requested

ISBN: 978-1-138-04366-4 (hbk)
ISBN: 978-1-138-04369-5 (pbk)
ISBN: 978-1-315-17297-2 (ebk)

Typeset in Bembo and Stone Sans
by Florence Production Ltd, Stoodleigh, Devon, UK
Printed in Great Britain by Ashford Colour Press Ltd

MIX
Paper from
responsible sources
FSC
www.fsc.org
FSC® C011748

For my beloved aunt, Marianne Meisels, of blessed memory

CONTENTS

PREFACE

In the course of Israel's 2014 operation "protective edge," four Israeli mothers of combat soldiers in elite units published a letter calling on Prime Minister Netanyahu to refrain from endangering their sons in order to minimize collateral damage to Gazans. These mothers, joined by a handful of Facebook supporters, were responding to reports that the IDF (Israel Defense Forces) rules of engagement place Israeli soldiers at considerable risk in attempts to spare enemy civilians. Specifically, the mothers complained about instructing soldiers to hold their fire in cases of doubt as to whether a person is a civilian or combatant.[1] The letter described the resultant risks to Israeli soldiers as unacceptable to their mothers, and closes by reminding the Prime Minister that "the lives of our sons, daughters, brothers and sisters—are more important than the lives of the enemy's civilians."[2] Subsequently, some bumper stickers emerged, stating that: "The lives of our soldiers take precedence over those of enemy civilians."

Far from a mass popular movement, the opening lines to the mothers' letter nonetheless expresses a common, near consensus, Israeli sentiment. Roughly translated: "No cause could be more just than fighting terrorist organizations that endanger the security of millions of Jews. We are proud of our sons for taking part in this important mission."[3]

To what extent should such convictions affect our rules of engagement? This is essentially the central divide within contemporary just war theory: should justice of cause and its urgency influence the way we fight? Nothing could be less theoretical for Israelis. If I were asked to describe the answer developed in the following chapters while standing on one leg, I would say: we should sympathize with the mothers, without incorporating their personal perspective into our military handbooks.

This book brings together various wartime issues I have been working on in recent years. My own Israeli perspective is undeniable, nor would I deny it if I could. Between 2012 and 2016, my research was supported by the Israel Science Foundation (Grant no. 45/12). The majority of chapters in this book are based on previously published articles, written roughly within or around this time frame. I thank the following journals for allowing me to re-use these materials here, as well as for the helpful comments and suggestions offered by their anonymous reviewers:

"Economic Warfare—The Case of Gaza," *Journal of Military Ethics*, Vol. 10, No. 2 (2011), 94–109.

"Preemptive Strikes—Israel and Iran," *The Canadian Journal of Law and Jurisprudence*, Vol. 25, No. 2 (July, 2012), 447–463.

"In Defense of the Defenseless—The Morality of the Laws of War," *Political Studies*, Vol. 60, No. 4 (December 2012), 919–935.

"Assassination: Targeting Nuclear Scientists," *Law and Philosophy*, Vol. 33, (2014), 204–234.

"Fighting for Independence—What Can Just War Theory Learn from Civil Conflict?" *Social Theory and Practice*, Vol. 40, No. 2 (April 2014), 304–326.

I am grateful to Tamar Caner for her research assistance on civil war, and useful discussion and comments on earlier drafts of Chapter 3.

Previous versions of the practical parts of this book, specifically Chapters 4–7, were presented at various workshops and seminars in Israel and abroad. Most memorably, my arguments on economic warfare in Gaza were presented at the Nuffield Political Theory Workshop in Oxford, and at the Law and Philosophy Workshop at the Hebrew University in Jerusalem. Drafts of Chapters 6–7, concerning Israel's dilemmas in the face of Iranian nuclear development, were presented at the *Faculty Seminar de Theorie Politique* at *Sciences Politique* during a short teaching stay in Paris in 2012, and at the Oxford Institute for Ethics, Law and Armed Conflict/Changing Character of War, lunchtime seminar. The latter forum is always invaluable to me in forming the final version of my arguments. I thank the participants of these seminars, among many others, for their critical comments on some very contentious issues.

Various friends and colleagues offered written comments and/or the opportunity for discussion and debate along the way. Both types of contribution have proved equally valuable. Special thanks are due to Yitzhak Benbaji, Eyal Benvenisti, Richard Bronaugh, Astrid von Busekist, Ariel Colonomos, David Enoch, Cecile Fabre, Chaim Gans, Alon Harel, Michael Gross, Robert Johnson, Seth Lazar, Judith Lichtenberg, David Luban, Jeff McMahan, David Miller, David Rodin, Guy Sela, Daniel Statman, Henrik Syse, Jeremy Waldron, Michael Walzer, Lea Ypi and Ruvi Ziegler.

Of those listed, many disagree with my views on Israel, others disagree with my traditional approach to just war theory; some object to both. To those who engaged with me in heated arguments and passionate debates, I am all the more grateful for the time and attention contributed to my work.

Notes

1. Protocol Additional to the Geneva Conventions of August 12, 1949, and relating to the Protection of Victims of International Armed Conflicts (Protocol 1, June 8, 1977), Article 50 (1) requires that "in case of doubt whether a person is a civilian, that person should be considered to be a civilian." www.icrc.org/ihl.nsf/7c4d08d9b287a42141256739003 e636b/f6c8b9fee14a77fdc125641e0052b079.
2. www.nrg.co.il/online/1/ART2/601/474.html.
3. Ibid.

INTRODUCTION

The existing laws of armed conflict, and the traditional rules of just war after which these laws are fashioned, comprise three basic principles: civilian immunity, the moral equality of soldiers and the independence of *jus in bello* (the laws regulating how a war is fought) from *jus ad bellum* (the legitimacy of a state engaging in war). All three of these tenets are gradually losing general support both in theory and in practice. All three require a renewed defense if the laws and customs of war are to withstand the ravages of time and to continue to command compliance. Why may we kill all combatants during combat, while all civilians remain immune from direct attack? If only defensive war is legitimate, how can the rights and liabilities of its individual participants remain independent of the justice of their cause? Why should soldiers fighting an aggressive war continue to enjoy immunity from prosecution for murder? And how can an unjust war fulfill the legal and moral requirements of necessity and proportionality? If a war is aggressive, futile and injurious, how can any of its measures be necessary and proportionate?

These are old philosophical issues, but they raise contemporary questions as increasing numbers of belligerents and bystanders begin to view the traditional rules and customs of war as obsolete. Terrorists defy civilian immunity and claim their right to target the citizens of democracies who vote, pay taxes and otherwise support regimes that the terrorists regard as oppressive. Governments question the immunity of civilians who condone terrorism, harbor terrorists, act on their behalf or serve as their human shields. When states resort to economic warfare—imposing sanctions, blockades or outright sieges on a population—civilians are placed at the forefront of the fight, as they are often the first to suffer.

States and paramilitary organizations alike increasingly view their justifications for war as lending them greater license with regard to its conduct. Terrorists invoke "liberation" and "last resort" as justifications for murdering civilians, while states defy the international legal prohibitions on torture, assassination and aggression in the name of self-defense. Philosophers, for their part, question the morality of modern legal arrangements. Some propose deeper moral principles of war that might replace our older moral norms and intuitions, and possibly effect changes in the laws of armed conflict. Contemporary just war theory is deeply divided on these issues. This book sets out to reaffirm the basic tenets of the traditional ethics of war and to lend them further moral support, subsequently applying them to a variety of practical issues.

The definitive account of just war theory in modern times appears in Michael Walzer's classic *Just and Unjust Wars*, which forms the theoretical point of departure both for its advocates and its critics.[1] Opponents of the just war tradition question whether its traditional tenets, reflected in our laws of war, correspond to any deep moral principles. This critical approach is represented most prominently in the work of Jeff McMahan, who denies that existing legal rules reflect the deep morality of war.[2] While traditional rules may be efficacious in regulating war, McMahan argues that they cannot represent an ethics of war because their corresponding moral principles are false: the reasons for fighting a war to begin with (just or unjust, defensive or aggressive) cannot be morally detached from the very license to fight and kill.[3] Accordingly, just and unjust combatants cannot be morally equal. If killing in war is justified as self-defense, then only soldiers on the defensive side can possess this license, while their aggressive opponents have no moral right to fight and kill. Finally, not all civilians are innocent or non-threatening, so there can be no deep moral justification for their automatic immunity as a group.

Morally speaking, McMahan argues, liability or immunity to harm in war ought to be judged case by case, on the basis of individual contribution and responsibility for injustice, in the same way as we judge liability in civilian life. According to McMahan, our traditional rules of war, as well as our international laws of armed conflict, are out of step with our everyday moral beliefs, though they may have their use in limiting the overall extent of suffering in war.[4]

These challenges are not easy to answer. They have been adopted and developed in various directions by a variety of contemporary scholars addressed in this book, such as Cecile Fabre and David Rodin. Some of these arguments, particularly on combatant inequality, have their roots in the writings of Francisco de Vitoria's "On the Laws of War". Writing in the sixteenth century, Vitoria denied that soldiers fighting on the objectively unjust side act permissibly when they fight and kill their opponents.[5] Gregory Reichberg argues that the contemporary separation between *jus in bello* and *jus ad bellum* is actually a modern development, and not the traditional view as Walzer presents it. He points out that

> From the thirteenth to the seventeenth centuries (Aquinas to Grotius), concerns that now go under the heading of *jus in bello* were in fact treated largely as an extension of *jus ad bellum*. On this understanding, belligerent rights attached only to the party that was possessed of a just cause. By virtue of its guilt, the opposing party possessed no such rights, and for this reason, there could be no set of *in bello* rules that applies to both sides, just and unjust, simultaneously.[6]

Consequently, many of Walzer's critics have dubbed their revisionist morality of war as "neo-classical," referring to his *Just and Unjust Wars* as the "orthodox (or traditional) account," of killing in war.[7] Revisionists also describe their critiques as "individualist," because they aim to supply a careful and precise account of individual rights and responsibilities in times of war, as opposed to the traditional understanding of war as essentially a collective enterprise.[8] The result is the emergence of not one but two reigning theories of the just war. Following the most prominent writers in both schools of thought, I refer to Walzer's account as the just war tradition, or traditional just war theory, and to his critics' accounts of the morality of war as revisionist theory.[9]

The first part of this book addresses the central theoretical challenges posed to traditional just war theory, and answers its critics. It offers a detailed defense of civilian immunity, the moral equality of soldiers and the related dichotomy between *jus ad bellum* and *jus in bello*, and argues for their moral coherence as an ethics of war. In this sense my project is "old school" (or "orthodox"). As such, it is distinct from the majority of contemporary accounts of the morality of war, most of which criticize the existing rules and question their moral validity. In a further sense, however, the book is also highly contemporary. While it affirms the just war tradition, it further applies it to an array of timely issues: civil war, economic warfare, excessive harm to civilians, preemptive military strikes, and assassination, which require applying just war theory in practice.

Two preliminary points are in order with regard to these practical sections of the book. First, while the theoretical analysis in Part I offers a moral argument for the traditional rules of practice, the revisionist, or "neo-classical," approach is never disregarded. These two competing ethics of war often complement each other, contributing different perspectives and helpful insights in hard cases.

Where these accounts are at odds with each other, the debate between them nonetheless assists our moral thinking on practical cases. Quite plausibly, both parties of opinion have a portion of the truth on their side, as John Stuart Mill thought most likely in cases of deep ethical disagreement.[10] Neither account is ignored or downplayed here, either in the discussions of theory or in those of the practice of war.

Second, the particular tactics and dilemmas of modern warfare considered in Part II of the book draw heavily on the Israeli experience. This is not merely a personal preference. For all the ongoing conflicts worldwide, the Middle East, particularly Israel, remains a source of international interest and concern. Within this region, Israel alone is home to free and open public debates of its military conduct. Israel has also been the focus of considerable academic attention from theorists of the just war worldwide.

In practice, Israel and its neighbors offer a variety of interesting military dilemmas for theorists to engage with. Bordering Israel in the north, Syria is the primary ongoing example of civil conflict discussed in Chapter 3. Israel's incursions into the Gaza Strip and its restrictions on Gaza's economy form the focus of discussions throughout Chapters 4 and 5. Iran is another big issue for Israelis.

Questioning whether early military strikes are ever justified, Chapter 6 considers the morality of a preemptive Israeli strike against Iran's nuclear facilities. Chapter 7 asks whether targeting scientists working on a nuclear project can ever be a legitimate alternative, or a complementary measure, to full-scale war.

More specifically, the book proceeds as follows: Chapters 1–3 set out the theoretical background for the subsequent analysis of these various issues. Chapter 1 reaffirms the "moral equality of soldiers" defending it against a renewed wave of philosophical criticism and lending it further support. So long as international conflicts lack an effective common authority to adjudicate disputes and administer justice, this first chapter argues, participants must remain equally at liberty to interpret and defend their natural rights as they see fit.

Moreover, for a variety of reasons, individual soldiers cannot be proved personally guilty of injustice, and ought therefore at least to be presumed innocent. Absent proof of individual liability beyond reasonable doubt, holding soldiers personally responsible for their nation's cause for war would amount to collective punishment. Respect for individual human rights requires recognizing soldiers' symmetrical standing in battle, fashioning them with equal permissions and liabilities, rather than penalizing or disabling some of them for their nation's collective causes.

Chapter 2 offers a moral justification of the traditional wartime immunities guaranteed by law to all civilians and prisoners. Some of these legal immunities appear artificial, even contradictory to moral reasoning, because many civilians and prisoners are both guilty of injustice and quite eminently dangerous.[11] McMahan suggests that sometimes these legal protections are senseless and inconsistent with our everyday moral thinking about guilt and innocence.[12]

Why refrain from directly targeting villagers who harbor terrorists, or require soldiers to risk their lives in order to separate terrorists from their civilian supporters? Why not torture a suspect who refuses to divulge life-saving information, thereby placing many innocent people in harm's way? Should we always refrain from killing prisoners, even if keeping them alive endangers soldiers on the defensive side and considerably hampers the advancement of a just cause? Why is it legal to kill innocent young soldiers, but illegal to assassinate their warmongering civilian leaders who control the army, or target the civilians who put them in power?

On some of these points, McMahan argues, the laws of war diverge significantly from its deep morality. While the legal protection of civilians and prisoners has merit as a rule, some civilians and prisoners (those fighting for injustice) may be morally liable to attack in an attempt to avert an unjust threat in which they are participants or for which they are responsible.[13] More generally, revisionist just war theorists suggest that the laws of war diverge significantly from its deep morality: at war's deepest moral level it is sometimes justified to violate these legal protections.[14]

As against this, I argue that the various legal protections in wartime do not diverge from morality at all. They are soundly based on the age-old moral prohibition on attacking the defenseless, which is both timeless and cross-cultural.

This commitment to the weak and vulnerable is not peculiar to any one moral or religious system and is as old as war itself. At the same time, it is not peculiar to war, and is also present in our everyday moral thinking, giving rise to familiar obligations toward the weakest members of society. Defending the defenseless, those who are otherwise helpless, weak and vulnerable, is a deeply moral principle in every sense. These moral obligations are well captured by the most basic tenet of traditional just war theory—blanket civilian immunity—and by the variety of legal protections guaranteed to non-combatants and prisoners in wartime.

Chapter 2 concludes that our moral commitment toward the defenseless supplies us with a significant point of convergence both between the law and morality of war and between *ad bellum* and *in bello* considerations. As for the latter, both *ad bellum* and *in bello* restrictions correspond to our moral obligation to defend the otherwise defenseless, though they correspond to it in different ways. Wars are currently justified only when they are pursued in self-defense, and perhaps also for humanitarian reasons. In other words, protecting the otherwise defenseless—whether locally or abroad—is the only legitimate reason for resorting to war. Subsequently, we require that wars be carried out in light of these same principles and that its participants refrain from assaulting defenseless persons, regardless of nationality or guilt.

The tenuous connection between *jus ad bellum* and *jus in bello* and the moral justification for their legal separation form the main subject of the third and final chapter of the theoretical part of this project. The chapter also paves the way towards the more practical sections of the book by selecting civil conflict as a case study in support of the traditional independence thesis. Crucially, this chapter points out that the laws applicable to civil wars maintain neither a full separation between *jus ad bellum* and *jus in bello* nor the related equality of combatants, upheld by international law for all interstate armed conflicts. Civil war presents an interesting real-world alternative to the traditional independence of *jus in bello* from just cause and the symmetrical rights of all combatants ("the independence-symmetry thesis"), criticized by "neo-classical" theorists of the just war, though it is admittedly not the type of case they have in mind.

Laws applicable to intrastate conflicts distinguish between rebels and soldiers, and deny rebels equal privileges, most notably prisoner-of-war rights if captured. Rebels, for their part, fight on to the bitter end with total disregard for the laws of war. The familiar results are disastrous. Civil wars are often interminable, recurrent, and particularly bloody and devastating, above all to civilians. It is admittedly arguable whether the partial abrogation of *jus in bello* independence is responsible for the savagery of contemporary civil wars; certainly it cannot be the entire explanation. Nonetheless, there is a lesson here for contemporary moral philosophers who question the traditional tenets of just war theory: in the real world, *jus in bello* dependence and combatant asymmetry appear to contribute to wartime disaster. The independence-symmetry thesis may well be necessary in order to limit the ills of war and save human life, as traditional just war theorists have always assumed, supplying an additional layer to their moral justification.

The discussion of civil war—its definition, causes, consequences and regulation —alongside the ongoing Syrian example set the scene for the second half of the book, which applies just war theory to practice. Kicking off with Israel's oft-criticized policies vis-à-vis the Gaza Strip, Chapters 4 and 5 consider the principle of proportionality that applies to military attacks, as well as various measures of economic warfare.

Chapter 4 discusses the restriction of proportionality in war in both its moral and its legal contexts, with reference both to the onset of war and to its conduct. The discussion of proportionality in this chapter also revisits the related debate concerning the military's responsibility to take "due care" to minimize civilian casualties, recently revived by just war theorists with specific reference to Gaza: are soldiers required to assume avoidable risks to themselves in order to minimize harm to enemy civilians, and if so to what extent? Is the military required to endanger its own soldiers beyond the degree necessary for attaining victory, in order to avoid excessive harm to non-combatants on the opposing side?

Finally, this chapter addresses the inevitable increase in civilian casualties experienced in "the war on terror," in which combat has moved from the traditional battlefield into civilian areas. It suggests that while the rules remain unchanged and binding regardless of the identity or conduct of the enemy, these changed battlefield conditions inevitably result in a far higher degree of collateral damage even when armies adhere to the rules.

Curiously, humanitarian law does not impose the restriction of proportionality, expressly or otherwise, upon the lawfulness of siege warfare or any other economic wartime measure.[15] Nevertheless, Chapter 5 suggests that it is legitimate to discuss these requirements as ethical restrictions on military conduct more generally, including its economic tactics, in a manner analogous to the legal restrictions on "attacks" in war. This chapter raises a wide range of principled questions surrounding sieges, sanctions and blockades.

More specifically, Chapter 5 reflects on the highly contested Israeli restrictions on the importation of civilian goods into the Gaza Strip. Beginning with Israel's unilateral withdrawal from Gaza and culminating in its recent easing of sanctions, Chapter 5 attempts to bring out the central issues of principle embedded in the political polemic: unilaterally terminated occupation; the responsibilities of a former, though recent, occupier; the semantic distinction between the terms "siege" and "sanction" and their respective ramifications; harm to civilians; necessity and proportionality.

In the specific case, the chapter suggests that Israel's restrictions on Gaza were not indefensible from the start as a first attempt to halt terrorism while avoiding full-scale conflict. In view of their ineffectiveness in achieving these goals, however, the harm they inflicted on civilians increasingly proved unnecessary and therefore also excessive. There could then be no justification for continuing to restrict the flow of purely civilian goods into Gaza, as Israel itself eventually recognized. Nonetheless, it is argued that Israel retains the right to search and regulate the passage of all relief supplies into Gaza, whether by land or by sea, as well as to secure its own borders for the safety of its citizens.

Chapter 6 looks at the contemporary just war theory literature on preventive war that has emerged largely in reaction to the US invasion of Iraq in 2003. The sanctions imposed on Iran and the debate over its nuclear program now suggest that a forward-looking perspective on preventive strikes would be more useful than the retroactive analyses offered thus far primarily with reference to the war in Iraq. With Iran as a major reference, this chapter addresses the various arguments for and against preventive war, indicating throughout that the various principled objections to early military action can be overcome in this case. Ultimately, the discussion suggests that, in principle, subject to credible intelligence information and requirements of proportionality, a unilateral Israeli strike against Iran could be justifiable as self-defense.

Full-scale war may not be the only available military option for preventing, or delaying, the development of dangerous nuclear programs. Since 2007, five scientists involved in Iran's nuclear program have been killed in mysterious circumstances. This is not the first time that nuclear scientists have come under direct attack. In the early 1940s, the United States considered assassinating German physicist Werner Heisenberg, believed to be working on an atomic bomb for Hitler. In January 1950, Egyptian theoretical physicist Dr Ali Mustafa Mosharafa was assassinated, possibly by agents of Israel's Mossad, which is said to have carried out a series of assassinations of prominent Arab scientists during the 1950s.

Scientists, like the rest of us, are protected by laws prohibiting murder and perfidious killing, and enjoy civilian immunity even during wartime. Moreover, powerful moral arguments oppose assassination policies specifically. Nevertheless, both contemporary theories of just war discussed at the outset of this book allow for the partial extension of combatant status to civilians who either pose a direct threat or who are responsible for unjust threats. Civilians who directly contribute to the business of fighting (on Walzer's account), or particularly blameworthy individuals (on McMahan's account), may lose their moral immunity from military attack.

Weapons manufacturers, their factories and employees are accorded less than absolute protection within either account of just war theory, and even under international law. Civilian immunity notwithstanding, orthodox just war theory, as well as the "neo-classical" morality of war, suggest that scientists who directly participate in the business of war may be liable to attack in exceptional circumstances in which their removal is dictated by urgent military necessity, such as contending with an existential threat. The various moral arguments against assassination on the one hand and the complex status of munitions workers on the other suggest that scientists involved in weapons manufacturing may in some cases be morally liable to direct harm, as well as being legally liable to proportionate collateral damage.

Concluding Part II of the book, this chapter exemplifies the need for the careful application of theory to practice, and demonstrates the interplay between the competing ethics of war. In this case, both accounts of just war contain insights that contribute invaluably to the ethical debate. The various conclusions of these chapters bring the book to a close, while debates over the controversial issues tackled throughout it naturally remain open.

Notes

1. Michael Walzer, *Just and Unjust Wars—A Moral Argument with Historical Illustrations* (New York: Basic Books, 1977).
2. Jeff McMahan, *Killing in War* (Oxford: Oxford University Press, 2009); Jeff McMahan, "The Ethics of Killing in War," *Ethics*, 114 (4) (2004), 693–733; Jeff McMahan, "The Morality of War and the Law of War," in D. Rodin and H. Shue, *Just and Unjust Warriors: The Moral and Legal Status of Soldiers* (Oxford: Oxford University Press, 2008), 19–43.
3. E.g. in "The Morality of War and the Law of War" (2008), 21–22.
4. McMahan, *Killing in War*, throughout.
5. Francisco de Vitoria, *On the Law of War*, in Anthony Pagden and Jeremy Lawrence (eds), *Vitoria: Political Writings* (Cambridge: Cambridge University Press, 1992), esp. 303–308. See also Francisco Suarez, "On War," in James Brown Scott (ed.) *Selections from Three Works of Francisco Suarez* (Oxford: Clarendon Press, 1944), esp. 845–846.
6. Gregory M. Reichberg, "Just War and Regular War: Competing Paradigms," in D. Rodin and H. Shue, *Just and Unjust Warriors: The Moral and Legal Status of Soldiers* (Oxford: Oxford University Press, 2008), 193–213, 193.
7. Cecile Fabre, *Cosmopolitan War* (Oxford: Oxford University Press, 2012), 73.
8. Michael Walzer, "Response to McMahan's Paper," 34 (1) *Philosophia*, 43–45, 43.
9. This is actually Jeff McMahan's terminology throughout most, or all, of his critical writing. See, for example: McMahan, "The Ethics of Killing in War," 693, and throughout; McMahan, *Killing in War*, e.g., 7–8, and throughout; and, more recently: Jeff McMahan, "Rethinking the Just War," *The New York Times*, November 11, 2012.
10. John Stuart Mill, *On Liberty*, in Geraint Williams (ed.), *Utilitarianism, On Liberty, Representative Government* (London and Vermont: Everyman, 1996), Chap. 2, pp. 113–120.
11. McMahan, *Killing in War*, 108, 221–235.
12. Ibid.
13. McMahan, *Killing in War*, 108, 221–235; McMahan, "The Morality of War and the Law of War," 19–43, 22.
14. McMahan, "The Ethics of Killing in War," throughout, esp. 722–723; McMahan, "The Morality of War and the Law of War" 21–22; McMahan, *Killing in War*, throughout, e.g. 32–37, 35, 38, 204–205.
15. The Hague Regulations (IV): Laws and Customs of War on Land, October 18, 1907, Article 23. Protocol Additional to the Geneva Conventions of August 12, 1949, and relating to the Protection of Victims of International Armed Conflicts (Protocol 1) 1977. Article 51 (5) B) and Article 57 (2) (a) (3). www.icrc.org/ihl.nsf/full/470?opendocument.

PART I

Just war theory

1

COMRADES IN ARMS

The equal innocence of soldiers

In classic accounts of just war theory, and in keeping with the laws of armed conflict (LOAC), killing soldiers in war is not murder. Soldiers are assumed to have lost their immunity from attack by virtue of the armed threat they pose to their adversaries.[1] All may be attacked and are equally permitted to kill, regardless of the respective cause they serve. The laws of war disengage principles governing the resort to war from those governing its conduct, with the result that soldiers obtain this unusual symmetrical license to kill one another in the course of war.[2] So long as they abide by the laws *in bello*, soldiers commit no crime—neither legal nor moral—when they fight in war and kill other soldiers. Consequently, as Michael Walzer puts it: "It is certainly possible for a just war to be fought unjustly and for an unjust war to be fought in strict accordance with the rules."[3]

This account of the moral equality of soldiers, along with the separation between *jus ad bellum* and *jus in bello*, has recently lost its consensus, receiving fierce criticism from moral philosophers. Opposition to moral equality is not new— it was raised by Francisco de Vitoria and Francisco Suarez in the sixteenth and seventeenth centuries and, far more recently, by Thomas Nagel[4]—but it is enjoying a lively renaissance, most notably in the prolific writings of Jeff McMahan and his followers.[5]

McMahan argues that Walzer's second proposition—that an unjust war can be fought in total compliance with the rules—is incoherent. Killing just combatants *in bello* cannot comply with a morally valid principle of distinction which would render the innocent, non-aggressive party non-liable to attack. On this view, soldiers fighting in self-defense are morally permitted to kill their aggressive adversaries, while the latter lack any moral justification for killing in pursuit of their collective aggression, and can at most retain a plausible excuse for doing so.[6]

This revisionist account of combatant inequality effectively leads to two interrelated conclusions. First, revisionists focus on liability to be killed in war, arguing un-controversially that soldiers who fight for an unjust cause are morally liable to *being killed* in battle. In fact, all versions of just war theory recognize a moral permission to kill unjust aggressors. The more controversial part of revisionist theory, distinguishing it from the traditional view, is that just soldiers remain non-liable to attack. Since soldiers on the just side are, by definition, non-aggressors, their adversaries cannot justify killing them in the name of self-defense. As a direct derivative thereof, unjust soldiers are morally blameworthy for participating in an unjust war, and in fact often guilty of murder for killing their non-liable innocent adversaries, whether or not they ought to be liable to punishment in the aftermath of war.

Prominent opponents of the traditional account nonetheless continue to affirm the practical logic in sustaining soldiers' legal symmetry.[7]

> Perhaps most obviously, the fact that most combatants believe that their cause is just, means that the laws of war must be neutral between just combatants and unjust combatants, as the traditional theory insists that the requirements of *jus in bello* are.[8]

For numerous practical reasons, such as epistemic difficulties in discerning justness of cause, a lack of a mutual arbitrator, the subjective belief of states and their soldiers in the justness of their cause, as well as the need for applicable and workable legislation that will mitigate the horrors of war, it is desirable that the law continue to insist on the equal application of *in bello* restrictions, regardless of just cause.[9]

McMahan also accepts many of the traditional arguments for freeing soldiers from legal repercussions for participating in an unjust war, but he regards such reasons as supplying excuses rather than justifications.[10] It might be unfair to hold individual young soldiers legally responsible for participating in their nations' unjust wars as their misperception of justice will have been manipulatively shaped by the great organs of state—education, public pressure, mass media, and the like.[11]

Not all revisionist moral philosophers address this complicated relationship between law and morality. Others suggest various intricate prescriptions for how their moral theories ought to inform future laws of war.[12] For the most part, revisionists do not recommend their moral theories translate directly into legal prescriptions that would necessarily discern the rights and duties of just from unjust combatants. Moreover, while unjust aggressors are liable to self-defensive harming during conflict, not all revisionists recommend that unjust soldiers should be held legally accountable or punished *post bellum*.

All revisionist just war theorists agree, however, that soldiers who kill in vain, in pursuit of an unjust cause, cannot possibly enjoy *moral* parity with their innocent adversaries who have been forced to kill defensively. On deep moral reflection—when we evaluate justness in war rather than contemplate its optimal regulation—we must acknowledge a stark incongruence between soldiers' legal equality and their moral disparity. As a matter of moral principle, if not always in practice, it does not stand to reason for just and unjust combatants to be bound by the same moral prohibitions and to enjoy the same moral permissions, it is argued. Far less sense to regard them theoretically as moral equals.[13]

This chapter attempts to reaffirm soldiers' traditional equality and lend it further moral support. The first section refutes the analogy between wartime aggression and domestic crime. John Locke argued that the crucial moral feature of war is the lack of a joint arbitrator to determine and administer justice among conflicting parties. This sets war entirely apart from our normal everyday moral judgments, suggesting a disanalogy between combatants on the allegedly unjust side and peacetime criminals pursued by the police.

The second section of this chapter suggests that, for many of the very reasons McMahan himself supplies, individual soldiers cannot be proved guilty of injustice regardless of the cause they serve, and are therefore presumed innocent, *morally* as well as legally. While these soldiers may not in fact be equal at some theoretically deep moral level, the moral presumption of innocents, I argue, renders them not only legally non-culpable, as many revisionist would agree, but also equal from any practical moral perspective.

Beyond that, McMahan argues that wholesale combatant liability, alongside blanket civilian immunity, contradicts the basic precepts of individualist morality applied in peacetime because the traditional distinction between combatants and civilians is based on class affiliation rather than personal responsibility. Understood as a doctrine of collective immunity and collective liability, the traditional principle of distinction is both false and repugnant, he argues.[14] As against this, I suggest that respect for individual human rights actually entails recognizing soldiers' symmetrical standing in battle, fashioning them with equal permissions and liabilities, rather than penalizing or disabling them for their nations' collective causes.

Finally, one point of terminological clarification that is also a point of substance: the principle applying equal rights and duties to warriors is often referred to as "combatant equality." Strictly speaking, it is actually "soldiers' equality" that is under discussion. Traditionally, only identifiable uniformed soldiers subject to a military chain of command, who carry their arms openly and abide by the laws of war, were accorded equal rights and protections by internationally accepted conventions of war and, subsequently, by the laws of armed conflict. After WWII, the Third Geneva Convention extended these privileges to militia members who fulfill the same conditions of overt warfare and law abidance.[15] Additional Protocol 1 controversially waives the uniform requirement in exceptional circumstances in which "an armed combatant cannot so distinguish himself," but it requires none-theless that such combatants clearly separate themselves from non-combatants by carrying their arms openly at all times.[16] Protocol 1 also requires membership in an armed force that enforces international law as a condition for attaining combatant status and lawful participation in armed hostilities.[17]

Many irregular combatants and all covert combatants—whether just or unjust—do not enjoy equal privileges, most notably prisoner of war (POW) rights when captured, though they are equally liable to wartime attack. This chapter defends the traditional principles, according to equal rights and obligations to uniformed soldiers as well as to those members of resistance movements who assume the risks of overt combat and abide by the laws of war. Following the authors addressed throughout, the paper refers to "combatant equality" as the accepted shorthand within the professional jargon for the principle of equality under consideration. Nowhere in my writing is this intended to include members of terrorist organizations who habitually abstain from the above requirements.

Cops and robbers

Early in *Just and Unjust Wars* Walzer cites and rejects a legal version of the opposition to combatant equality, as it was put by the chief British prosecutor to the court at Nuremberg:

> The killing of combatants is justifiable . . . only where the war itself is legal. But where the war is illegal . . . there is nothing to justify the killing and these murders are not to be distinguished from those of any other lawless robber band.[18]

More recently, McMahan has suggested that, as a matter of deep morality, a combatant on the aggressive side may not attack a combatant on the defensive, just as a bank robber may not attack a policeman or an armed guard. McMahan firmly rejects combatant equality along with the underlying idea that one makes oneself liable to defensive attack simply by posing a threat to another. A soldier fighting an aggressive war cannot be morally permitted to kill his just adversary in self-defense, any more than a bank robber is justified in killing a guard or policeman who threatens him by resisting the robbery.[19] The unjust soldier, just like the bank robber, is liable to being killed in self-defense, while the just soldier, like the policeman, is not. Moreover, and necessarily, the unjust soldier is at least morally liable for the murder of the innocent, though for practical reasons peculiar to war we might not hold him legally liable in the way that the bank robber is.

Traditionally, however, as Walzer comments, this is not the way in which we judge a soldier who fights for his government: "He is not the member of a robber band, a willful wrongdoer, but a loyal and obedient subject and citizen."[20] Walzer rejects any analogy between the collective wartime crime of aggression and domestic crime, asserting the traditional view of soldiers as moral equals.[21] At first glance such symmetry in the *jus in bello* seems irrational, as one of its advocates concedes, "because the normative considerations that determine the justice of the war are withheld from determining the overall normative status of those actually fighting the war."[22] This appears to negate common sense, because it deviates so dramatically from ordinary everyday morality.

This lack of analogy between war and domestic life is, however, deeply rooted in the liberal tradition. Social contract theories advocate political community precisely in order to end a state of war, or prevent degeneration into a state of war. The last thing one would then expect to find within civil society is anything at all resembling, or even remotely analogous to, a wartime situation. Domestic law and its enforcement are precisely the antithesis of war. It is the very possibility of war that we try to avoid by creating a civil society.

Nonetheless, Hobbes notoriously suggested such an analogy between criminal activity and war, upholding a symmetrical license to kill threatening adversaries in times of conflict regardless of just cause. Hobbes maintained that all subjects within a political community, whether guilty or innocent, retain an inalienable right to resist being killed, so that individuals are at liberty to resist their sovereign if he or his agents come to arrest or kill them. The sovereign, for his part, maintains a symmetrical right to pursue the criminal. In such a case a Hobbesian state of nature (i.e., a state of war) re-emerges with respect to the relationship between the accused and his sovereign, in which both parties maintain an equivalent right to kill one another and are equally liable to be killed.[23]

McMahan denies the existence of a morally symmetrical right to self-defense against threatening agents regardless of just cause, noting that Hobbes was one of the last people to accept this idea.[24]

> He [Hobbes] believed that the murderer has a natural right to kill the police officer in self-defense. But he conceded that this right is not a *moral* right; hence even his quite radical view does not support the *moral* equality of combatants.[25]

Morally speaking, McMahan argues, the correct criterion of liability to attack is not posing a direct threat, but rather moral responsibility for an objectively unjustified or wrongful threat.[26]

In fact, however, endorsing combatant equality does not entail adopting a Hobbesian view on domestic crime conceding that a robber is not entitled to defend himself by shooting at the police, nor does it imply moral subjectivism. We no longer share Hobbes's understanding of domestic law and political community— the nature of our relationship with the sovereign—or view our disagreements with the authorities as a private state of war or analogous to it. Instead, it is the absence of a joint arbitrator in most genuine situation of war, rather than the rejection of moral objectivism, that renders the situation unique and its participants morally equal, at least from any practical human perspective on morality rather than a god's eye view.

Locke may be more helpful here than Hobbes was. While Locke certainly recognized the moral distinction between aggressive and defensive force, he observed that the very essence of war is the lack of superior authority to determine and enforce justice. In war, as in any other state, there are offenders and victims, innocent and guilty. Absent a joint arbitrator, however, individuals have no choice but to interpret natural law for themselves, and they must act as judges in their own quarrels regarding their natural rights, primarily their right to self-preservation.[27] Thus, one may kill a thief though he robs only one's coat or one's horse, "because the aggressor allows not time to appeal to our common judge, nor the decision of the law, for remedy in a case, where the mischief may be irreparable."[28]

In war, as in peace, there is an aggressor and a defender. Unlike disproportionally killing a horse thief in the state of nature, however (where the thief is presumably precluded from responding in kind), the disputed question in international wars is often precisely who the aggressor is. Referring to the complicated territorial dispute that led to war between Israel and the Ammonites, recounted in the Book of Judges, Locke comments: "Had there been any such court, any superior jurisdiction on earth, to determine the right between *Jephtha* and the *Ammonites*, they had never come to a State of War, but we see he was forced to appeal to *Heaven*. . . "[29]

In contemporary contexts, McMahan's bank robber analogy is admittedly more compelling in cases of humanitarian intervention (such as Kosovo, East Timor, Sudan and Libya), in which the United Nations may be viewed as the international authority employing its police force, and their opponents as criminals. It is tempting to concede that the soldiers of Serbia, Sudan, Libya, or Indonesia had no more right to defend themselves against international troops than a criminal has to defend himself against the police.[30] Wars authorized by the United Nations are however, at most, an exception to the deficiency in joint authority more commonly experienced in war. Interestingly, even in these cases the UN Security Council has never used the fact that forces were acting under UN authority as a reason for proposing unequal application of the laws of war.[31]

Apart from the fact that most wars do not have this structure of a humanitarian intervention, several further points are noteworthy. First, international intervention, when it occurs, addresses egregious violations of *jus in bello* that are far more discernable than justice of cause, both factually and morally, and universally agreed on prior to the outbreak of conflict. The international responsibility to protect is limited to combating blatant war crimes and crimes against humanity, and not to arbitrating and enforcing *jus ad bellum* among warring parties who abide by the laws of war.[32] Second, combatants who target civilians are not merely like bank robbers, but in fact clearly murderers. And even in such cases, the authority to intervene by force of arms has been exercised by the UN only scarcely and selectively. While all this may be a step in the right direction, it does not yet indicate the existence of a joint international arbitrator capable of adjudicating justice of cause, settling disputes in an effective and consistent manner. Occasional, inconsistent and mostly late international efforts to stop mass murder are not typical cases of war and cannot serve as the basis for any far reaching analogies between soldiers in wartime and an arresting police force or the criminals they pursue.

In the more common cases of war, the lack of superior jurisdiction on earth and the subsequent inevitability of judgment in one's own cause characterize a state of war, separating it for the worse from peacetime conditions. The lack of an available overarching authority for determining justice of cause sets soldiering apart from any other violent activity, such as crime, piracy, or modern terrorism. Regardless of the root cause, all non-state violence is subject to the laws of states, as well as to agreements among states. By contrast, the moral status of a war itself—just or unjust—is rarely a provable matter; often it remains subject to political dispute to be manipulated by the strong or determined retroactively by the victor.[33] In extremely clear-cut cases of aggression, those responsible for the war ought to be punished in its aftermath, if a sufficiently objective court can be established to determine personal responsibility. Mostly, though, the lesson to be learned from Locke is that, absent a common judge, determining whether one is under attack and whether to respond by force of arms and to what extent is largely a matter of personal conscience.

> Whether another hath put himself in a State of War with me . . . Of that I my self can only be Judge in my own Conscience, as I will answer it at the great Day, to the Supreme Judge of all Men. [34]

Judgments of conscience can be objectively true or false, but for the most part their truth value will remain an indeterminate matter of contention among men who do not share a common jurisdiction.

Crucially, the independence of *jus ad bellum* from *jus in bello* and according combatant equality are not based on moral subjectivism nor on any "political realism." Most realists would argue that morality is inapplicable in war, comparing war to a Hobbesian state of nature in which moral relations are impossible.[35] No theory of the just war could adopt such a stance without also abandoning the idea of morally just conduct within war. Once "anything goes," *jus in bello* would be equally inapplicable to combat, except as a practical legal expedient towards mitigating the horrors of warfare. Instead, just war theory affirms the existence of objective justice with regard to war's causes, as well as to the moral rules that apply within it. At the same time, it recognizes that without any power on earth to determine justice and enforce it, the heavenly level of objective truth is immaterial to the earthly regulation of human conduct in war.

Needless to say, Walzer's objection to the British prosecutor's argument at Nuremberg is not based on moral skepticism with regard to Nazi aggression. The idea of "just cause" is integral to any just war thinking and not only to its revisionist versions.[36] The party that should not have waged war obviously has no moral right to fight and ought not to have been fighting to begin with. Conceding the obvious, it is less clear how it spills over into the common real-life situation of war in which both sides appear on the battlefield claiming justice for their cause and God on their side.

Vattel made this point back in the eighteenth century.

> War cannot be just on both sides. . . . However, it can happen that the contending parties are both in good faith; and in a doubtful cause it is, moreover, uncertain which side is in the right. Since, therefore, Nations are equal and independent, and can not set themselves up as judges over one another, it follows that in all cases open to doubt the war carried on by both

parties must be regarded as equally lawful, at least as regards its exterior effects until the cause is decided.[37]

Admittedly, not all causes are doubtful and not all contending parties necessarily act in good faith. Nevertheless, Vattel's words about the absence of judges still hold. Thus, many just war theorists deny that *jus ad bellum* is helpful in regulating wartime situations. This is also one of Henry Shue's powerful arguments against McMahan's morality of war, in which he points out that it offers little guidance for action in actual combat. Requiring unjust combatants to refrain from going to war offers no guidance at all to soldiers who remain unaware of their injustice, or to just soldiers who already regard their opponents as unjust.[38] If the unjust were to admit their guilt and go home, then there would be no war (and hence no morality of war) of which to speak. As Locke pointed out, if there were a superior jurisdiction, or court, to determine the right of the matter, "they had never come to a State of War."[39]

Like Walzer, Shue argues that war is too different from domestic morality to allow any helpful analogies.[40] Comparisons involving domestic criminals facing the police—presupposing a peacetime criterion of individual moral liability to attack—are particularly bad arguments by analogy, Shue argues:

> In ordinary life, everyone—both the cops and the robbers—are civilians, and "civilians" has its meaning by contrast with "combatants." Combatant is a role unique to warfare, is created by the laws of war and is given a technical definition by the LOAC . . . It is impossible to be a combatant in the strict sense specified in the laws of war outside war any more than one can be a shortstop outside of baseball . . . The norms of combatancy are constituent norms.[41]

McMahan objects precisely to the way in which just war theory carves out a separate ethical sphere for soldiers, rendering the latter morally equal to one another regardless of the cause they serve. But what it seems he cannot do is to compare the status of just combatants to that of the police. Our relationship with the state sovereign and its domestic law enforcement agencies, even in times of conflict, is the very antithesis of war, neither constituting a private case of war nor being analogous to it. Civil society along with its law enforcement agencies is constituted precisely in order to avoid, or end, a state of war.[42] As Walzer notes when comparing war to armed robbery: "Indeed it is the contrast rather than the correspondence that illuminates the war convention."[43]

On anything *but* a Hobbesian account, nothing could be less analogous to war than the availability of the police. The only remotely plausible analogy between war and ordinary life concerns situations, such as Locke's horse thief, in which law enforcement agencies are temporarily unavailable. Even this analogy, however, goes only so far. War is not merely a temporary suspension of law and the availability of its agents. In war, by contrast, it is often unclear who the aggressor is and which is in fact the rightful party.

Revisionism suggests that this wartime indeterminacy about right and wrong is merely a superficial matter of proof, whereas the moral facts remain constant in the world of true justice, possibly determinable at some later date. So while deep disagreement and the absence of an arbiter might justify granting all soldiers *legal* equality (because—lacking an impartial judge—unjust soldiers possess epistemic excuses for their erroneous moral beliefs), it cannot in fact establish their equal *moral* standing.[44]

This fine distinction between fact-relative and evidence-relative moral reasoning, however, may not be entirely tenable when it comes to establishing *jus ad bellum*, or the moral status of soldiers. Non-negotiable disagreements between warring parties are rarely reducible to epistemic arguments over evidence. Wars all too often represent contesting concepts of justice and even contests about the very nature of rightful authority itself. Moreover, personal responsibility is a further issue, to which presumptions of innocence and the requirement of proof normally apply.

Presumed innocent

Assume now that a nation is indisputably engaged in a war of aggression against its neighbor and that this moral fact is a discernable matter. Should soldiers be expected to inquire into the justness of their war and held morally responsible for participating if the war turns out to be objectively unjust? To take the outstanding case, should German WWII veterans be held morally responsible for participating in Nazi aggression? While their liability to be killed at the time is uncontroversial, their moral inequality and personal responsibility for joining Nazi forces and killing allied soldiers remain a source of contention.

Yitzchak Benbaji has suggested that the moral justification for combatant equality is based on a division of labor similar to the division that exists within the criminal justice system: soldiers are not required to inquire into the justness of their war in the very same way as jailors and executioners are exempt from inquiring into the guilt or innocence of individuals who have been sentenced by a court of law. By analogy, Benbaji argues, the appropriate division of labor within societies with regard to war places the duty to consider *jus ad bellum* in the hands of political leaders, rendering soldiers on either side equally justified in fighting and free of guilt for doing so.[45] Like lawyers, jailors, and executioners, soldiers are justified in deferring to the relevant authority in matters of justice, rather than exercising their own discretion in these matters.

McMahan disputes this analogy. Officers of the court are justified in deferring to judicial decisions because courts are institutions dedicated to the goal of establishing the truth and producing just outcomes, whereas governments are not. In order for courts to fulfill their just function, lawyers and jailors must play their part well. Lawyers are justified in defending culpable aggressors as part of a system considered "overall . . . the best way to balance the risks of punishing the innocent and freeing the guilty."[46] By contrast with courts, McMahan notes, governments notoriously act in a self-interested manner rather than in a justice-oriented fashion.

Soldiers therefore have no right to defer to political judgments, knowing full well that governments have a bad track record where justice is concerned, and consequently act impermissibly when they blindly follow their governments into an unjust war.[47]

Moreover, as of 2017 (subject to several conditions), the ICC will have jurisdiction over crimes of aggression.[48] How would such a determination of aggression affect the *moral* standing of individual soldiers and officers who nonetheless believe in the justness of their nation's war, or who continue to participate regardless of just cause?

The following suggests that many of the reasons that rule out the legal culpability of most soldiers equally preclude their moral condemnation during war or in its aftermath. Individuals who cannot be proved guilty beyond some minimal threshold have a right to be regarded as our moral equals. Notwithstanding the incommensurability of war and peace, suspected criminals in both spheres are presumed not-guilty until proven otherwise, regardless of the objective truth at any deep moral level. If unjust combatants are analogous to bank robbers or murderers (as revisionist just war theory asserts and traditionalists deny) they are then to be presumed equally innocent unless proved individually guilty. Regardless of their complicity in prosecuting an aggressive war, soldiers and civilians on the unjust side remain innocent because they cannot be proved personally responsible for its injustice to any significant degree. Quite apart from the indeterminacies of just cause, this section questions any attribution of moral guilt to ordinary soldiers and officers on the unjust side.

Most lawyers and many philosophers agree that soldiers ought not to be held *legally* culpable for their nations' aggressive wars. The ICC regards only top political and military leaders as potentially prosecutable perpetrators of aggression, recognizing the impracticability of gathering evidence against every individual involved in war, as well as the injustice of trying a small minority of ordinary participants selectively. McMahan himself concedes this much: "Even if there were a just and impartial international court there would still be powerful objections to any attempt to punish combatants merely for fighting in an unjust war."[49] Unjust combatants are culpable to varying degrees and it would be entirely impossible to provide fair trials to them all. Trying a randomly selected number of unjust combatants would result in comparative unfairness and would be unlikely to provide a significantly deterrent effect, especially as most would have substantial excuses, resulting in relatively mild punishment.[50]

David Rodin, among others, goes further by suggesting that unjust combatants ought to be held accountable after the war is over: ". . . soldiers who fight in an unjust war have no right to use force against just combatants and should be held responsible for unjust killing *post bellum*. . ."[51] Either way, all revisionists insist that unjust combatants are not morally innocent, on par with their just adversaries. Ordinary soldiers on the unjust side are not only liable to wartime attack, but also morally reprehensible for killing their innocent opponents, and ought not to be assumed otherwise as they have been by traditional theory and practice.

Arguing for the wartime immunity of unjust civilians, on the other hand, Cecile Fabre applies a presumption of innocence to most non-combatants. Ordinary civilians who contribute to an unjust war (e.g., by electing a warmongering leader, paying their taxes, and so on), Fabre argues, ought nonetheless to remain immune from direct attack. This is because war is an action involving thousands of individual agents within which it is impossible to establish whether the contribution of any ordinary civilian on the unjust side falls above or below a marginal threshold of contributory responsibility for the unjust threat. Consequently, she argues, civilians on the unjust side are not liable to direct targeting because the extent of their contribution to injustice cannot be established. At most, they may be liable to lesser harms than killing as well as to indirect "collateral" damage.[52]

Defending the immunity of unjust civilians, Fabre suggests that under conditions of epistemic uncertainty "we ought to err on the side of caution, and proceed on the assumption that those agents are innocent."[53] One of the reasons subsequently supplied for this cautionary principle is that "agents generally ought to be regarded as (causally) innocent of wrongdoing until proven (causally) responsible for it."[54] Note that this presumption of innocence appears to hold regardless of any "deep moral level" at which warmongering civilians are, presumably, patently unequal to their peaceful counterparts on the just side. Nonetheless, Fabre maintains that ordinary civilians on the unjust side are not liable to being killed because their responsibility for injustice cannot be proved to be more than marginal, and they are therefore to be presumed innocent. Contra Fabre, however, this same presumption of innocence is in fact entirely extendable to most soldiers as well, serving to strengthen the traditional thesis on the moral status of combatants rather than its revisionist version which her argument is designed to support.

Unlike civilians, soldiers are admittedly direct contributors to the execution of war. Like McMahan and Rodin, Fabre rejects combatant equality, maintaining that soldiers who choose to fight and kill for an unjust cause render themselves liable to wartime attack, while their just adversaries remain morally immune from harm. Fabre's "innocent until proven guilty" argument is not intended to apply to unjust soldiers who actively participate in an aggressive war and kill just combatants, thereby, she assumes, contributing directly to an injustice beyond the threshold necessary for holding them liable to attack. Moreover, no one but a pacifist would argue for the wartime immunity of unjust combatants. Nevertheless, the same presumption of innocence that Fabre attributes to unjust civilians is in fact extendable to most combatants as well, establishing their innocence and subsequent moral parity with their adversaries, though all remain liable to wartime attack by virtue of the threat they pose. Wartime liability is entirely compatible with equal innocence.

Given the tender age of most soldiers, the extent of their contribution to the initiation of war—whether just or unjust—will normally be infinitesimally small. Most likely their impact on the onset of war is less than that of most civilians, as many soldiers are too young even to have voted for the leaders in power. If civilians who contribute to the onset and continuation of war cannot be judged sufficiently responsible for injustice, as Fabre maintains, it is then unclear how young soldiers can be.

Numerous soldiers contribute only marginally to the execution of war; for the most part they do so less freely and willingly than older civilians. Once enlisted, many of the men and women who don military uniform will never see the battlefield, and of those who do, a great number of them will never even fire their gun, let alone kill anyone at all.[55] Armed and outfitted, the non-firers are indistinguishable from their comrades and liable to defensive attack by their enemy. Taken individually, neither the firers nor the non-firers could possibly be convicted of committing or attempting murder, nor is their personal contribution to the collective enterprise—aiding and abetting injustice—provably more than marginal.

Assigning a definite, non-negligible degree of personal responsibility for collective aggression to individual young soldiers in wartime, and to an extent that falls clearly above the relevant contributory threshold, appears extremely implausible.[56] Legally, Christopher Kutz points out that "given the fog of war and the organizational complexity of the enterprise, most combatants would have to be charged as accomplices in murder rather than as direct perpetrators."[57] Regarding punishment, Kutz argues, legal controversies over complicity, alongside excuses such as duress and epistemic limitations, would be entirely insurmountable outside a complex system of social regulation and under the pressures of war.[58]

Furthermore, international political judgment is often determined only in the aftermath of war. In practice, Kutz adds, such determination will depend on the identity of the actor and the interests of other states; it will inevitably be affected by the success/failure of the military campaign and manipulated by the strong in accordance with their interests: "Success may, *ex post*, rewrite the norms of permissible warfare."[59] Consequently, Kutz continues, there can be no transparent criteria for culpability and no realistic prospect of supplying soldiers with advance warning of their complicity in a crime of aggression. Moreover, in all likelihood, punishment for participation in aggressive war would be meted out selectively and unequally as a form of victor's justice.[60]

In view of the absence of fair warning, the lack of transparent criteria for criminality, and the foreseeable horizontal unfairness in the distribution of punishment, alongside the difficulties surrounding crimes of complicity and co-conspiracy, Kutz concludes that punishing soldiers for participating in aggressive wars cannot be legitimate: "There are simply not enough normative facts to underwrite liability."[61]

The absence of normative facts to underwrite liability goes deeper than any practical political or institutional obstacle to applying legitimate punishment. Taken together with the presumption of innocence, these various deficiencies amount to a clear case against asymmetry, as a matter of moral principle. If there is no sufficient basis for determining the liability of soldiers for *ad bellum* offences, then skepticism, or suspension of judgment, is not only the most appropriate legal response, as Kutz argues, but also the most appropriate moral response.

In the absence of provable guilt, all soldiers are equally innocent from anything but a god's-eye perspective. This is not a legal technicality, but rather a further matter of deep morality within the limitations of human knowledge. At their very worst, soldiers are analogous to suspected criminals whose crimes cannot be ascertained beyond reasonable doubt and ought therefore to be treated as on a par with the innocent. Absent sound evidence of personal guilt, we have no moral right to treat another person as anything but our equal. This is all the more so where the alleged crimes in question were committed in the course of activities that precisely mirror our own.

Mirror image

Objective justness and injustice notwithstanding, Tony Coady points out regarding war that

> Not only is it likely that both sides of a violent conflict will believe themselves to have just cause, but this subjective fact often also mirrors objective features of the situation leading up to war, even if the mirroring is subject to distortion.[62]

Walzer's classic depiction of the moral equality of soldiers captures the various aspects of this mirroring. Walzer explains the emergence of the war convention as the product of mutual respect and recognition among soldiers, based originally on aristocratic chivalry and later mostly on the joint servitude of soldiers mobilized by the modern state.[63] Young soldiers, whether conscripts or volunteers, will be similarly motivated by patriotism, obedience and an understandable belief in the justness of their own cause.[64] Once at war, Walzer tells us most crucially, they recognize each other as equally " 'poor sods, just like me,' trapped in a war they didn't make."[65] Or as Dan Zupan puts this, "Combatants find themselves in the same hell, a hell created by someone else and about which they have little control."[66]

If enemy soldiers are "as blameless as oneself,"[67] killing anyone in war may be murderous when considered at the deepest moral level. Where no atrocities against civilians are involved, war is often a tragic contest between essentially innocent combatants who are equally innocent victims.[68] Unlike the bank robber whose criminality is manifest, ordinary soldiers are neither patently guilty of injustice nor can they been personally convicted of any crime. If killing innocent aggressors is impermissible, then most killing in war may be impermissible. The strengths of pacifism notwithstanding, combat inevitably involves the reciprocal killing of "poor sods," without which there would be no war about which to moralize.

Once the fighting begins, soldiers on the battlefield share their basic moral predicament with each other. Soldiers are not only equally threatening; but also equally locked in an unusual situation that is unfamiliar to their civilians at home but identical to that of their opponents behind enemy lines. Arrayed against opposing troops, and defending themselves against enemy fire, soldiers face a reality that is unique to the business of soldiering, uniting them with their adversaries and separating them from the home-front. Their respective causes, even the relative strengths of their armies, are irrelevant to them as individuals when they stand against each other in the realities of battle. The symmetrical danger they face, alongside their comparable training, equipment, skill, and experiences, renders opposing soldiers each others' mirror image, regardless of the cause they serve. While their nations' cause for war may be just or unjust, the individual soldiers on either side aim mostly for survival.[69] As Shue comments: "War is not about killing people who are morally liable to be killed; it is about killing people who may otherwise kill you."[70]

Attributing blame to young soldiers who have been unfortunate enough to come of age at a time of armed conflict would add to the tragedy of warfare rather than mitigating it. Moreover, any denial of self-defense to "unjust soldiers" (regarding just soldiers as non-liable to their attack) or attribution of guilt to individual soldiers, would be not only tragic but also unjust, because such liability could be assigned only on the basis of collective affiliation rather than individual responsibility. All soldiers go to war for similar reasons, and those who fight in the cause of justice mostly do so with no more moral reflection than those who fight unjustly. Whether one turns out eventually to have been fighting on the just or unjust side may be largely a matter of luck.[71] Even where collective injustice is manifest (as was undoubtedly the case with Hitler's Germany), it is widely acknowledged that most individual soldiers will have at least one of several exonerating excuses for participation, particularly within totalitarian regimes. Far from advancing the individualist morality applied in peacetime, distinguishing among combatants on the basis of their nations' causes for war would in fact amount to collective punishment.

As noted, apart from the difficulties in establishing *jus ad bellum*, assigning personal responsibility for injustices to individual combatants would require concrete evidence (who fired and killed whom on the battlefield), which would be virtually impossible to gather in the fog of war. Establishing individual responsibility for prosecuting an unjust war would entail determining levels of contribution, which will often be lower in the case of young soldiers than in the case of their older civilian compatriots. Attributing guilt to soldiers merely for joining the armed forces, or participating in its activities, would have to be based on the difficult areas of conspiracy and complicity. Determining the extent of moral blameworthiness, let alone legal culpability, would require examining each and every individual case for possible excuses and justifications. In the absence of all this informative fact finding (unlikely under conditions of war), any distinction between just and unjust soldiers can be based only on their collective's political goal and their national affiliation. In McMahan's own words:

> Even if they are a minority, some unjust combatants are not culpable. And among those who are culpable, some are significantly more culpable than

others. Collective punishment would therefore be unjust . . . But it would be entirely impossible, for obvious reasons, to provide fair trials for all the members of an army.[72]

Trials aside, regarding one set of soldiers as one-sidedly liable to attack in battle and un-entitled to defend themselves, attributing blame to individual soldiers and war veterans, as well as recommending their moral condemnation, are all forms of social and political penalties. Doctrines of collective liability are morally false and repugnant, as McMahan rightly asserts.[73] Contra McMahan, however, it is not a traditional distinction based on combatant/non-combatant affiliation, but actually asymmetric distinction—attributing guilt to individuals by virtue of association—which is morally questionable in this respect. Denying individual self-defense to soldiers on one side cannot be anything but collectively assigned liability based on their national affiliation.

As opposed to this, the traditional rules uphold soldiers' individual rights by fashioning them with equal permissions and liabilities which reflect the objective similarities in their predicament, rather than penalizing or disabling them for their nations' collective cause back home. On anything but an essentially collective theory of guilt and punishment, all soldiers in similarly threatening circumstances must be symmetrically entitled to defend their own lives and those of their fellows, most notably and tragically at the expense of killing others who are just like them.

Accidental enemies

Determining justness of cause is the very issue of contention between warring parties, with no accepted or effective arbitrator for their dispute. Often it is the very nature of judge and justice that forms the crux of the conflict. This is the essence of war that sets it apart from peacetime conditions. International institutions notwithstanding, there is nothing remotely analogous to a 911 number to dial in the case of foreign aggression. In extreme cases of mass atrocity crimes, one may try to call on the United Nations. They might or might not answer the call, and will (at best) arrive on the scene relatively late.

Objective justice does not vanish from the scene even under these near-anarchical conditions. It clearly dictates some basic rules of combat, most fundamentally the rule against targeting defenseless civilians, protecting them from slaughter. Such principles, defended in the following chapter, are widely accepted (though not always adhered to) cross-culturally, and lend themselves to legal agreement among states before any fighting begins. The justice of the war itself, on the other hand, is difficult to determine and impossible to agree upon prior to or during conflict. In the absence of a joint referee (or a pronouncement of judgment by a heavenly voice), justice cannot be determined and administered, even where aggression appears manifest.

Assigning individual responsibility to soldiers on the unjust side for killing just soldiers would be impossible, and therefore cannot be required by morality. Absent individually incriminating evidence, soldiers must be regarded as innocent, at least by any theory that rejects collective punishment. This is itself a point of deep morality rather than merely of law or practicality: under conditions of epistemic uncertainly we ought to err on the side of caution, not merely in order to spare the innocent false legal conviction, but also because we lack sufficient ground on which to pass *moral* judgment.

The relevant normative facts are not only insufficient to underwrite legal liability, as Kutz argues, but also insufficient to underwrite moral liability. Passing judgment without foundation, withholding the presumption of innocence, and attributing guilt without sufficient proof are *moral* wrongs. All this is particularly objectionable where unfounded judgment is passed collectively, and with regard to actions which closely resemble those of all other soldiers, on either side. If the rules of war ought to reflect peacetime morality, this requires treating all human beings in like cases as equals except where personal guilt can be established. Absent provable guilt, all soldiers remain honorable adversaries as they in fact often perceive each other to be. Perhaps they are after all, as Rousseau described them, "enemies only by accident."[74]

Notes

1. Michael Walzer, *Just and Unjust Wars—A Moral Argument with Historical Illustrations* (New York: Basic Books, 1977), 34–47, 42, 127–128, 145.
2. Walzer, ibid, 34–41, esp. at 36, 41, and 127. And The Preamble to Additional Protocol I. www.unhchr.ch/html/menu3/b/93.htm
3. Walzer, *Just and Unjust Wars*, 21.
4. Francisco de Vitoria, "On the Law of War," in Anthony Pagden and Jeremy Lawrence (eds), *Political Writings* (Cambridge: Cambridge University Press), esp. 303–308; Francisco Suarez, "On War," in *Selections from Three Works* (Oxford: Clarendon Press, 1944), esp. 845–6; Thomas Nagel, "War and Massacre," 1 *Philosophy and Public Affairs* (1972), 123–143, 123.
5. Jeff McMahan, *Killing in War* (Oxford: Oxford University Press, 2009); Jeff McMahan, "The Ethics of Killing in War," *Ethics*, 114 (4) (2004), 693–733; Jeff McMahan, "The Morality of War and the Law of War," in D. Rodin and H. Shue, *Just and Unjust Warriors: The Moral and Legal Status of Soldiers* (Oxford: Oxford University Press, 2008), 19–43; David Rodin, *War and Self-Defense* (Oxford: Oxford University Press, 2003); David Rodin, "The Moral Inequality of Soldiers: Why *jus in bello* Asymmetry is Half Right," in Rodin and Shue, *Just and Unjust Warriors*, 44–68; Cecile Fabre, *Cosmopolitan War* (Oxford: Oxford University Press, 2012), esp. 71–81, s. 2.3.2.
6. McMahan, *Killing in War*, 38.
7. Most notably McMahan himself, in, for example, "The Morality of War and the Law of War," 27–30. See also Fabre, *Cosmopolitan War*, 74.
8. McMahan, "The Ethics of Killing in War," 730.
9. McMahan, "The Morality of War and the Law of War," 27–30; "The Ethics of Killing in War," 700, 725.
10. Ibid.
11. McMahan, *Killing in War*, 104–154. And Walzer, *Just and Unjust Wars*, 39–40, 127.
12. E.g. Rodin, The Moral Inequality of Soldiers: Why *jus in bello* Asymmetry is Half Right," in in Rodin and Shue, *Just and Unjust Warriors*, 44–68; Adil Ahmad Haque, "Law and Morality at War," 8 (1) *Criminal Law and Philosophy*, 79–97.

13. McMahan, *Killing in War*, esp. Chapters 1–2; "The Ethics of Killing in War," 695–708 and *passim*. Rodin, "The Moral Inequality of Soldiers" ibid, 44–68, argues that soldiers (just and unjust) ought to be equally bound by the same restriction, but should not enjoy equal licenses. Going further than McMahan, Rodin begins to question legal, and not only moral, equality. See also, David Rodin, "Two Emerging Issues of Jus Post Bellum: War Termination and the Liability of Soldiers for Crimes of Aggression" in Carsten Stahn and Jann K. Kleffner (eds.) *Jus Post Bellum—Towards a Law of Transition From Conflict to Peace* (The Hague: Asser Press, 2008), 68–76.

14. McMahan, *Killing in War*, 209–210.

15. Convention (III) relative to the Treatment of Prisoners of War, Geneva, August 12, 1949, Article 4.2. www.icrc.org/ihl.nsf/FULL/375

16. Protocol Additional to the Geneva Conventions of August 12, 1949, and relating to the Protection of Victims of International Armed Conflicts (Protocol 1, June 8, 1977), Article 44(3). www.icrc.org/ihl.nsf/7c4d08d9b287a42141256739003e636b/f6c8b9fee14a77fdc 125641e0052b079

17. Ibid, Article 43.

18. Walzer, *Just and Unjust Wars*, 38.

19. McMahan, "The Morality of War and the Law of War," 21–22.

20. Walzer, *Just and Unjust Wars*, 39.

21. Ibid, 127–128.

22. Christopher Kutz, "Fearful Symmetry," in Rodin and Shue, *Just and Unjust Warriors*, 69–86, 81, 69.

23. Thomas Hobbes, *Leviathan*, R. Tuck (ed.) (Cambridge: Cambridge University Press, 1991), ch. XXI, esp. 109, 112–113.

24. McMahan, "The Ethics of Killing in War," 698–699; *Killing in War*, 14, 88.

25. McMahan, *Killing in War*, 14.

26. Ibid, 32–37, 35, 38, 204–205; McMahan, "The Ethics of Killing in War," 722–723; "The Morality of War and the Law of War," 21–22.

27. John Locke, *Two Treatises of Government*. Peter Laslett (ed.), (Cambridge: Cambridge University Press, 1960), *Second Treatise*, Ch. III, §16, §19, §20, §21.

28. Ibid, §19.

29. Ibid, §21, referring to the Book of Judges, 11: 11–29. Locke chose his historical examples well, illustrating the inability to determine or administer *jus ad bellum* in the absence of a joint arbitrator. In this Biblical case, the Ammonites demand a piece of territory "from the Arnon to the Jabbok, all the way to the Jordan" that had belonged to them in the distant past and had subsequently been conquered by the Amorites and then taken from the latter by the Israelites when they came up from Egypt (Judges 11:13). At the time of the Exodus, the Israelites had requested the right to pass through the lands in the area in order to reach their destination in Canaan. They were not only refused, but also attacked by Sihon king of the Amorites and other neighboring kings who viewed their emerging presence as a threat. In the course of their defensive war (following an Amorite attack on their civilian population), the Israelites seized the lands in question: "Heshbon, Aroer, the surrounding settlements, and all the towns along the Arnon" (Judges: 11:26). The Israelites claimed the land had been delivered into their hands by God in the course of a war that had been forced upon them unjustly by the Amorites, and that they had, in any event, been holding the disputed territories ever since, living in them for what was by then some 300 years. While the Ammonites no doubt believed they had a just claim to the territory as its original occupiers (preceding the Amorites and having been dispossessed by them), the Israelites argued that they had obtained the land with God's help in the course of a defensive war, and added that the Ammonites had never contested the conquest over the past hundreds of years. As against this complicated political background, Jephta (and later John Locke) exclaims: "Let the LORD, the judge, decide the dispute this day between the Israelites and the Ammonites" (Judges 11:27). Moreover, the case involved contesting views over the very nature of judge and justice—the true

God of the Israelites, vs. the false Ammonite god Chemosh. In the end the Israelites win a spectacular victory. (Judges 11:33). See also: Samuel Moyn, "John Locke on Intervention, Uncertainty, and Insurgency," in Stefano Recchia and Jennifer M. Welsh (eds.) *Just and Unjust Military Intervention – European Thinkers from Vitoria to Mill* (Cambridge: Cambridge University Press, 2013), Chapter 5, 113–131.

30. Michael Gross, *Moral Dilemmas of Modern War* (Cambridge: Cambridge University Press, 2010), 207–213.
31. Adam Roberts, "The Principle of Equal Application of the Laws of War," in Rodin and Shue, *Just and Unjust Warriors*, 226–254, 231, 244–248.
32. For the responsibility to protect, see UN General Assembly, 2005 World Summit Outcome, A/60/L1, paragraphs 138–140, esp. 139.
33. Kutz, "Fearful Symmetry," 83.
34. Locke, §21.
35. Cf. McMahan, *Killing in War*, 36.
36. C.A.J (Tony) Coady, "The Status of Combatants," in Rodin and Shue, *Just and Unjust Warriors*, 153–75, 164.
37. Emer de Vattel, *The Law of Nations or Principles of Natural Law Applied to the Conduct and Affairs of Nations and Sovereigns*, translated by Charles G. Fenwick (Washington D.C., Carnegie Institute, 1916) (new edition: William S. Hein, Buffalo, N.Y. 1995; 1. edition: London 1758), Book III, Chapter III, §39–§40, p. 247.
38. Shue, "Do We Need a 'Morality of War'?," in Rodin and Shue, *Just and Unjust Warriors*, 85–111, esp. 105, 107–109.
39. Locke, §21.
40. Shue, 87–111, esp. 95, 97–111, 100.
41. Ibid, 100–101.
42. Locke, §124–126.
43. Walzer, *Just and Unjust Wars*, 127.
44. On the distinction between fact-relative and evidence-relative reasoning applied to the morality of war, see Adil Haque, "Law and Morality at War," 83: . . . the morally best laws of war tell soldiers what they ought to do in what Derek Parfit (2011) calls the evidence-relative sense. The morality of war, in addition, tells soldiers what they ought to do in the fact-relative sense . . . As Parfit observes, while wrongness in the evidence relative sense enjoys greater practical significance, wrongness in the fact-relative sense enjoys logical and justificatory priority.
45. Yitzhak Benbaji, "The War Convention and the Moral Division of Labor," 59 (237) *The Philosophical Quarterly*, October 2009, 593–617; Yitzhak Benbaji, "The Responsibility of Soldiers and the Ethics of Killing in War," 57 (229) *The Philosophical Quarterly*, October 2007, 558–572; Yitzhak Benbaji, "A Defense of the Traditional War Convention,"118 (3) *Ethics*, April 2008, 464–495. For further analogies between wartime responsibility and the social division of labor: Dan Zupan, "A Presumption of the Moral Equality of Combatants" in Rodin and Shue, *Just and Unjust Warriors*, 214–225, 218–224.
46. McMahan, *Killing in War*, 67. Judith Lichtenberg, "How to Judge Soldiers Whose Cause is Unjust," in Rodin and Shue, *Just and Unjust Warriors*, 112–130, 126.
47. McMahan, *Killing in War*, 67–68.
48. www.icc-cpi.int/en_menus/icc/about%20the%20court/frequently%20asked%20ques tions/Pages/14.aspx
49. Ibid, 191.
50. McMahan, ibid.
51. Rodin, The Moral Inequality of Soldiers: Why *jus in bello* Asymmetry is Half Right 44–68, 45. David Rodin, "Two Emerging Issues of Jus Post Bellum: War Termination and the Liability of Soldiers for Crimes of Aggression," 68–76.
52. Fabre, *Cosmopolitan War*, 76–78.
53. Ibid, 77.
54. Ibid, 77–78.
55. Many, if not most, soldiers are "non-firers." See Walzer, *Just and Unjust Wars*, 139.

56. Shue, "Do We Need a 'Morality of War'?," 100. See also, Michael Walzer, "Response to McMahan's Paper," 34 (1) *Philosophia*, 43–45, 43.
57. Kutz, "Fearful Symmetry," 82.
58. Kutz, "Fearful Symmetry," ibid.
59. Kutz, "Fearful Symmetry," ibid, 83.
60. Kutz, "Fearful Symmetry," ibid, 82–84; Rodin and Shue, *Just and Unjust Warriors*, 8.
61. Kutz, ibid, p. 83.
62. Coady, "The Status of Combatants," 164–165.
63. Walzer, *Just and Unjust Wars*, 34–35.
64. Ibid, 127. Walzer, "Response to McMahan's Paper," 44.
65. Ibid, 36.
66. Zupan, "A Presumption of the Moral Equality of Combatants," 220.
67. Walzer, 36.
68. I am assuming here that one may kill an innocent aggressor/innocent threats in self-defense. See also Lichtenberg, "How to Judge Soldiers Whose Cause is Unjust," 115. Some would disagree, e.g. Rodin, *War and Self-Defense*, 88.
69. Lichtenberg, "How to Judge Soldiers Whose Cause is Unjust," 114–115.
70. Shue, "Do We Need a 'Morality of War'?," 100.
71. McMahan himself concedes this point, *Killing in War*, 3, 188.
72. McMahan, *Killing in War*, ibid, 191.
73. McMahan, *Killing in War*, 209–210.
74. Jean-Jacques Rousseau, *The Social Contract and Discourses* (London and Vermont: Everyman, 1993), Book 1, Chapter 4.

2

IN DEFENSE OF THE DEFENSELESS

The morality of the laws of war

Traditional just war theory distinguishes between principles governing the resort to war and those governing its conduct. Assuming the moral equality of combatants, it regards all soldiers as liable to attack; and it categorically prohibits direct assaults on non-combatants and prisoners of war. The laws of war license the killing of all combatants during armed conflict while prohibiting assaults on all those unengaged in hostilities.[1] Revisionists question these three basic tenets: the independence of *jus ad bellum* from *jus in bello*; the moral equality of soldiers, and the blanket immunity granted to civilians and prisoners of war (POWs). The three are connected, and all are worthy of further consideration.

This chapter takes issue with the revisionist critique of non-combatant immunity. As against the prevailing moral and legal norms, revisionism suggests that some civilians and prisoners may be morally liable to wartime attack.

Civilian immunity is the bedrock of the just war tradition and the linchpin to understanding its inner logic as a coherent moral system. In defending this principle, I suggest that the laws of armed conflict (LOAC) do not diverge significantly from any deep morality of war, as revisionist just war theorists argue. The rules of war—moral as well as legal—are grounded in an age-old commitment to protect the defenseless, and can go only so deep without rendering them totally inapplicable to belligerent action. Moreover, this moral guideline—defending the defenseless—supplies a moment of union between *in bello* rules and *ad bellum* justness, as is well reflected in international law.

My argument proceeds as follows: the first section revisits the issue of liability versus immunity in war, focusing on McMahan's critique of non-combatant immunity. The second section suggests that the very justification for war, such as it is, along with the rules of engagement in it, reflects our moral obligation towards the defenseless and vulnerable. Revisionists reject the separation between *ad bellum* justness and *in bello* rules, arguing that at the deepest moral level the two ultimately converge. Crucially, this second section suggests that our commitment to protecting the weak and vulnerable represents a point of convergence between the justness of war and the particular rules governing its conduct.

The remainder of this chapter looks more closely at some of these specific rules of just engagement, and the way in which they reflect our commitment to those who are literally at the mercy of the military. These sections include discussion of civilian immunity; contemporary concerns about terrorism and torture; POW rights, and the protection of parachutists. Finally, the penultimate section attempts to anticipate and answer some predictable objections to my overall argument.

Immunity to attack

Why may we kill combatants during war while all civilians remain immune from direct attack? As Walzer observes, "the theoretical problem is not to explain how immunity is gained, but how it is lost. We are all immune to start with; our right not to be attacked is a feature of normal human relationships."[2] Jeremy Waldron makes a similar point with regard to civilian immunity:

> We have worked too long with a model that assumes that the default position is that you can kill anyone you like in wartime and that people have to be argued out of *that* if civilians are to be given immunity.[3]

The default position is the moral prohibition on murder—"Thou shalt not kill"—and the challenge is to explain what justifies the privileging of certain killings in wartime that would otherwise be murder.[4]

As we saw in Chapter 1, soldiers have traditionally been assumed, by Walzer and others, to have lost their immunity from attack by virtue of the threat they pose to their adversaries. Civilians and prisoners, on the other hand, retain, or regain, their natural immunity, because, unarmed, they pose no direct threat to anyone.[5] By contrast, revisionists deny that one makes oneself liable to defensive attack simply by posing a threat to another, suggesting instead that liability to harm ought to be assigned on the basis of individual responsibility for an unjust threat, just as it is in civilian life.[6] Consequently, they reject combatant equality, maintaining that only unjust soldiers are morally liable to attack.

In keeping with this same revisionist criterion, and as its flip side, civilians and prisoners cannot enjoy the blanket immunity from assault that the laws of war accord them. In principle (morally speaking), either may be liable to attack, even if rarely, in an attempt to avert an unjust threat.[7] Certain civilians (e.g., politicians or key figures, voluntary human shields) may be responsible for an unjust war, or an unjust threat in the course of war, even if they pose no active immediate threat in battle. Removing this unjust threat, subject to requirements of necessity and proportionality, may justify causing harm to specific civilians responsible for instigating the injustice.

Similarly, captured combatants may be liable to harm if "harming them would significantly contribute to the achievement of the just cause, or if refraining from harming them would expose just combatants to significantly greater risks."[8] After all, prior to their capture, they were partly responsible for the unjust threat. This would presumably also be true for the rule against shooting down pilots who are evacuating their plane in distress while they are parachuting in mid-air, if the pilot had been fighting on the unjust side and where killing him would significantly contribute to the just party's military cause.[9]

In practice, McMahan concedes, cases of morally justified attacks on non-combatants will be rare, and the laws of war ought not to reflect this possibility. Nevertheless, he argues that in principle, and under certain conditions, some civilians and prisoners may be morally liable to attack.[10] Ultimately, here again McMahan distinguishes between "the deep morality of war" on the one hand, and the laws of war on the other. On the deeper, purely moral, level, he argues, some civilians— those responsible for unjust threats—may be liable to deadly attack, while innocent soldiers—those on the just side who are acting purely in self-defense against aggression—are not liable to murderous assault. Nonetheless, he recognizes good reasons for maintaining the laws of war as they stand.[11]

Much has been written on the utility of maintaining the laws of war as we know them, whatever their deviation from objective moral requirements, most notably the protection of civilians. Walzer points to the utilitarian arguments for fighting limited wars, regardless of justness of cause on either side.[12] Whatever the causes and their relative justice, there is obvious moral merit in narrowing the cycle of violence by limiting the scope of legitimate targets.[13] It would be highly imprudent to grant greater license to kill civilians to the party with a just cause, as almost everyone believes his or her own cause to be just. Such license would therefore likely increase, rather than diminish, civilian suffering and the overall "hellishness" of war. Furthermore, there is also a *post bellum* consideration: fighting limited wars in accordance with the rules reduces the likelihood of long-lasting bitterness and resentment that would result in endless acts of retaliation. Perceiving one's enemy as having fought honorably, and in accordance with the reciprocal rules, leaves open the possibility of peace.[14]

McMahan himself accepts most of these arguments for maintaining the conventional legal requirements, including the protection accorded to all civilians and prisoners.[15] However, on his account we must acknowledge and accept a stark incongruence between the laws of war and the true morality thereof. At the deepest moral level, he insists, liability in wartime is determinable only with reference to individual responsibility for an unjust threat, rather than by their formal classification as civilian or combatant.[16] While there are good moral reasons for maintaining existing legal immunities despite their divergence from the pure requirements of morality, this incongruence ought nonetheless to be acknowledged.

I shall contribute nothing here to these points about the unquestionable utility of *in bello* rules or about the obvious moral value of mitigating the horrors of war and its aftermath. The following questions McMahan's basic proposition that, if considerations of practicality are left aside, morally speaking there is little justification for the laws of war as they stand, "for the corresponding moral principles are false."[17] Particularly with regard to civilian immunity, I argue, there is far more congruence between the laws of war and deep moral principles than revisionists would have us believe. The same, I will suggest, is true of the protection of all prisoners of war and parachutists in distress, which appears entirely conventional by nature.[18]

Just cause and just war

Wars, Henry Shue observes, "are competitions in lethal violence and destruction."[19] They signify the breakdown of peacetime activity along with any peaceful arbitration of disputes. Consequently, both Shue and Walzer argue that the morality of war cannot accurately reflect a peacetime criterion of liability to assault.

Even if, contra Shue and Walzer, the morality of war ought to reflect a peacetime criterion of liability, this criterion could not be the one McMahan proposes, licensing the killing in war of those who are responsible for unjust threats.[20] As Jeremy Waldron points out, "There is no general moral permission to kill those who are guilty of injustice."[21] Domestic peacetime rules, moral as well as legal, do not permit killing anyone responsible for an unjust threat, anymore than they permit harming all those perceived to be threatening.

According to Shue, the lack of a perfect analogy between the license to kill combatants in wartime and any domestic peacetime rules neither point to a deficiency in the laws of war nor to any splitting of moral requirements into various tiers, as McMahan suggests. There is no *necessary* divergence between the morality of war and the laws of war (though perhaps some laws could be morally better). It is the situations—peacetime versus wartime—that differ dramatically. For one thing, Shue notes, attributing individual responsibility in war is literally impossible. "Since war consists of mutual assaults on an organized and massive basis, any assumption of the applicability of any criterion of individual liability is thoroughly implausible."[22] Shue takes his cue from Walzer's own response to McMahan:

> What Jeff McMahan means to provide . . . is a careful and precise account of individual responsibility in time of war. What he actually provides, I think, is a careful and precise account of what individual responsibility in war would be like if war were a peacetime activity.[23]

Worse still is the fact that wars do not effectively arbitrate between just and unjust parties even at the collective level, though we love to believe that they do. We might conceive of wars as extensions of old-fashioned duels, exclaiming: "May the best man win!," but even this call crowns the better swordsman or marksman as the winner, and not necessarily the more virtuous. Wars are communal contests of brute force in which "God fights on the side with the best artillery," as Napoleon observed. It is the stronger, not necessarily the worthier or less blameworthy, who ultimately prevails.

How could such large-scale contests of force, entailing massive killings of anonymous individuals regardless of personal responsibility, ever be justified to begin with? Shue suggests that "wars are sometimes justified, or excused, perhaps in defense of the otherwise defenseless."[24] Whether or not the wholesale killing of combatants in wartime is ultimately justifiable, wars are legally defensible, and widely accepted as legitimate, when they are undertaken either in our own self-defense against aggression or in defense of our compatriots. In the case of humanitarian intervention, war is undertaken in defense of others who face mortal peril and are otherwise helpless.

In the post WWII era, I take this to be the relatively uncontroversial conventional wisdom on *jus ad bellum*, as is well reflected in The UN Charter system. While essentially aiming to avoid war altogether, Chapter VII of the Charter recognizes the right to self-defense as the only exception to the prohibition on the unilateral recourse to armed force.[25] Arguably, we might add humanitarian intervention as an additional just cause for war. It is indeed difficult to see what could either justify or excuse the large-scale costs of modern warfare aside from defending members of our political community who would otherwise be left vulnerable to armed attack, or else the protection of distant strangers who are, absent our intervention, rendered defenseless victims of assault.

Once engaged in battle, we require that fighting be carried out in keeping with the duty to refrain from assaulting others who cannot defend themselves. If, as McMahan argues, considerations governing the justness of the war and those governing its conduct necessarily converge at the deepest moral level and are not independent of one another, their point of congruence is, I suggest, this moral commitment to the defenseless.

Moreover, positively rescuing the otherwise defenseless, as in preventing genocide, as well as defending one's own compatriots, may in itself be a moral obligation. Aside from self-defense, "Thou shalt not stand idly by the blood of thy neighbor" justifies the privileging of certain (though not all) killings in wartime that would otherwise be murder.[26] Correspondingly, once a war has begun the most fundamental *in bello* moral principle mirrors the *ad bellum* duty of protection by prohibiting attacks against the defenseless.

McMahan views the laws of armed conflict as diverging significantly from the deeper morality of war. Once we identify the correct underlying moral principle as concerning defenselessness, however, we begin to see a closer (though, importantly, imperfect) convergence between the laws of war and the morality thereof. Furthermore, this is where some linkage between *jus in bello* and *jus ad bellum* begins to present itself: both ought to be guided by our concern for defenseless persons.

A skeptic may argue that the very essence of warfare is generally about trying to find a vantage point from which one's enemy is effectively defenseless and thus vulnerable to our attack. Anyone injured or killed by a bullet was, in effect, defenseless with respect to that bullet. On this understanding, even Goliath was defenseless in the face of David's slingshot, as he proved vulnerable to the lethal attack. This, however, is clearly not the notion of defenselessness implied in Shue's original suggestion, nor is it the meaning I employ here in arguing that defending the defenseless is the fundamental moral principle of just war. There is a subtle notion of fairness, or reciprocity, involved in the suggestion that our duties towards the defenseless form the moral underpinning of the laws of war. There will always be a winner and a looser; but there should not be a perpetrator and a victim.[27] The playing field may be unequal, but the traditional war convention (and the laws that followed) at least minimally "allows for a 'fair fight' by means of protecting the utterly defenseless from assault."[28]

Who are to count as defenseless, or vulnerable, for the purposes of immunity in war? In the following sections, I suggest that the categories of people protected by the laws of armed conflict correspond roughly to some traditional moral intuitions about vulnerability in wartime. Most notably, the principle of distinction recognizes that soldiers generally have a fair chance of defending themselves in battle, while civilians do not.

Civilians

I argued in Chapter 1 that the similarity in predicament experienced by soldiers provides a significant layer of justification for their equal treatment, both legally and morally. This resemblance also supplies a further reason for regarding attacks on unsuspecting and untrained civilians as morally worse than killing combatants.[29] Soldiers are well trained and prepared to expect attacks and to respond in kind. They are not only threatening by virtue of their status, but also equipped to protect themselves and each other from counter threats, in ways in which most civilians are not.[30] If war "is about killing people who may otherwise kill you,"[31] the defenseless are individuals who can neither kill you nor defend themselves when you try to kill them.

In his discussions of non-combatant immunity, Seth Lazar points out several aspects of civilian vulnerability in wartime: non-combatants lack the protective material equipment and professional military training that soldiers receive. Soldiers are psychologically prepared for attack and trained to respond to danger. Civilians retain normal expectations of going about their business unhindered. Civilians are psychologically ill-equipped to deal with the frustration of these reasonable expectations. Crucially, combatants act cooperatively, and are protected by their unit acting together. That is the whole point of having an organized military. Their action is organized collectively and their comrades in arms are both duty bound and psychologically conditioned to look out for one another. Civilians are not organized to protect themselves and others in any similar manner. That is in fact what their military is for.[32]

The specific rules protecting non-combatants are not an inadequate legal mechanism for minimizing injustice in war, approximating, but always falling short of, the true requirement to pursue unjust aggressors. Restraints *in bello* do not aim imperfectly at a criterion of liability which licenses attacks on those morally responsible for unjust threats, and no one else. Rather, they restrain an unusual exception to the prohibition on killing in general. The rules of just engagement uphold a moral prohibition on attacking defenseless and otherwise vulnerable individuals, regardless of their moral responsibilities or the indirect threat they pose. Moreover, they reflect this moral commitment rather accurately by providing for the immunity of unarmed civilians.

However objectionable it may be to kill soldiers, killing unarmed civilians is worse.[33] Lazar points out that radical vulnerability is in itself often understood to generate responsibilities. "This is one explanation of why adults have duties to protect children, and at a societal level, of why we have a duty to look after the weak and most vulnerable among us."[34] At least some recognition of familial and social obligations towards the weak and vulnerable seems common enough to human societies.

In the context of war, the prohibition on attacking the defenseless, held morally independent of just cause, is nearly as old as war itself, and pre-dates any theorized version of its morality. Recall the grave sin of the Amalekites as described in the book of Deuteronomy:

> Remember what Amalek did to you on your way as you came out of Egypt, how he attacked you on the way when you were faint and weary, and cut off your tail, those who were lagging behind you, and he did not fear God.[35]

While the retaliation on the part of the Israelites against their Amalekite enemies (commanded by God to blot out the name of Amalek) notoriously ignored any principle of distinction, this does not in itself invalidate the nature of the original condemnation: ". . . how he attacked you on the way when you were faint and weary, and cut off your tail, those who were lagging behind you."[36]

The sin of the Amalekites was not their unjust cause, about which (in the eyes of the Israelites) there could be no doubt. Rather, put anachronistically, it was their violation of *in bello* requirements—the rules of just engagement—against attacking the defenseless from the rear rather than facing the army. It was the assault on the weak and weary at the tail of the Israelite camp—the women, the children, and the elderly–rather than the lack of just cause (presumably shared by all of Israel's enemies) that warranted the condemnation of Amalek in particular: "and he did not fear God."[37]

This concern for the vulnerability of defenseless non-combatants regardless of their collective cause is not particularly Judeo-Christian.[38] Paul Berman's *Terror and Liberalism* cites Sayyid Qutb's understanding of the concept of Jihad as containing a similar ethical dimension.

> He [Qutb] quoted Mohammed's successor, Abu Bakr, the first Caliph, who told his army "Do not kill any women, children or elderly people." Qutb quoted the Koran, which says: "Fight for the cause of God those who fight against you, but do not commit aggression. God does not love aggressors."

. . . Writing about Muhammad and his companions, he said, "These principles had to be strictly observed, even with those enemies who had persecuted them." Jihad did have its rules. It was fastidious.[39]

Qutb's aggressors are not liable and culpable for pursuing an unjust cause. They are combatants fighting for a holy cause who nonetheless fail God by killing women, children, or the elderly—members of the most vulnerable echelons of society. Here it is clear that the rules about discrimination have nothing to do with just cause. They would stand on their own even if the Almighty Himself were to name the just party in war, or declare a Jihad.

Needless to say, the prohibition on attacking the defenseless has never been universally complied with. (Nor, for that matter, have our obligations towards the radically vulnerable in peacetime society ever been entirely discharged either). There is no shortage of examples throughout history (as well as in Walzer's *Just and Unjust Wars*) of direct attacks on civilians even in the course of just wars. Often, as in the case of modern terrorism, rules designed to protect defenseless civilians are invoked one-sidedly by those who would use them as justification of their own cause, as well as for the protection of their own civilians, but not others. At times, talk of protecting the defenseless is hypocritical; but even hypocrisy attests to the validity of a principle and its demand for compliance.[40]

Shue refers to "the primitive moral prohibition against assault upon the defenseless."[41] This primeval commitment to the helpless and vulnerable may be expressed in a variety of morally intuitive rules or criteria, as it has been throughout the ages. Walzer cites an ancient Indian text which includes among protected persons "Those who look on without taking part, those afflicted with grief . . . those who are asleep, thirsty or fatigued . . . ."[42] These are the weak and the weary. While the details vary from place to place, Walzer speaks of the frequent protection of "those people who are not trained and prepared for war, who do not fight or cannot: women and children, priests, old men, the members of neutral tribes, cities or states, wounded or captured soldiers."[43] Similarly, Qutb lists "women, children, the elderly, and those devoted to religious activity, such as priests and monks of all religions and ideological persuasions."[44] Members of these categories are not necessarily blameless or entirely unthreatening, as McMahan would be quick to point out. They include prisoners and the wounded on the unjust side. Priests may incite people to violence; women, even in traditional societies, may actively support an unjust cause. Nonetheless, they have customarily been protected by a wide variety of moral codes rather than merely by modern laws.

Walzer describes the general underlying principle at work in all these judgments as connecting immunity from attack with military disengagement. "What all these groups have in common is that they are not currently engaged in the business of war."[45] They are, as we call them, *hors de combat*. This is precisely the meaning of "innocent" non-combatant with which McMahan takes issue: those who are currently doing no harm, who are non-threatening, and who do not contribute to the prosecution of the war.[46] It is easy to imagine members of these traditionally protected categories who are in fact highly threatening: civilians who allow irregulars into their homes and villages serving as their human shields; mothers who send their sons on terrorist suicide missions; citizens who vote, pay taxes and otherwise support the foreign policies and wars of unjust regimes, and so on.

Far more crucially than being non-threatening or disengaged from the business of war (which many are not) is the fact that all these people are defenseless and unarmed: "Those people who are not trained and prepared for war, who do not fight or cannot."[47] Sometimes this is expressed in terms of protecting women and children; the latter in particular are traditional paradigms of the weak and vulnerable. Any such rule is destined to be imperfect. Within irregular popular resistance movements, for example, minors are often armed and actively employed in war. But given the necessity to frame the laws with reference to large categories of individuals, civilian immunity appears to capture our duty towards the defenseless as well as it can. Protocol 1 Article 51 (3) states that: "Civilians shall enjoy the protection afforded by this section, unless and for such time as they take a direct part in hostilities."[48] Civilians may pose a threat, at least indirectly. They are not necessarily blameless, or non-culpable for various aspects of the ongoing conflict. What they are, for the most part—as they stand unarmed, disorganized and ill-equipped at the outskirts of direct combat—is utterly vulnerable and defenseless.

Politicians are an exception. Often they take a direct part in hostilities—initiating war, giving the orders, even serving as commander-in-chief. When such politicians are indisputably unjust, the argument about the divergence of the law from deep morality certainly has its moment of truth. Something like this, however, regarding officials of state, was already noted by Walzer in his discussion of political assassination back in *Just and Unjust Wars*.[49] More crucial for the account I have given here is the fact that high-ranking politicians are not defenseless. Their personal bodyguards are probably better armed and equipped than the average soldier. Their legal protection is largely artificial, though it has some very good utilitarian justifications. It serves to protect diplomacy and political alternatives to war. At the deepest moral level politicians' immunity would not hold up in the rare "Hitler-like" cases, where the injustice committed was entirely discernible.[50]

As for ordinary civilians, legal restraints *in bello* appear entirely congruent with the fundamental moral principles that govern the conduct of war, and are independent of the important moral principles that govern the war's overall justness. They are designed to protect those who are not going to kill you (regardless of their moral responsibilities) and who cannot defend themselves if you try to kill them. Any force used against the defenseless, Lazar points out, is likely to be particularly lethal because there is little non-combatants can do in response. This is a further reason to regard their attack as worse than attacks on combatants. "Vulnerability is a force multiplier."[51] Our moral obligation to protect the defenseless, regardless of cause or the indirect threat they may pose, appears particularly clear in the absolute ban on torture, especially in the age of terrorism, and in our condemnation of terrorism itself.

Terror and torture

The fundamental prohibition on attacking the defenseless is the basis of Henry Shue's original argument against the use of torture,[52] but it has not received the kind of attention it deserves within recent debates about killing in war. Defenselessness also forms part of the basis on which we condemn, or ought to condemn, all terrorism against civilians regardless of cause.

There is a striking equivalence between torture and the terrorism it often purports to combat from the perspective of the vulnerability of the intended victims. The victim of torture (or terror) is disarmed, and in that sense is totally defenseless. Terror and torture are, at least to this extent, moral parallels: both involve direct and deliberate assaults against the defenseless; both use, and misuse, helpless individuals in order to attain political ends.

To some, like McMahan, this condemnation seems morally counter-intuitive. A captured terrorist, as well as some potential victims of terrorism, may well be morally responsible for an unjust threat. Furthermore, a captured terrorist will often withhold information that could significantly contribute to removing an unjust threat.[53] Similarly, deliberately killing civilian supporters of an unjust regime might substantively contribute to the achievement of a just cause, such as ending a war or freeing a nation. In both cases, refraining from harming the proposed victim would expose just combatants, as well as innocent civilians, to significantly greater risks. In the absence of a principled moral ban on directly assaulting the defenseless, absolute prohibitions on terror, and perhaps even torture, appear at times to diverge from purely moral requirements.

McMahan endorses a legal ban on terrorism, and the legal protection of civilian immunity. He also points out that any purely moral license to target liable civilians will be rare (subject to necessity, proportionality, effectiveness, justness of cause, and so on). Nonetheless, his point remains that "civilian immunity is contingent rather than absolute."[54] As for torture, McMahan supports this legal ban as well, but he thinks that in some cases it diverges from morality. From a purely moral perspective, a person may be liable to torture if this is necessary for averting an unjust threat which that person is most probably responsible for, or implicated in, creating: "In these rare cases of morally justified torture, the torturer would be, paradoxically, a martyr to a higher morality."[55]

Admittedly, an interrogated terrorist, albeit unarmed, may pose a very realistic and at times even immediate threat to his torturers and their compatriots. The information withheld from the interrogators might be construed as an ongoing threat, often more deadly than, and at times as immediate as, that of a fully armed opposing soldier. It has been suggested that the prisoner's continued silence constitutes part of his attack.[56] Jeremy Bentham made this point when he argued in defense of torture that when a prisoner declined to do what justice requires of him, what is in the interest of the community at large, he is in effect committing an ongoing offence against society. "Every moment that he persists in his refusal he commits a fresh offence, of which he is convicted upon much clearer evidence too than can be obtained in almost any other case."[57]

More significant than being unthreatening or innocent, however, which the intended victim of torture may not be, is the fact that he is radically vulnerable to his assailant. Shue raises and rejects the suggestion that supplying information, thus avoiding the torture, constitutes a form of defense. Even a knowledgeable terrorist, Shue argues, is defenseless and helpless in the face of torture because the betrayal of one's ideals, values, and friends, whatever their moral worth, is such a dishonorable alternative and a violation of one's own integrity, effectively a denial of one's very self, that it cannot reasonably count as an escape route.[58]

Less controversial is the indisputable fact that an ignorant (or partially ignorant) victim of torture has no possible escape route whatsoever, as he lacks the information with which to satisfy his interrogators. There is no way of differentiating in advance between an uninformed victim and a dedicated enemy who is withholding valuable life-saving information. And even the knowledgeable terrorist can have no guarantee that the torture will cease if he divulges information. The vast inequality in the relationship with his interrogators does not enable any such assurance.[59] So while a terrorist suspect bound to a chair may be guilty and possibly poses a threat to the innocent, as McMahan envisions, he is nonetheless fundamentally vulnerable in very significant ways.

Viewed from the perspective of the victim's vulnerability, it is questionable whether there is any moral level at which one is entitled to be more relaxed about killing defenseless civilians or torturing prisoners because their military is pursuing an unjust cause, or because of their indirect part in that threat. Civilian victims of terrorism, however influential within an unjust regime, are defenseless in a variety of significant ways discussed in the previous section. This is a large part of the moral rationale for their protection, and it stands regardless of cause or individual political responsibility. As for potential victims of torture, they are at the mercy of their interrogators, and as such are entirely vulnerable. It is difficult to see how their torturers could possibly be martyrs to any level of morality at all. If any counter-examples to the prohibition on torture ever appear intuitively compelling in extreme and rare situations of dire peril, they could at most be excusable in terms of "extreme emergency" or political "dirty hands," rather than being morally commendable, or even justifiable.[60]

POWs and parachutists

The basic prohibition against attacking the defenseless grounds a series of additional restrictions in war. Securing prisoner of war (POW) rights and prohibiting shooting at parachutists in distress,[61] just like the absolute legal prohibition on torture and the targeting of civilians, are cases in point. None are maintained artificially as distinct from justness of cause for purely utilitarian reasons or merely to safeguard combatants' mutual interests. All represent a basic moral commitment that stands regardless of justness of cause at any level of morality.

McMahan suggests that in some rare incidents the execution of unjust prisoners would be morally permissible.[62] This would necessarily also license the background threat of their execution, which is a significant psychological form of torture. But what is true of non-combatants is true of POWs as well. POWs are radically vulnerable to their captors who literally hold their captives' lives in their hands. This generates a responsibility to protect prisoners, regardless of any unjust cause they may have served and however beneficial it might be for the just side to murder their prisoners.

Granted, the specific rules regarding POWs have not been in place since time immemorial. Aristotle notoriously believed that barbarian captives in war ought to be enslaved.[63] Waldron points out that "Grotius observes that the permissibility of killing prisoners used to be taken for granted at least in certain circumstances, but that now civilized countries no longer follow that rule."[64] But as Waldron explains, such change may well indicate moral progress rather than the arbitrariness of the various rules.[65]

Moreover, recall that McMahan takes a radically individualist approach to war, claiming that the same principles that govern individual conduct outside of war also govern individual conduct in war. Crucially, he denies that conditions of war make any significant difference to the application of the fundamental moral principles that govern the permissibility of killing and injuring. Consequently, it remains unclear what this license to kill prisoners of war is comparable to in normal everyday life. Domestic law does not license the killing of imprisoned criminals responsible for creating unjust threats, even if such executions would significantly contribute to averting an unjust threat to innocent civilians or to the police, (e.g., by way of deterring others, removing a symbol of, or "martyr" to, their cause, or in order to sever the convict's continuing ties to the outside world).

On the present account, there could also be no license, for example, at any level of morality, for shooting at a parachutist who is in distress during a forced descent, on the grounds that he is parachuting in the pursuit of an unjust cause. In fact, such an act would be morally despicable, as well as illegal, regardless of cause.[66] A pilot who uses an ejector seat when evacuating his plane may not be targeted, though he can of course be detained as a POW and must be offered that option. He is assumed, in the words of Protocol 1, to be "in distress;" in other words, he is quite helpless. Attacking him during his descent would be not only, or even primarily, a breach of conventional rules but also a clear violation of a basic moral prohibition on assaulting the defenseless or vulnerable.

Defending the defenseless?

We are left with the horrors of war, as it inevitably places civilians in danger. This is, as Walzer puts it, the central feature of wars' hellishness, and it is not precluded by the rules concerning non-combatant immunity.[67] As for combatants, they are legally targeted in a variety of situations in which they are not only materially innocent but also materially defenseless. The laws of armed conflict permit the bombardment of strictly military targets, though the victims of bombardment, soldiers and civilians alike, may have little effective defense against such attacks.[68]

All combatants may be attacked during armed conflict at any time, whether in fact they pose an immediate threat or are idly standing by, simply because they have the particular status of combatants.[69] "It is not against the rules of war as we currently understand them to kill soldiers who look funny, who are taking a bath, holding up their pants, reveling in the sun, smoking a cigarette."[70]

Many civilians are killed in war and so are some vulnerable soldiers. The laws also protect some civilians, namely political leaders, who are relatively well-equipped to defend themselves. Clearly, the laws of war do not supply a comprehensive defense of the defenseless, nor am I suggesting that they do; I doubt this is even their intent. War, at least modern war, would not allow that, virtually by definition. This is Walzer's and Shue's point about the nature of war versus the nature of peacetime activity.[71] For all the importance of the various restrictions on harming the defenseless, war remains a massive display of force aimed at large groups of people.

When considering McMahan's critique of civilian immunity, Waldron points out that the laws *in bello*, like any positive norm, must take account of considerations of legal technicality and implementation which may make such immunity look odd by any standards of moral philosophy. The LOAC are designed to apply in circumstances of deep dissent on issues of justice and guilt, and can therefore be administered effectively only by using simple and non-controversial category-based distinctions such as "combatants" versus "civilians," though these are admittedly over-and under-inclusive by purely moral standards. The laws of war cannot be over-demanding if they are to command any compliance at all in circumstances of panic, anger and great danger.[72] Furthermore, these laws cannot require combatants to make inquiries into their individual adversaries' moral standing; "laws designed to govern conduct in the fog of war cannot take account of every detail that a deep moral theory will take account of."[73]

All this goes to the heart of McMahan's argument about the existence of a *necessary* divergence between the laws of war and the deep morality of war. It also concedes too much to McMahan. These same observations about the nature of war may do away with any alleged incongruence between law and morality, even as they point directly to it. It is not an incidental feature of war that it is a situation of deep dissent, great danger, anger and panic. These are not contingent features of war that the law, as opposed to morality, has to account for. This is precisely what war *is*, and any level of its regulation—moral as well as legal—would have to address that. Furthermore, the essence of war is not merely that it is a situation of deep dissent, anger and panic. It is also essentially a collective activity and any regulation has to address this feature as well.

There is no deep moral level at which wars are otherwise, while the law, regrettably, has to apply to real-world contingencies in the fog of war. The morality of war, and not only its legality, must be equally applicable to the belligerent scenario in order to be action guiding. Even if the deepest level of morality is confined to evaluating justness in war, rather than guiding action within it, there is still no escaping the very essence of the subject matter under consideration. Otherwise, the moral rules in question are not rules of war at all (neither deep nor superficial); they are then, as Walzer suggests, the morality of war under peacetime conditions.[74]

I have argued contra McMahan that defending the defenseless gives a better account of the morality of war than any criterion which distinguishes individuals who are morally responsible for unjust threats from those who are not. I also maintain that protecting the defenseless is a somewhat easier principle to apply and comply with than McMahan's criterion of distinction would be. It does not involve inquiries into the personal guilt and innocence of enemy combatants and civilians, nor does it require discerning the objective justice of the war. Admittedly, defenselessness does not render all individual civilians total immunity from lethal harm, while some combatants are relatively defenseless and yet may still be attacked under the laws of war. Sometimes defenselessness is insufficient to render legal immunity (as in the case of the naked soldier); rarely immunity is granted to individuals with ample means of defending themselves (political leaders). Bearing this in mind, how then can we argue in good faith that the laws of war successfully reflect any moral obligations toward the defenseless and vulnerable?

I sincerely doubt whether there is any deep morality of *war* that could require the absolute protection of every defenseless individual during wartime, any more than it could protect all of the innocent. This would be the morality of the impossible. As with McMahan's argument, here too there are two possible explanations for this partial anomaly between the moral criterion for protection—in this case defenselessness—and actual immunity. The first is purely practical; the second refers more fundamentally to the collective character of war.

As for the former, although some combatants may be temporarily defenseless while exceptional civilians may be capable of defending themselves, combatants are generally equipped for self and collective defense, while civilians are almost always defenseless.[75] One cannot strictly specify any entirely sufficient test on either side (combatants or civilians) and so some workable compromise has to be made about practical epistemological burdens in discrimination. On this account, the "combatants versus civilians" compromise is admittedly imperfect at reflecting any deep moral distinction and leaves outliers in both camps. It has nonetheless proved itself useful, and probably as good as we can get.

Second, and quite apart from the practical real-world inapplicability of a law to protect all the defenseless in wartime, it seems odd even at the theoretical level to regard their absolute protection as the "deep morality of war" from which the laws of war necessarily diverge for practical reasons. This would be a McMahan-type argument, albeit with a different criterion of liability (i.e., kill only the threatening and well prepared; protect all the defenseless). But I do not think that even at the "deep moral level" there could possibly be such a "morality of war," any more than there could be a deep morality of war that permitted the killing only of those responsible for unjust threats. The LOAC apply to large categories of people because wars are essentially fought, and endured, by large groups of people. This is a feature of war which any moral theory has to account for. Wars are not pinpointed attacks carried out on a large scale. War is an activity which essentially involves massive deadly attacks against collectives; it is incompatible with a moral requirement to protect people on an individual basis, according to any criteria. War simply is not the type of activity that lends itself to this type of *moral* restraint. This, as Walzer observed long ago, is essentially why war is hell.

Concluding remarks

The laws of armed conflict have many morally advantageous consequences, as they serve to mitigate the horrors of war. This, however, could not be their sole justification since this goal could be attained by almost any restriction on the scope of violence. The laws of war have a much older and deeper moral justification. They prohibit direct attacks on certain types of people who are by their very nature defenseless and vulnerable, helpless or in distress, and therefore entirely at the mercy of the military. In all these cases, we want to tell the military to run along and pick on someone their own size, so to speak, and never to hit a man when he's down, regardless of cause. McMahan may think this is all just quaint chivalry, but this may actually be as deep as the morality of war can go without prohibiting war altogether.

The legal restrictions *in bello* reflect this age-old commitment toward the defenseless in a variety of specific, albeit very limited, ways that are peculiar to the distinct character of war. While this principle has never attained universal compliance, it has received widespread recognition cross-culturally. This is the deep morality of war, such as it is. It is the fundamental moral rationale that underlies the rules of conduct in war. The laws of just engagement are not a second-best solution to discerning the justness of cause in order to get at the individuals responsible for injustice, while at the same time protecting all those who are just. We should not be looking for the morality of war by analogy with individual conduct outside war. The same fundamental moral principles apply, but peacetime conditions do not obtain in war.[76]

Aside from this difference between war and peace, there is also no license to kill morally responsible individuals in civilian life; so the laws of war could not, even by analogy, reflect such a criterion of liability.[77]

Finally, in contemporary just war thinking as well as international law, resort to war is justified only in self-defense or resisting aggression, and perhaps also for humanitarian reasons. In other words, wars are justified only on the basis of protecting the otherwise defenseless. Subsequently, we require that they be carried out in keeping with the duty to refrain from assaulting others who cannot defend themselves. This is precisely the category of people that any just military is supposedly fighting for, rather than fighting against. If we must persist in looking for a deep moral connection between *ad bellum* and *in bello* considerations, this is probably where we should look. Both *ad bellum* and *in bello* restrictions correspond to our moral commitment to defend the otherwise defenseless, though they correspond to it in different ways. If, at the deepest moral level, considerations governing the justness of the war and those governing its conduct necessarily converge and are not independent of one another, this is their point of union.

Notes

1. Michael Walzer, *Just and Unjust Wars* (New York: Basic Books, 1977), 42. George P. Fletcher, *Romantics at War—Glory and Guilt in the Age of Terrorism* (Princeton & Oxford: Princeton University Press, 2002), 107–108; Yoram Dinstein, *The Conduct of Hostilities Under the Law of International Armed Conflict* (Cambridge: Cambridge University Press, 2004), 95.
2. Walzer, *Just and Unjust Wars*, 145.
3. Jeremy Waldron, *Torture, Terror and Tradeoffs—Philosophy for the White House* (Oxford: Oxford University Press, 2010), 109–110.
4. Waldron, ibid.
5. Ibid.
6. Jeff McMahan, "The Morality of War and the Law of War," in: D. Rodin and H. Shue, *Just and Unjust Warriors: The Moral and Legal Status of Soldiers* (Oxford: Oxford University Press, 2008), 19–43, 21–22: "The correct criterion of liability to attack in these cases is not posing a threat, nor even posing an unjust threat, but moral responsibility for an unjust threat."
7. McMahan, *Killing in War*, 108, 221–235.
8. McMahan, "The Morality of War and the Law of War," 22.
9. For this rule, see: Protocol 1 to the Geneva Conventions (1977) Article 42 (1) and (2).
10. McMahan, *Killing in War*, Chapter 5, 203–235. McMahan, "The Morality of War and the Law of War," 22.
11. Ibid.
12. Walzer, *Just and Unjust Wars*, 132–133.
13. This objective is clearly stated in the preamble to The Hague Convention: Laws and Customs of War on Land (Hague IV) October 18, 1907. http://net.lib.byu.edu/~rdh7/wwi/hague/hague5.html
14. Walzer, *Just and Unjust Wars*, 132.
15. McMahan, "The Morality of War and the Law of War," 27–30; *Killing in War*, 234–235.
16. McMahan, "The Morality of War and the Law of War," 21–22; See also: McMahan, "The Ethics of Killing in War," 722–723; McMahan, *Killing in War*, 35, 38.
17. McMahan, "The Morality of War and the Law of War," 21–22, ibid. See also: Seth Lazar, "Just War Theory: Revisionists Versus Traditionalists" *Annual Review of Political Science* (2017, forthcoming), 20.4–4.18: "Revisionists argue that international law is at its best a pragmatic fiction—it lacks deeper moral foundations," 4.1.
18. On the importance of conventions, specifically the rule about civilian immunity, see: Jeremy Waldron, "Civilians, Terrorism and Deadly Serious Conventions," in Waldron, *Torture, Terror and Tradeoffs*, Chapter 4, pp. 80–110.
19. Henry Shue, "Do We Need a 'Morality of War'?," in Rodin and Shue (Eds.) *Just and Unjust Warriors* (Oxford: Oxford University Press, 2008), 87–111: 95.
20. McMahan, "The Ethics of Killing in War," 722–723; McMahan, The Morality of War and the Law of War" 21–22; McMahan, Killing in War, 32–37, 35, 38, 204–205.
21. Waldron, 108.
22. Shue, "Do We Need a 'Morality of War'?," 100.
23. Michael Walzer, "Response to McMahan's Paper," 34 (1) *Philosophia*, 43–45, 43.
24. Shue, "Do We Need a 'Morality of War'?," 87.
25. See: Charter of the United Nations, Chapter VII: Article 51. www.un.org/en/documents/charter/chapter7.shtml. The power granted to the UN Security Council in articles 24, 25 and in Chapter VII of the Charter, to authorize collective action to maintain or enforce international peace and security also appear entirely congruent with the underlying moral principle I am arguing for here.

26. For a detailed, though highly qualified, defense of such an obligation, see: Cecile Fabre, "Mandatory Rescue Killing," 15 (4) *Journal of Political Philosophy*, 363–384. More recently: Cecile Fabre, *Cosmopolitan War* (Oxford: Oxford University Press, 2011), Chapter 5: "Humanitarian Intervention," 166–207, section 5.3, "The Duty to Intervene," 178–187. See also Shue, "Do We Need a 'Morality of War'?," 105, on Rwanda.
27. Henry Shue, "Torture," 7 (2) *Philosophy and Public Affair*, (1978), 124–143, 129–130.
28. Shue, "Torture," ibid, 129.
29. Cf: Seth Lazar, *Sparing Civilians* (Oxford: Oxford University Press, 2015), 1–22; 112–114.
30. Lazar, *Sparing Civilians*, ibid, esp. 112–115. *Seth* Lazar, "Necessity, Vulnerability, and Noncombatant Immunity," unpublished manuscript (2010), cited with permission from the author.
31. Shue, "Do We Need a 'Morality of War'?," 100.
32. Lazar, *Sparing Civilians*, Chapter 5: "Vulnerability and Defenselessness," esp. 112–115.
33. Lazar, *Sparing Civilians*, ibid, Chapter 1: "Killing Civilians is Worse than Killing Soldiers," 1–22; and 114–115.
34. Lazar, "Necessity, Vulnerability, and Noncombatant Immunity," (2010), 16; see also: Lazar, *Sparing Civilians*, 107–108, and Seth Lazar, "Just War Theory: Revisionists Versus Traditionalists," 4.13.
35. *Deuteronomy*, 25: 17–18.
36. *Deuteronomy*, 25: 18.
37. *Deuteronomy*, 25: 18.
38. Alia Brahimi, *Jihad and Just War in the War on Terror* (Oxford: Oxford University Press, 2010), 174–8.
39. Paul Berman, *Terror and Liberalism* (New York & London: Norton, 2003), 98.
40. Walzer, *Just and Unjust Wars*, 20.
41. Shue, "Torture," 125.
42. Walzer, *Just and Unjust Wars*, 43.
43. Walzer, ibid.
44. Brahimi, *Jihad and Just War in the War on Terror*, 175.
45. Walzer, *Just and Unjust Wars*, 43.
46. McMahan, "The Ethics of Killing in War," 695.
47. Walzer, *Just and Unjust Wars*, 43.
48. Protocol 1 added to the Geneva Conventions, 1977, Chapter II: Civilians and Civilian Population: Article 51(3). Admittedly, the criteria for direct participation are extremely controversial. This has been a serious issue of contention, for example, regarding Israel and the United States' policy on targeted killing. Much of the debate circles around the question of who counts as a direct participant in hostilities, and so many of the usual issues surrounding the combatant/civilian distinction simply re-surface. (See e.g.: Kristen Eichensehr, "On Target? The Israeli Supreme Court and the Expansion of Targeted Killing," 116 (8) *The Yale Law Journal* (2007), 1873–1881. My argument here does not attempt to settle such disputes. It is limited to arguing that the general ideal or moral principle reflected in the LOAC is the protection of defenseless persons, rather than the protection of the innocent. It does not suggest that every defenseless individual is always successfully protected from all harm, nor does it suggested that no controversy exists as to whom, precisely, counts as defenseless and who does not.
49. Walzer, *Just and Unjust Wars*, 200.
50. Walzer, ibid, 199–200. The law accounts for some such exceptions as tyrannicide. In any event, politicians retain the responsibility for the war itself. Unlike with soldiers, their war is their crime. (Walzer, ibid 37–38).
51. Lazar, "Necessity, Vulnerability, and Noncombatant Immunity," (2010), 16. See also: Lazar, *Sparing Civilians*, 115.
52. Shue, "Torture," 129.
53. McMahan, *Killing in War*, 108.
54. McMahan, ibid, 231.

55. Jeff McMahan, "Torture, Morality and Law," *Case Western Reserve Journal of International Law*, 37 2/3 Law Module (2006), 241–248, 248.
56. David Sussman, "What's Wrong with Torture?," 33 (1) *Philosophy and Public Affairs*, (2005), 1–33, 16–8.
57. W.L. Twining and P.J. Twining, "Bentham on Torture," 24 (3) *Northern Ireland Legal Quarterly* (1973), 305–356, 312.
58. Shue, "Torture," 135–136.
59. Shue, "Torture," 135–136. This concern for the ignorant victim of torture was already raised by Bentham, who admitted that this worry poses a serious objection to the use of torture in general. Bentham cautioned that torture could be appropriately inflicted only after serious precautions have been taken to assure that the victim of torment is indeed capable of complying. Alternatively, Bentham suggests, there may be rare cases in which the public interest in preventing a harm is so great, that it outweighs the dangers of torturing the innocent and legitimizes the torture of a suspect whom we are fairly sure, though not certain, is capable of preventing the large scale harm. (Twining, 1973, 312–314).
60. Michael Walzer, "Political Action: The Problem of Dirty Hands," 2 (2) *Philosophy and Public Affairs* (1973), 160–180, 167.
61. Protocol 1 added to the Geneva Conventions, 1977, Article 42 (1).
62. Jeff McMahan, "Killing in War: A Reply to Walzer," 34 *Philosophia* (2006), 47–51, 49; McMahan, "The Morality of War and the Law of War," in: Rodin and Shue (eds.), *Just and Unjust Warriors*, 19–43, 22, 36.
63. Aristotle, *Politics*, T.J. Saunders (ed.), trans. T.A. Sinclair (London: Penguin, 1992), 1255a–1255b.
64. Waldron, *Torture, Terror and Tradeoffs*, 103.
65. Ibid.
66. Protocol 1 added to the Geneva Conventions, 1977, Article 42 (1): "no person parachuting from an aircraft in distress should be made the object of attack during his descent."
67. Walzer, *Just and Unjust Wars*, 156.
68. Combatants are not invincible. They are considerably vulnerable to certain types of attack, such as aerial bombardment and predator drones. I think Seth Lazar meets this challenge concerning heavy artillery as well as anyone can: First, combatants are nonetheless far better equipped to protect themselves and each other from a wide range of threats than civilians are. They are well-trained to take shelter, and to maximize this use of cover. Combatants can often return fire in response, while civilians cannot. Soldiers are also better emotionally prepared for attacks. Crucially, they are organized and taught to act as a unit for their mutual protection. Second: when particular types of weapons actually render combatants as vulnerable as non-combatants, this supplies good reason to regard their use as fundamentally problematic, as many of us do in the case of nuclear weapons. Lazar, *Sparing Civilians*, 115–117. See also Lazar, "Just War Theory," 4.13.
69. Walzer, *Just and Unjust Wars*, 142. See also, Fletcher, *Romantics at War*, 107–108; Dinstein, *The Conduct of Hostilities Under the Law of International Armed Conflict*, 95.
70. Walzer, *Just and Unjust Wars*, 142.
71. Walzer, "Response to McMahan's Paper," 34 (1) *Philosophia*, 43; Shue, "Do We Need a 'Morality of War'?," 89.
72. Waldron, 93–95.
73. Waldron, ibid, 94.
74. Walzer, "Response to McMahan's Paper," *Philosophia*, 43.
75. Cf. Lazar, "Just War Theory," 4.3: "Civilians are typically more vulnerable and defenseless than soldiers."
76. Walzer, "Response to McMahan's Paper," 43; Shue, "Do We Need a 'Morality of War'?," e.g. 100.
77. Waldron, 108.

3

FIGHTING FOR INDEPENDENCE

What can just war theory learn from civil conflict?

Chapters 1 and 2 offered a theoretical defense of combatant equality and civilian immunity in war, regardless of the justice of its cause. The overarching thesis encompassing both these aspects is that the principles governing the conduct of war are independent of those governing the initial resort to war. Arguing about war on this purely theoretical level may have limited practical implications. As we have seen, revisionist just war theorists widely acknowledge some practical reasons for maintaining existing legal arrangements, mostly reserving their critique of traditional rules to the realm of deep moral inquiry.[1]

Nonetheless, revisionist theorists believe their alternative morality of war—attributing rights and liability in war based on just cause—can be practically significant. Quite plausibly, it is argued, granting equal rights and status to all soldiers, regardless of the justice or injustice of their nation's cause, has encouraged young men throughout the ages to go to war un-hesitantly, motivated by patriotism, national partiality, and deference to political authority.[2]

Put plainly, the argument in hand suggests that a soldier who believes that fighting for his country is morally permissible regardless of the cause for which he fights might be more inclined to participate in a war than one who believes that participation is morally permissible only if his nation's cause is just. Given the latter belief, participation in a war is a morally risky act. In general, we do not want to be murderers. And many soldiers pride themselves on being more than thugs–they are warriors with honor fighting for their homeland. If they are told that participating in an unjust war would make them murderers, they might take a second look at the cause for which they are fighting. Variants of this practical argument, opposing *jus in bello* independence on the grounds that it encourages participation in war regardless of just cause, appear in several contemporary accounts of the just war.[3]

This chapter addresses the independence of *jus in bello* from *jus ad bellum* in this more pragmatic and contemporary light. It looks to non-international armed conflict, in which the traditional independence thesis is not fully maintained by law, and considers whether introducing a similar dependence of *jus in bello* on *jus ad bellum* into the Laws of International Armed Conflict would be morally advantageous in terms of minimizing participation in unjust wars.

The purpose of this chapter is twofold. First, it presents the urgent case of civil war, relatively neglected by just war theorists, along with the normative issues that pertain to this type of conflict and its participants specifically. Second, it suggests that this civil war perspective offers fresh support for the central doctrine of traditional just war theory—the third and final tenet defended in this part of the book—namely that the just war category of *jus in bello* ought to be judged independently of the just war category of *jus ad bellum*.

Introduction

Most armed conflicts since 1945 have been civil wars, and the overwhelming majority of wartime casualties following WWII have occurred within them.[4] By stark contrast, the voluminous writing on just war theory in the last few decades has concentrated almost exclusively on international conflicts.[5] To take the classic case, Michael Walzer's *Just and Unjust Wars* makes little mention of civil war, apart from its references to the Lieber Code (1863).[6] It is often pointed out that this very first codified set of rules for the conduct of the armed forces in war was written at President Lincoln's request as a guide for the Union's army during the US civil war.[7] While this code was not always adhered to, and its future impact proved to be largely on international armed conflict, it is nonetheless noteworthy that it was designed to apply specifically to a civil war. Governments confronted with internal struggles have rarely followed President Lincoln's example. As I write these lines, civil conflict rages in neighboring Syria, where no apparent restraint is shown by the warring factions and where no end is in sight.

Legally, only a small part of humanitarian law applies to non-international armed conflicts, while all of international humanitarian law applies during international armed conflicts. The laws that apply to non-international armed conflict—those laid down in Article 3 common to the Geneva Conventions (1949) and, more recently, Protocol II (1977)—aim to uphold civilian immunity and the rights of the sick and wounded, as well as prohibiting torture and further excesses in wartime.[8] These existing laws suffice to condemn all sides to the Syrian conflict (and many other conflicts), branding them war criminals. They do not, however, apply the full set of laws *in bello* applicable within international armed conflicts to non-international strife.

Crucially, the laws applying to civil wars do not maintain full separation between *jus ad bellum* and *jus in bello* or the related equality of combatants, upheld by international law for all interstate armed conflicts. Notably, they do not equally accord to all captured combatants the rights of prisoners of war. As opposed to the law of international armed conflict, the laws applicable to civil conflict leave rebels unprotected from interrogation, prosecution, and punishment for the mere fact of their participation in the fighting, even if they fight overtly and refrain from targeting civilians.

Francois Bugnion of the International Committee of the Red Cross (ICRC) argues persuasively that such selective application of the laws of war to non-international armed conflicts is inadequate, ineffective and even counterproductive in protecting civilians caught up in civil strife: ". . . the combatants, who risk incurring the most severe penalties for the mere fact of having taken part in hostilities, are hardly motivated to comply with the laws and customs of war."[9]

This chapter refers to civil war primarily as a case study for considering the morality of war more generally. It suggests that the relatively under-theorized case of civil war supports the traditional "independence thesis"—separating just cause for war from the rules of its conduct—often criticized by contemporary moral philosophers. As against these critiques, I argue that the level of destructiveness and general lack of compliance with *jus in bello* exhibited in most civil wars support the moral case for maintaining the stark separation between *jus ad bellum* and *jus in bello*, at least within international armed conflict. Whatever the philosophers' examples show, civil war supplies a concrete demonstration of what actually happens where independence does not wholly apply. Without the total independence of *jus in bello* from just cause and the symmetrical immunities of combatants, all wars might be as bloody and devastating as non-international armed conflicts, with no hope of maintaining the protection of those who are *hors de combat*. The plight of Syrians is no exception to the lot of civilians in most civil wars.

The argument proceeds as follows. The following section defines civil war, touching on the multiple causes and typical consequences of civil conflict. The subsequent section describes existing international legislation pertaining to non-international conflict and its inadequacy in regulating conduct in civil wars. Finally, I present civil conflict as a practical rebuttal to contemporary moral skepticism about the traditional independence thesis.

Civil wars

Definition and causes

As opposed to the relatively scarce literature on civil conflict within just war theory, there is by now a considerable body of empirical literature on civil wars. Definitions of civil war revolve around its two central features: first, it is a *civil* war, fought within the boundaries of a single state, unlike international forms of armed conflict; second, it is a civil *war*, distinguished by its level of violence from lesser forms of domestic strife.

While definitions vary, civil war is typically defined as an internal armed conflict within the territory of a sovereign state, carried out between forces of that state and at least one other organized armed group capable of inflicting harm.

It is widely accepted that in order to count as a full-fledged civil war the conflict must substantially threaten the sovereign's effective control of the state, and result in a casualty count that exceeds a certain threshold, usually placed at 1000.[10] A minority of definitions include politically motivated war among factions within a community, even where the regime itself is not party to the conflict.[11]

The 2010–11 regime change in Egypt, for example, satisfied most of these definitional requirements but nonetheless did not count as civil war because it did not reach the threshold death toll. Subsequent events in Egypt in 2013 may have satisfied the casualty count but nonetheless were not recognized by either local or international authorities as constituting a civil war. On all accounts, criminal violence, sporadic political violence, and even genocide (in which the state is not threatened and the victims are defenseless) do not on their own count as civil wars, though they may take place within the context of civil conflict.[12]

Civil wars are not defined in terms of their causes and consequences, though both issues feature prominently in the empirical literature, exhibiting more variety and controversy than the definitional issues. Diverse studies of the origins and causes of civil war display roughly three theoretical approaches: ethnic, economic, and those that point to a state's structure and features as the central explanation for civil conflict.[13]

The ethnic approach to civil war focuses on the dynamics and demography of ethnic groups and suggests that multiethnic societies are particularly prone to civil conflict due to ethnic or and/or religious cleavages.[14] Critics of this approach argue that diverse ethnicity may breed low-level hostility between groups within one state, but does not suffice to lead people into war. At most, ethnicity and ethnic sentiment are vehicles of civil war, facilitating recruitment of group members into the rebel army, rather than forming the basis for war.

As against the ethnic approach, the predominant explanation of civil wars emphasizes economic factors as the central feature leading up to civil conflict. Paul Collier describes the lethal cocktail:

> If a country is in economic decline, is dependent on primary commodity exports, and has a low per capita income and that income is unequally distributed, it is at high risk of civil war.[15]

Poverty and inequality breed frustration and despair among young men, rendering them an easy target for paramilitary recruitment because they have nothing to do and little to lose. States in which these conditions predominate are likely to be nondemocratic and incompetent, incapable of countering rebel violence and inadvertently even encouraging it.[16] When these states are resource-rich, their natural wealth provides a source of funding for the rebels, who can realize their motivation to fight only when they are economically strong. At the same time, greed and resentment, combined with the availability of natural resources such as oil, supply a central motivation to enlist in the hope of enjoying the spoils of war in its aftermath.[17]

Other scholars deny that either ethnicity or inequality suffice in themselves to explain civil war, suggesting a wider variety of internal features that put states at risk of civil war.[18] These include poverty, but importantly also a country's demography, geography, and various political features.[19] According to Fearon and Laitin, large states that are politically weak and unstable, wealthy in natural resources (particularly oil), inhabited by large populations with a lower than average per capita income, spread out across a vast territory that includes mountainous and non-contiguous terrain, jungles and remote peripheries cut off from the center, are at high risk of experiencing internal conflict and civil war. These internal features are favorable to rebels, enabling them to organize, strengthen and remain hidden from the authorities, and are thus conducive to civil war, regardless of any ethno-religious hostilities or inequality.[20]

Uncovering the causes of civil war is a particularly complex task.[21] Anke Hoeffler suggests reasonably that "[m]any explanatory variables are endogenous and it is probably better to refer to correlates of war, rather than causes."[22] Some variables may be difficult to proxy, or lack sufficient empirical evidence. Others allow for multiple interpretations, while still others are highly correlated with each other or depend on their interaction.[23]

Civilians

While the causes of civil war are multifarious and difficult to gauge, their typical consequences are easy enough to observe: civil wars typically last longer than international wars, and are more devastating, particularly to the civilian population.[24] The average duration of civil wars is 7 years, as opposed to 6 months in the case of interstate wars.[25] Most fatalities in interstate wars occur among the military, whereas most casualties in internal conflict are civilians.[26] Civil wars wreak havoc within a community and rarely end in a negotiated settlement. Usually they are concluded by military victory.[27] They are also likely to recur within the first decade after their conclusion.[28]

Civil wars are mostly asymmetrical, fought unconventionally, and lack a traditional battlefield.[29] "A few civil wars mix irregular and conventional warfare (e.g., Russia, China, Vietnam), while a very small number are fought fully, or predominantly as conventional wars (e.g., Spain)."[30] Not unrelated is the high casualty rate among civilians that characterizes virtually all civil wars. There are many obvious reasons for this, not least of which is that such wars are fought entirely within the boundaries of their society.[31] Irregular tactics place civilians at greater risk (e.g., when insurgents hide in their midst, live off the land) or even exploit non-combatants outright in order to gain military advantage.[32] Allen Buchanan has pointed out recently that revolutionaries "often face a stark choice: the use of morally impermissible coercion against the people they seek to liberate or failure."[33]

When the conflict is ethnic, Paul Gilbert notes, "The principle of civilian immunity is often ignored. . .because the opposing ethnic group becomes defined as the enemy."[34] Civilians also suffer indirectly from the breakdown of society and from the long-term social and economic costs of war.[35]

Once again, civilian immunity is the cornerstone of traditional just war thinking and humanitarian law. War carried out among non-combatants (not only civil war) requires paying particular attention to this principle. This is true regardless of kinship or cultural national ties, and for purely circumstantial reasons. When battles are fought within a community, minimizing harm to civilians will require a stricter application of the rules than in wars conducted on the battlefield. Guerrillas and partisans fighting among civilians, as well as the armies drawn in to pursue them, are duty-bound to protect non-combatants of all nationalities from the danger they themselves inflict in the vicinity of civilians.[36]

As for the protection of compatriots specifically, it is widely accepted that governments are under special protective obligations towards their own citizens. (This consensus, I will suggest, also translates into a similar obligation for rebels towards the beneficiaries of their actions). Anti-rebel forces act on behalf of the government whose legitimacy depends on upholding its citizens' rights. Writing of civil war, Vattel points out that:

> . . . we must, in the first place, recollect that all the sovereign's rights are derived from those of the state or of civil society, from the trust reposed in him, from the obligation he lies under of watching over the welfare of the nation, of procuring her greatest happiness, of maintaining order, justice, and peace within her boundaries.[37]

Governments who kill, or unduly endanger, their own non-combatants not only defy the more general and universal obligation to refrain from killing civilians, but also violate their special obligations towards their own population whom they are sworn to protect. If civil wars pit brothers and sisters against each other, states that kill their own defenseless citizens are like parents who kill their children. They transgress the universal prohibition against murder, and additionally violate their special obligation to protect. These special obligations supply further reasons to condemn parents who harm their own children, or states that kill their own civilians.

Rebels and freedom fighters, as well as governments, also have special obligations to protect members of the population they profess to be fighting for, above and beyond the general duty to refrain from murdering civilians. This special duty to protect, again, has little to do with nationalism and stands alongside the general obligation to minimize harm to all those who are *hors de combat*. Like governments, rebels derive any legitimacy they may have from the welfare of their people. Regardless of whether national ties confer stronger moral obligations towards fellow members, rebels have special protective obligations towards their civilian co-nationals because they claim to act for them and in their name.[38]

Above and beyond the care and caution required of any combatants who fight among civilians, states have special responsibilities towards their citizens, as do militants with regard to the population they claim to represent. In short, when war sets neighbor against neighbor outside the traditional battlefield, greater vigilance is required on all sides in order to uphold the moral principles that underlie the laws of war.

The reality in civil war is diametrically reversed. Civilians caught up in civil conflict lack all the support and protections normally enjoyed by non-combatants in wartime. They lack national solidarity, the support of their neighbors and co-nationals and the protection normally accorded by the state sovereign and military. A primary concern of governments engaged in international wars is to protect their civilian population and to distance the fighting from the home-front. By stark contrast, civil wars are carried out mostly among civilians by parties concerned primarily with victory at all costs. On the revolutionary side, Buchanan notes, overcoming military inferiority and pursuing victory frequently requires insurgents to use violence against their own population, for example, in order to recruit others, enhance support and participation, consolidate and coordinate the revolutionary leadership, and so on.[39]

In all these ways, civilians are often physically abandoned by both the rebels and the sovereign, remaining utterly defenseless, as well as emotionally forsaken by many who were hitherto their friends and neighbors and now find themselves in opposing camps. The social fabric that was once the anchor of their lives becomes the source of great suffering and pain.[40]

Perhaps above all, civil wars are fought largely outside any structure of rules,[41] let alone any stricter application of civilian immunity. Bugnion lists multiple factors that contribute to the prolonged and enhanced violence experienced in civil wars alongside their devastating effect on civilians. Crucially, he suggests that "it would be a mistake not to also take into account the rudimentary state of the rules applicable to non-international armed conflict."[42] International humanitarian law applies only partially to such conflicts, and in practice is rarely adhered to at all.

International humanitarian law applicable in non-international armed conflict—Common Article 3 and Protocol II

Common Article 3

Article 3 common to the four Geneva Conventions of 1949 was the first international legal provision for humanitarian protection in the case of armed conflicts that are not of an international character.[43] The Article applies broadly to non-international armed conflicts, avoiding the complicated distinctions drawn between them in the previous section.[44]

Dubbed a "miniature convention,"[45] Article 3 applies a subset of the Geneva Conventions to non-international armed conflicts. Its minimalism reflects the reluctance of the contracting parties to restrict their sovereignty, particularly the authority to put down uprisings within their jurisdictions and to punish rebels.[46] Consequently, the Article refrains from applying to non-international strife the full set of laws applicable to international armed conflict, and does not regulate the actual conduct of hostilities—the methods and means of warfare.[47] Instead, it aims to afford persons who are *hors de combat* with a minimum of humanitarian protections.

Article 3(1) guarantees the rights of non-participants to humane treatment, prohibiting violence to their life and person, particularly murder, mutilation, cruelty, and torture.[48] The Article further prohibits hostage taking and outrages upon dignity, specifically humiliating and degrading treatment.[49]

Article 3(1)(d) reaffirms the general prohibition on extra-judicial execution and requires due process, specifically prohibiting sentencing and executions "without previous judgment pronounced by a regularly constituted court, affording all the judicial guarantees which are recognized as indispensable by civilized peoples."[50]

Finally, Article 3 briefly guarantees the right of the wounded and sick to be collected and cared for.[51]

Mindful of the rudimentary nature of the safeguards guaranteed in this article, its drafters added that

> The Parties to the conflict should further endeavor to bring into force, by means of special agreements, all or part of the other provisions of the present Convention.[52]

Aware of the natural fear of governments of acting in any way that might be construed as granting legitimacy to those rebelling against it by recognizing their war rights, the article closes with the assurance that

> The application of the preceding provisions shall not affect the legal status of the Parties to the conflict.[53]

The humanitarian provisions of Article 3 apply to all parties "regardless of whether the revolutionary authorities have made any declaration of intent to comply."[54] They also apply equally to all, regardless of the origin and causes of the conflict, thereby maintaining some separation between justice of cause and the rules of engagement. Nonetheless, this separation does not extend to fashioning insurgents with Prisoner of War (POW) status if they fall into the hands of their enemy.[55]

Rebels are not afforded immunity from interrogation and prosecution in exchange for fighting overtly and abiding by the laws of war, such as the Geneva Conventions accord to Prisoners of War. Anthony Cullen points out with respect to the final clause of Article 3, "there is no provision in the body of international humanitarian law that would prevent a government from treating rebels or insurgents in a non-international armed conflict as ordinary criminals."[56] Though torture is specifically prohibited, interrogation is not. Irregulars who have been taken captive are not entitled to remain silent, unlike captured soldiers who need only state their name, rank, and serial number. Nor are rebels immune from trial and sentencing for their participation in the conflict, including the implementation of the death penalty, so long as these proceedings accord with the requisite judicial guarantees: "An insurgent combatant does not enjoy immunity when charged with having taken up arms, as do members of the armed forces in a conflict between states; on the contrary, he may be punished for having violated the national law."[57]

Furthermore, no provisions are laid down in Article 3 for regulating the situation that prevails at the end of a civil conflict, or specifying the rights of participants once the fighting has ended. Naturally, this omission will be particularly troubling to those combatants who ultimately find themselves on the losing side.[58] Nothing in article 3 prevents trial by the victors in the aftermath of war, providing judicial guarantees are observed.

Protocol II

Additional protocol II (1977) "develops and supplements Article 3," by clarifying its requirements and elaborating on its humanitarian provisions "without modifying its existing conditions of application."[59]

As for these "conditions of application," the vague term "armed conflict not of an international character," employed in the common Article, had been criticized for leaving the applicability of international humanitarian law largely dependent on the willingness of states to recognize the existence of an "armed conflict" within their territory.[60] To take an outstanding contemporary example, Syrian President Assad continues to maintain that there is no civil war in Syria. Instead, he persists in claiming that Syria is plagued by criminal gangs of terrorists, attempting to disrupt law and order and forcefully take over the state, and that they must be stopped at all costs.

As against this, Protocol II lays down four objectively verifiable criteria for its material field of application and applies automatically to non-international armed conflicts

> . . . which take place in the territory of a High Contracting Party between its armed forces and dissident armed forces or other organized armed groups which, under responsible command, exercise such control over a part of its territory as to enable them to carry out sustained and concerted military operations and to implement this Protocol.[61]

The Protocol excludes "internal disturbances and tensions," and has been criticized for setting too high a threshold for its application, applying to nothing less than full-scale civil war.[62] While the Protocol offers a wider net of humanitarian protections than those guaranteed in Common Article 3, its objective requirements, such as a threshold level of violence, narrow its scope of application in relation to that of the pre-existing Common Article.[63] Moreover, unlike Article 3, Green points out, Protocol II has not yet hardened into customary international law and "it creates treaty law only for those states who ratify and accede to it," which some of the major powers have not.[64] Furthermore, the Protocol's lack of international measures of enforcement and its inability to oversee its provisions have earned it the title of "warrior without arms."[65]

As for content, Protocol II fleshes out the principles of humanitarian protection sketched only roughly in Common Article 3, and takes initial strides towards regulating the methods and means of warfare in internal conflict.[66] The final Articles to the Protocol concern the protection of the civilian population, civilian objects and installations, echoing the legal provisions applicable to international conflicts.[67]

Provisions are also set out for humanitarian aid offered by impartial international organizations such as the Red Cross. However, such relief action remains contingent on the consent of the high contracting parties concerned, with the unfortunate result that states may reject offers of humanitarian relief to their civilian population.[68]

Regarding penal prosecution of participants in hostilities, Article 6 of the Protocol specifies the judicial provisions guaranteed by Common Article 3(1)(d): independence and impartiality of the courts, the right of defense and the right to be present at one's trial, individual responsibility, non-retroactivity, presumption of innocence, the right to remain silent, and the right to information on judicial remedies.[69] It also prohibits the pronouncement of the death penalty on persons under 18 at the time of the offense and the execution of pregnant women and mothers of young children.[70] Finally, Article 6(5) calls for, but does not require or impose, a general amnesty at the end of hostilities.[71]

For all its specificity, the Additional Protocol does not substantially alter the international legal framework for regulating internal armed conflict. It expands on the humanitarian provisions granted in Article 3, but applies less broadly. Even when it applies, civilians remain far more vulnerable than they are within interstate wars, while rebels are denied virtually all rights and status as combatants. Protocol II does not place specific restrictions on the type of weapons that may be employed by the parties to the conflict including some that are prohibited within international conflicts and by customary international law, such as poison gas. This results in the absurdity that states are not specifically prohibited from employing weapons against their own citizens which they are prohibited from using against foreign nationals (though the general prohibitions of customary international law apply to civil conflict as well). Perfidy is another example of means and measures prohibited specifically with regard to international conflict, but unrestricted by Protocol II.[72]

Most notably, Bugnion points out that: "Protocol II did not fundamentally change the relationship between *jus ad bellum* and *jus in bello* established by Article 3."[73]

> Protocol II, like Article 3, establishes a separation between *jus ad bellum* and *jus in bello* as far as the obligations it creates are concerned. Nevertheless, as it . . . affords combatants no immunity from prosecution for the mere fact of having participated in the hostilities, Protocol II—again like common Article 3—establishes that separation only to a limited extent.[74]

Rebels may be interrogated, tried, and punished for treason, both during the conflict and in its aftermath. Unlike soldiers, who can stand trial only for war crimes, rebels may be prosecuted by their governments for the mere fact of their belligerence. In fact, all combatants in civil war, not only rebels, risk prosecution by the victors, simply for having fought for the cause that is ultimately judged (by the victorious party) to have been unjust.[75]

Just war theory and the independence-symmetry thesis

The law applicable to non-international armed conflict presents an interesting alternative to the traditional separation between *jus in bello* and *jus ad bellum*. It represents a wartime regime in which one side to an armed conflict is held responsible for the outbreak of hostilities and judged to be pursuing an illegal cause. Individuals who partake in this illegal course of action are consequently culpable for their participation, whether they kill civilians or combatants or merely conspire to do so. A rebel is not immune from trial for treason on the grounds that he refrained from targeting civilians any more than a bank robber is immune from prosecution for murder if he kills an armed guard but refrains from shooting the customers at the bank.

Conversely, the laws of international armed conflict mirror traditional just war theory, starkly separating the causes and aims of the war from the rules of engagement in it, holding soldiers responsible only for the latter. Yet, as we have seen, an increasing number of contemporary just war theorists do not attribute equal moral status to all soldiers. Revisionists argue that the principles governing the conduct of war ought *not* to be judged independently of those governing the initial resort to war and that just combatants cannot be morally equal to unjust combatants.

For the most part, this revisionist moral critique is not intended to translate into a revision of the laws of war, and generally concedes the consequential bene-fits of *jus in bello* neutrality and its independence of just cause.[76] The primary revisionist concern is to refute the moral truth of the independence-symmetry doctrine. Nonetheless, at least one of Jeff McMahan's arguments against maintaining the independence-symmetry thesis is distinctly pragmatic: "If it is correct that it is wrong to fight in a war that lacks a just cause, this has considerable practical significance. Unjust wars can occur only if enough people are willing to fight in them."[77]

> [T]he widespread acceptance of the moral equality of combatants has facilitated the ability of governments to fight unjust wars. Wars are now and have always been initiated in the context of the general and largely unquestioned belief that the moral equality of combatants is true. If that background assumption were to change—if people generally believed that participation in an unjust or morally unjustified war is wrong—that could make a significant practical difference to the practice of war.[78]

McMahan suggests that the independence-symmetry doctrine may have an adverse effect on people's moral beliefs and encourage their willingness to go to war without inquiring into its legitimacy. If moral philosophers were to abandon the independence thesis, perhaps forewarning potential combatants of the injustice of their future aggression, prospective participants might be reluctant to take up arms for fear of incurring moral culpability and possible legal repercussions. It would then be more difficult to recruit combatants, resulting in fewer wars and less suffering.[79]

Despite this, McMahan does not as yet recommend the prosecution of soldiers for participating in unjust wars, acknowledging that ". . . *at present*, there are decisive reasons not to hold unjust combatants liable to punishment."[80] Combatants fearing punishment might be reluctant to surrender, thus prolonging the conflict. Facing prosecution for their mere participation, they might feel they had nothing to lose, and perhaps something to gain, from abandoning all restraint and committing any "war crimes or atrocities that might increase their chances of victory and thus of immunity to punishment."[81] Nevertheless, McMahan believes that "conditions could change in a way that would make it desirable to threaten unjust combatants with punishment."[82]

Specifically, McMahan envisions the establishment of an international court that would provide an authoritative interpretation of *jus ad bellum* and supply prospective participants with advance guidance regarding the legality of their war.[83] Such a court would serve to minimize unjust wars by deterring participation in them, as it would "put soldiers on notice that the war in which they have been commanded to fight, or in which they are at present fighting, is an illegal war and that they can be held legally accountable for participating in it."[84]

Civil wars give cause to doubt this. Rebels are informed precisely of the illegitimacy and illegality of their participation in hostilities by both national and international law. The latter permits and regulates their trial and execution even if they abide by the rules of *jus in bello*. In spite of such warnings, the twentieth and twenty-first centuries have seen no shortage of recruits to fight in civil wars.

The unequal status of combatants in civil wars is admittedly not the product of a deep moral evaluation of their aims and causes, and is not determined by an impartial international court dedicated to judging justness of cause in each case. Nonetheless, internal armed conflict is a recurrent type of war in which the rights of combatants, their privileges, liabilities, and culpability are legally determined initially by both national and international law in relation to the cause they serve. Despite this authoritative stance, individuals are not deterred from participating in these wars; instead they are deterred from abiding by the rules of engagement.

If the civil wars of the past eight decades are anything to go by, authoritative warnings about the illegality of international conflicts, even if these could be attained, would have little, if any, effect on the frequency of war. Warning participants of the illegality of their war would probably have the sole effect of greatly enhancing and prolonging the horrors of war, as is already the case in non-international armed conflicts. Any arguments purporting to minimize the ills of unjust wars by authoritatively establishing their illegality and the culpability of their participants would have to take the example of civil war into account.

McMahan maintains throughout that at the deepest moral level—when war is contemplated by philosophers rather than pragmatically regulated by lawyers—the independence of *jus in bello* and the equality of combatants are unsustainable. "By fighting in a war that lacks a just cause, unjust combatants are acting in a way that is objectively wrong."[85] David Rodin goes further down this road, suggesting that soldiers who fight an unjust war, thereby killing combatants on the just side, are not only morally blameworthy but should also be held legally responsible, subject to criminal investigation and potentially liable to punitive sanction.[86] Unlike McMahan, who designates the prosecution of unjust combatants to a futuristic international court dedicated to determining *jus ad bellum*, Rodin aspires more imminently "to align both legal norms and legal institutions more closely with moral considerations."[87]

On a practical note, Rodin denies that "unjust combatants will have no *incentive* to comply with currently accepted *in bello* prohibitions if they are not granted equal war privileges."[88] This is because, even if merely participating in an unjust war were to become a culpable offense, harming civilians would still be *worse*.[89] Unjust combatants would still have an incentive to refrain from killing civilians in order to avoid incurring the greater culpability, just as a bank robber who murders an armed guard retains the incentive to refrain from capriciously killing unarmed customers in order to avoid the enhanced charge of aggravated murder.[90]

Regarding the common concern about victors' justice, Rodin agrees with McMahan that the appropriate authority for the prosecution and punishment of unjust combatants ought to be international, adding that "the International Criminal Court clearly has the form of authority that would be required to punish unjust soldiers."[91]

Finally, Rodin also raises and rejects the objection, conceded by McMahan, that asymmetry contributes to prolonging conflicts because "fear of punishment might encourage unjust combatants to continue fighting beyond the point at which they might otherwise have surrendered, thus prolonging the war unnecessarily."[92] As against this, Rodin asserts that

> In reality, the opposite seems true. If *post bellum* punishment was the norm, it would be possible for the international community to bring strong pressure on unjust combatants to surrender by offering to reduce or suspend punishment providing they surrender or defect . . .[93]

Given that civil conflict has been the most prevalent form of warfare since 1945, however, *post bellum* leniency may not supply a sufficient incentive to surrender. Rebels know from the start that they can avoid punishment (not only reduce or suspend it) if they refrain from fighting altogether. Nevertheless, most remain uninspired to abstain and seem unlikely to change their minds unless they are fairly certain of defeat.

In this model of combatant asymmetry, rebels also remain undeterred from killing non-combatants precisely because, as rebels, they are culpable for their participation anyway. This stands to reason and is unlikely to be altered by a moral distinction between harming combatants on the just side and harming non-combatants, or even by the legal distinction between culpability for murder and culpability for aggravated murder.[94] Whatever the case with bank robbers, gradations of criminal activity may not be effective in wartime. Absent the equal immunities of soldiers, combatants are liable to prosecution on grave charges if they lose, but will get off scot free if they win. From a pragmatic perspective, they had better do whatever it takes, and for as long as it takes, in order to win the war.

McMahan and Rodin are not alone in enlisting practical arguments against traditional independence. Anthony Coates specifically addresses pragmatic-consequential justifications for the independence-symmetry thesis. Centrally, Coates acknowledges the danger feared by advocates of independence of encouraging excessive moral zeal if obligations in war are dependent on the justice of their cause. Nevertheless, he believes that the threats to restraint in war posed by *jus ad bellum* are avoidable, while the independence of *jus in bello* is both impossible and undesirable.[95]

Independence is impossible, according to Coates, because political and cultural reasons for fighting will necessarily affect the way the war is fought. (The Nazi's, e.g., could not separate their racial beliefs from the war in which they fought–distinguishing between the status and rights of soldiers on the Western and Eastern fronts). Independence is undesirable because, far from diminishing the threat to restraint in war, the independent application of *jus in bello* actually makes matters worse by permitting soldiers to kill in war regardless of cause.[96]

It is a traditional mistake, Coates argues, to assume that *jus ad bellum* has a justifying effect whereas *jus in bello* has a restraining function, so that emphasizing *jus in bello* independently of just cause will necessarily limit war. *Jus in bello* is not purely restrictive, but is also entitling—it permits killing on both sides, regardless of cause. This all too easily grants soldiers the right to kill, rather than restraining war by forcing them to take the resort to war seriously.[97] "If the rights and obligations of war . . . are so easily granted and acquired, what incentive is there to take *ad bellum* . . . seriously?"[98]

Coates presents a complex proposal for the critical reconstruction and application of *jus ad bellum* which, he argues, will do better at combating the dangers of wartime excesses than the independence of *jus in bello* does.[99] He clearly intends his thesis to be realistic, suggesting that subordinating *jus in bello* to *jus ad bellum* will, at least in the long run, limit and perhaps eventually eliminate the occurrence of war.[100]

Coates' proposal is a far cry from the legal regime applicable to civil conflict. Nonetheless, the experience of combatant asymmetry and the dependence of *jus in bello* on *jus ad bellum* in civil war cannot be ignored or downplayed. Occurring five times as often as interstate war, this paradigm of combatant liability lends itself to little moderation or settlement. Judging by civil conflict, it is quite possible that combatant liability for mere participation actually has a degenerating effect, increasing rather than diminishing the level of violence and prolonging its duration.

It is difficult to see how matters could possibly get worse than this. Most civil wars are carried out with no restraint, perhaps largely because rebels are answerable for the illegality of their cause: they have little to gain in terms of avoiding punishment by adhering to *jus in bello* and much to lose tactically by restraining themselves by its rules. Instead, they must fight for victory to the bitter end, and at all costs to civilians, in order to escape punishment.

What can just war theory learn from civil conflict?

Civil war is the most prevalent and costly form of warfare in the modern era, and should command the full attention of theorists contemplating the morality of war. The circumstances of most civil conflict—its civilian setting alongside the special relationships among its participants—suggest a call for stricter *in bello* restrictions than those that already apply to the traditional interstate battlefield. In practice, the reverse is true: only a subset of humanitarian law applies to internal conflict, and what does is rarely adhered to.

One reason suggested for this lack of adherence is the discriminatory nature of the applicable rules—differentiating as they do between the rights and duties of rebels versus soldiers. This is not likely to change, nor does this chapter suggest that it necessarily should. States are understandably reluctant to grant equal combatant status to rebels and to restrict their right to put down insurrection within their jurisdictions. More generally, any legitimization of irregulars by placing them on a par with soldiers poses its own dangers to civilian immunity. Even where irregulars abide by the rules of war they still endanger civilians by fighting among them, living and hiding in their midst, thereby forcing their opponents to pursue them among the civilians.[101]

Nonetheless, just war theorists ought to be acutely aware of civil conflict as an exemplar of combatant inequality, and draw out its possible lessons for the morality of war more generally. This is particularly true for contemporary philosophers who criticize the traditional tenets of just war theory, specifically those who profess to make practical-pragmatic or consequential arguments against the traditional independence-symmetry thesis. Whatever else remains to be said of civil war, it is a real-world example of combatant asymmetry. While the experience of civil war might not be unequivocally conclusive in determining the moral case for independence and symmetry and the dangers of dispensing with them, it might still be more instructive than purely philosophical hypotheses on the morality of war. It does not precisely represent the type of asymmetry that revisionist theorists have in mind, but it is more informative than bank robbery.

In the widespread case of civil conflict, the dependence of *jus in bello* on the origins and causes of war and the culpability of combatants appear counter-productive in minimizing the ills of war. National and international forewarnings about the illegality of one party and authoritative notice, alerting potential participants about their future culpability, do nothing to advance these restrictive goals and possibly even defeat them.

Just war theorists debating interstate war have something to learn from this experience. The wholesale violence and destruction exhibited in civil conflicts indicates good moral reason for retaining the independence of *jus in bello* and the equality of combatants, at least where this already applies. Whether or not the laws governing civil war ought to resemble the laws of international armed conflict (LOIAC), it might be unwise to move in the opposite direction, that is, away from the independence-symmetry in the international sphere.

No doubt, at the deep moral level (at any moral level) it is objectively wrong to kill people without just cause. Not all moral philosophers regard just war theory as directly action-guiding, concentrating instead on the moral evaluation of war and its conduct. Nevertheless, theorists who contemplate the deep morality of war also recommend their theories in terms of their practical advantages. These theories must then also account for some superficial factors, such as hundreds of thousands of civilian deaths in Syria, and scrutinize their proposals in light of such experiences.

Ruthless regimes and unruly rebels who care little for their people are unlikely to adhere to any set of rules. Nevertheless, a moral code of interstate war must realistically consider incentives for complying with *jus in bello* rather than contriving counter-incentives. The moral rules of war, as well as its laws, ought to be devised with an eye on their application. If they are particularly unlikely to be obeyed in the absence of *in bello* independence and combatant equality, resulting in civilian slaughter, what use is a morality that suggests otherwise? Independence and symmetry may be essential to limiting war and preventing conflicts from dragging on interminably.[102]

One explanation for this is that *jus in bello* is internally structured to operate in an all-of-a-piece manner. Addressing international humanitarian law, Bugnion argues that "it is impossible to separate the rights from the obligations deriving from this body of law," as in conferring only obligations and no rights to combatants of the aggressor state.[103] Thus, emblems that protect medical facilities also protect their adversaries by assuring them that such facilities may not be used for hostile acts; the status of POW protects both sides, because it not only confers rights but also restricts the category of persons who can engage in hostilities while being entitled to claim this status if captured. Distinction protects soldiers as well as civilians, by warning civilians that they cannot take up arms without losing their immunity.[104]

Michael Walzer said as much back in *Just and Unjust Wars*: distinction by means of external insignia protects civilians but it is also a two-way street: "Soldiers must feel safe among civilians if civilians are ever to be safe from soldiers."[105] This is a central reason for denying irregulars the war rights of soldiers, because they do not abide by the rules that serve to maintain the safety of civilians. But it is also a reason for maintaining the equal rights of all lawful combatants, regardless of cause, because their compliance serves to protect civilians and restrict the horrors of war.

On this understanding, independence and symmetry are not merely simple incentives designed to enhance adherence to civilian immunity, but are in fact part and parcel of these immunities. The three basic tenets of just war theory— the independence of *jus in bello* from *jus ad bellum*, combatant equality, and non-combatant immunity—taken together operate as one coherent set of rules for protecting civilians in wartime. They may not be separable in the way that revisionist just war theorists envision. As Bugnion concludes, "The law of war consists of a set of balances between rights and obligations; if these balances are upset, what remains is not a unilateral application of the law but lawlessness and anarchy."[106]

The connection between asymmetry and anarchy within civil conflict is admittedly indeterminate. Nonetheless, it is a point to be noted by just war theorists before dispensing with the independence of *jus in bello* and combatant equality in the international sphere as well. The rights and immunities attached to the independence-symmetry thesis, omitted from the existing laws of civil conflict, may be entirely indispensable to guaranteeing non-combatant immunity and ought to be upheld, at least within international conflicts, partly for this reason. Absent the symmetrical immunity of all combatants from prosecution for the mere fact of participation, the entire framework of *jus in bello* appears to fall apart, as is most often the case in civil conflict. This is not easily remediable with regard to internal insurrections, but it ought not to be replicated in the international arena.

Notes

1. Jeff McMahan, *Killing in War*, (Oxford: Oxford University Press, 2009), 27–30, 108–110, 234; Jeff McMahan, "The Ethics of Killing in War," 114 (4) *Ethics* (2004), 693–733, 700, 725, 730. Cecile Fabre, *Cosmopolitan War* (Oxford: Oxford University Press, 2012), 74.
2. McMahan, *Killing in War*, ibid, 6–7, 192.
3. McMahan, ibid; Anthony Coates, "Is the Independent Application of *jus in bello* the Way to Limit War?" in David Rodin and Henry Shue (eds.), *Just and Unjust Warriors* (Oxford: Oxford University Press, 2008), 176–192, esp. 184–186; David Rodin, "The Moral Inequality of Soldiers: Why *jus in bello* Asymmetry is Half Right," in Rodin and Shue, *Just and Unjust Warriors*, 44–68; David Rodin, "Two Emerging Issues of Jus Post Bellum: War Termination and the Liability of Soldiers for Crimes of Aggression" in Carsten Stahn and Jann K. Kleffner (eds.) *Jus Post Bellum—Towards a Law of Transition From Conflict to Peace* (The Hague: Asser Press, 2008), Chapter 3, 53–76, esp. 62–76;
4. Stathis N. Kalyvas, "The Logic of Violence in Civil War: Theory and Preliminary Results," *Estudio*/Working Paper 2000/151 (June, 2000), 1–45: www.march.es/ceacs/publicaciones/working/archivos/2000_151.pdf. James D. Fearon and David D. Laitin, "Ethnicity, insurgency, and civil war," 97 (1) *American Political Science Review*, 75–90, 75. Fabre, *Cosmopolitan War*, 130–165, 130. Stephen P. Lee, *Ethics and War an Introduction* (New York: Cambridge University Press, 2012), 240–275, 240–241. Antonio Cassese, *The Human Dimension of International Law*, (New York: Oxford University Press, 2008), 112.
5. Noteworthy recent exceptions to this focus on international are: Fabre and Lee, ibid, on civil wars. On revolutionary wars and insurgencies, see: Allen Buchanan "The Ethics of Revolution and Its Implications for the Ethics of Intervention," 41 (4) *Philosophy and Public Affairs* (2013), 291–323 (also noting that "The recent flowering of just war theory has not yet explicitly extended its reach to revolutions . . .," Buchanan, 291); Michael L. Gross, *The Ethics of Insurgency—A Critical Guide to Just Guerrilla Warfare* (New York: Oxford University Press, 2015); Christopher J. Finlay, "Legitimacy and Non-State Actors," 18 *Journal of Political Philosophy* (2009), 287–312; Christopher J. Finlay, *Terrorism and the Right to Resist—A Theory of Just Revolutionary War* (Cambridge: Cambridge University Press, 2015).

6. Michael Walzer, *Just and Unjust Wars* (New York: Basic Books, 1977), 96–67, 143, 305, 345. Fabre, ibid, 131.

7. Fabre, ibid. Francois Bugnion, "*Jus ad Bellum, Jus in Bello* and Non-International Armed Conflicts", in *The YearBook of International Humanitarian Law* T.M.C Asser Press, Vol. VI (2003), 167–198. www.icrc.org/eng/assets/files/other/jus_ad_bellum,_jus_in_ bello_and_non-international_armed_conflictsang.pdf. pp. 1–43, 17.

8. Convention (III) relative to the Treatment of Prisoners of War. Geneva, August 12, 1949. Conflicts not of an international character; Article 3. www.icrc.org/ihl/Web ART/375-590006 Protocol Additional to the Geneva Conventions of August 12, 1949 and relating to the Protection of Victims of Non-International Armed Conflicts (Protocol II), June 8, 1977. www.icrc.org/ihl.nsf/7c4d08d9b287a421412567390 03e636b/d67c3971bcff1c10c125641e0052b545?OpenDocument

9. Bugnion, "*Jus ad Bellum, Jus in Bello* and Non-International Armed Conflicts", 1–43, p. 30.

10. Stathis N. Kalyvas, "Civil War," in *The Oxford handbook of Comparative Politics*, Carles Boix and Susan C. Stokes (eds.), (New York: Oxford University Press 2007), Chapter 18, 416–435, esp. 417–418; Stathis N. Kalyvas, *The Logic of Violence in Civil War* (Cambridge UK: Cambridge University Press, 2006), 17. Melvin Small, and J. David Singer, *Resort to Arms: International and Civil Wars 1816–1980.*" (Beverly Hills, CA: Sage Publications 1982), 210. Nicholas Sambanis "What Is Civil War? Conceptual and Empirical Complexities of an Operational Definition," 48 (6) *Journal of Conflict Resolution* (2004), 814–858, 816–821; Paul Collier, Lani Elliott, Håvard Hegre, Anke Hoeffler, Marta Reynal-Querol, Nicholas Sambanis, *Breaking the Conflict Trap: Civil War and Development Policy* (Oxford: Oxford University Press 2003), 11. James D. Fearon., and David D. Laitin, "Ethnicity, insurgency, and civil war," 97 (1) *American Political Science Review*, 75–90, 76. Anke Hoeffler, "On the causes of Civil War" in *The Oxford Handbook of Economics of Peace and Conflict* (Oxford Handbooks, 2012), 179–204. Sambanis suggests a threshold of 500–1000; Fabre, 135, places it at 500.

11. E.g. Fabre, 134–135.

12. Fabre, 132–133.

13. Kalyvas, "Civil War," 419; Hoeffler, "On the causes of Civil War," 179–204; Fabre, 135–136.

14. Fearon, and Laitin, 78; Lee, 241, 243–244.

15. Collier in: *Breaking the Conflict Trap* (2003), 4.

16. Ibid, 4, 53–78.

17. Paul Collier and Anke Hoeffler, "Greed and Grievance in Civil War," 56 *Oxford Economic Papers* (2004), 563–595; Fabre, 135; Leif Wenar, "property Rights and the Resource Curse," 36 (1) *Philosophy and Public Affairs*, 2–32.

18. Fearon and Laitin, 75.

19. Ibid, 78–88.

20. Ibid.

21. Kalyvas, *Civil War*, Chap. 18, 426.

22. Hoeffler, "On the causes of Civil War," 24; Fabre 136.

23. Ibid.

24. Fabre, 135, 157; Collier et al. *Breaking the Conflict Trap* (2003), 11; Kalyvas, *The Logic of Violence in Civil War*, 18.

25. Collier and Hoeffler, "Greed and Grievance" 563–595. Patrick M. Regan, "Third-Party Interventions and the Duration of Intrastate Conflicts" 46 (1) *Journal of Conflict Resolution* (2002), 55–73.

26. Kalyvas, *The Logic of Violence in Civil War*, 54.

27. Collier et al. *Breaking the Conflict Trap*, 11; Roy Licklider, "The Consequences of Negotiated Settlements in Civil Wars, 1945–1993," 89 (3) *American Political Science Review* (1995), 681–687.

28. Mason, T. David, and Patrick J. Fett, "How Civil Wars End: A Rational Choice Approach" 40 (4) *Journal of Conflict Resolution* (1996), 546–568; Barbara F. Walter, "The

Critical Barrier to Civil War Settlement," 51 (3) *International Organization* (1997), 335–364; Errol A. Henderson and J. David Singer, "Civil War in the Post-Colonial World, 1946–1992," 37 (3) *Journal of Peace Research* (2000), 275–299; Kalyvas, *The Logic of Violence in Civil War*; Fearon and Laitin, "Ethnicity, Insurgency, and Civil War," 75–90; Collier and Hoeffler, 563–595; Lacina, Bethany, "Explaining the Severity of Civil Wars." 50 (2) *Journal of Conflict Resolution* (2006), 276–289.

29. James D. Fearon, "Why Do Some Civil Wars Last So Much Longer Than Others?" 41 (3) *Journal of Peace Research* (2004), 298; Lee, 258–259. On lack of traditional battlefield: Kalyvas, *The Logic of Violence in Civil War*, 83.

30. Kalyvas, "Civil War," 427.

31. Collier et al., *Breaking the Conflict Trap*, 11.

32. Lee, 258–265.

33. Buchanan, "The Ethics of Revolution," 291–323, 296 and throughout 296–314.

34. Paul Gilbert, "Civilian Immunity in the 'new wars'," in Igor Primoratz *Civilian Immunity in War* (Oxford: Oxford University Press, 2007) 201–216, 205.

35. Collier et al., *Breaking the Conflict Trap* (2003), 11, 12–32; Fabre, 157.

36. For a discussion of the responsibilities of insurgents and soldiers who fight among civilians, See: Michael Walzer, "Coda: Can the Good Guys Win?," 24 (1) *The European Journal of International Law* (2013), 433–444.

37. Emerich de Vattel, *The Law of Nations or Principles of Natural Law Applied to the Conduct and Affairs of Nations and Sovereigns* (1758), Book III, Chapter 18, "Of Civil War," Par. 287. www.lonang.com/exlibris/vattel/vatt-318.htm

38. Fabre, 159–160, suggests conversely that the war's potential beneficiaries are possibly more liable to be killed collaterally than foreign civilians "precisely because the former civilians are meant to benefit from the war in a way that the latter are not. Far from tightening constraints on the resort to war, the special relationship might well loosen them."

39. Buchanan, "The Ethics of Revolution," 291–323, 293–303. Both Buchanan and Gross, *The Ethics of Insurgency*, argue that just insurgents or revolutionaries fighting oppressive regimes will have to bend the rules *in bello* in order to have a fighting chance of winning, or satisfying the *ad bellum* reasonable chance of success condition. Buchanan argues that especially where the just cause for revolution is clearest, revolutionaries will be under stronger pressures to engage in wrongful behavior. Nevertheless, he does not propose relaxing *jus in bello* in the case of revolutionary war. By contrast, all throughout his *Ethics of Insurgency* Gross suggests that the laws of armed conflict ought to be adjusted more extensively, and interpreted more liberally, in order to accommodate just insurgents, enabling them to fight legally. My limited point here is that any mixture of *jus in bello* with *jus ad bellum* will further reduce protection to civilians, as is already the case in civil wars, and ought not to be emulated in the laws of international armed conflict.

40. See the descriptions of "intimate violence" in Kalyvas, *The Logic of Violence in Civil War*, 330–331, 333.

41. Collier et al., *Breaking the Conflict Trap*, 11.

42. Bugnion, 30.

43. Leslie C. Green, *The Contemporary Law of Armed Conflict* (Manchester: Juris Publishing, Manchester University Press, Third Edition, 2008), 72–73. Anthony Cullen, *The Concept of Non-International Armed Conflict in International Humanitarian Law* (Cambridge: Cambridge Studies in International and Comparative Law, Cambridge University Press, 2010), 25.

44. Green, ibid, 346. Cullen, ibid, 29–51, esp. 49–50.

45. Cullen, ibid, 86; Bugnion, 23; Cassese, 117.

46. Bugnion, 20–26, 31.

47. Cullen, 59–60; Cassese, 117.

48. Convention (III) Article 3(1)(a). Green, 73, 346–347.

49. Ibid, Article 3(1)(b) (c)

50. Ibid, 3(1) (d). Green, 347; Bugnion, 25.
51. Ibid, 3 (2).
52. Article 3, ibid.
53. Ibid. See also Cullen, 55–56; Bugnion, 33.
54. Green, 347.
55. Bugnion, 24–29 (esp. 24–25), 39.
56. Cullen, 56.
57. Cullen, 58.
58. Bugnion, 25–26, 29.
59. Protocol II, Article 1. Cullen, 86–87. Bugnion 26–27.
60. Cullen, 57–61.
61. Protocol II, Article 1(1); Cullen, 102–107.
62. Ibid, Article 1(2). Cullen, 102–112, esp. 111; Akande, 54; Green, 348–349.
63. Cullen, ibid.
64. Green, 348.
65. Cassese, 124.
66. Protocol II, Articles 4–12; Cullen, 87; Green, 351.
67. Protocol II, ibid, Articles 13–17.
68. Ibid, Article 18; Cassese, 123.
69. Ibid, Articles 6(2) & 6(3). See also Bugnion, 28; Green, *The Contemporary Law of Armed Conflict*, 357.
70. Ibid, Article 6(4).
71. Ibid, Article 6(5).
72. Cassese, 122–123.
73. Bugnion, 27–29, 27.
74. Bugnion, ibid, 29.
75. Bugnion, 29.
76. McMahan, *Killing in War*, 108–110, 234. Conversely, several of his proposals suggest practical legal application, e.g. pp. 31, 153–154.
77. McMahan, ibid, 6.
78. Ibid, 6–7.
79. Ibid.
80. Ibid, 189–192, 192.
81. Ibid, 190–191. See also Fabre, *Cosmopolitan War*, 74–75.
82. McMahan, Ibid, 192.
83. Ibid, 153–154, 190–192; McMahan, "The Morality of War and the Law of War," 19–43; 41–43.
84. McMahan, *Killing in War*, 192.
85. Ibid.
86. Rodin, "The Moral Inequality of Soldiers," 44–68, 45, 46, 53. Rodin, "Two Emerging Issues of Jus Post Bellum," 68–76.
87. Rodin, "The Moral Inequality of Soldiers," 63–64.
88. Rodin, ibid, 61; "Two Emerging Issues," 74.
89. Ibid.
90. Rodin, "The Moral Inequality of Soldiers," 61.
91. Rodin, ibid, 63; Rodin, "Two Emerging Issues," 74–75.
92. McMahan, "The Morality of War and the Law of War," 19–43, 30; Rodin, ibid, 62; Rodin "Two Emerging Issues," 74.
93. Rodin, "The Moral Inequality of Soldiers," 62.
94. Rodin, ibid, 61.
95. Coates, 177–188, 182–186, and throughout.
96. Coates, 182–186.
97. Coates, 184–186.
98. Coates, 185.
99. Coates, 186; Shue and Rodin, 17.

100. Ibid.
101. Walzer, *Just and Unjust Wars*, 179–181; and: Walzer, "Coda: Can the Good Guys Win?," esp. 436–437.
102. The classic argument favoring conventional independence of *in bello* from *ad bellum* justice in international conflicts is best stated by Walzer: any relaxation of the rules *in bello* based on justice of cause would be claimed by both sides. Consequently, "There will not be any rules at all unless they apply in the same way to both sides." (Walzer, *Can the Good Guys Win*, 439). In the remainder of this section I pursue a different, additional, argument towards the same conclusion.
103. Francois Bugnion "Just War, Wars of Aggression and International Humanitarian Law" 847 (84) *The International Review of the Red Cross*, pp. 523–546. www.icrc.org/eng/assets/files/other/irrc-847-2002-bugnion-ang.pdf, pp. 1–26, 16.
104. Ibid.
105. Walzer, *Just and Unjust Wars*, 182.
106. Bugnion, "Just War", 16–17. See also Walzer, "Can the Good Guys Win," 439.

PART II

Just war theory in practice

The preceding discussion of civil conflict and its suggested implications completes the first part of this book and its particular defense of the three interrelated tenets of traditional just war theory and international law. With a renewed defense of the traditional rules in hand, Part II moves on from the case of internal strife to consider further issues of contemporary belligerency and military measures, to wit: proportionality, sieges and sanctions, preventive and preemptive military action, targeted killing, and assassination.

4
PROPORTIONALITY AND RISK

Despite criticism from revisionist circles considered in the last three chapters, the laws and customs of war remain firmly divided into the two categories tradition-ally viewed as distinct: *jus ad bellum* governs the initial resort to war, while *jus in bello* regulates its conduct. Following just war theory, the laws of international armed conflict (LOIAC) assume traditional *jus in* bello neutrality, applying equally to both parties independently of their respective causes.[1] In Michael Walzer's words: "War is always judged twice, first with reference to the reasons states have for fighting, secondly with reference to the means they adopt."[2]

In keeping with this traditional independence-symmetry thesis, traditional just war theory also "contains two proportionality conditions that say that a war or an act in war is justified only if the damage it causes is not excessive" in relation to its benefit.[3] The first requires that the initial resort to war be a proportionate, non-excessive, response to the harm it purports to combat. The second applies to specific tactics resorted to within an ongoing conflict, and requires that the harm they cause to civilians remain proportionate in relation to their military goal.[4] Only the second, *in bello*, proportionality rule has been clearly incorporated into international legal documents.

The following two sections consider each of these standards separately, in both their moral and legal contexts, setting out the general terms for discussion and disagreement. Accusations of "disproportion" have been leveled against the conduct of armed forces in various conflicts, most recently against Israel's various incursions into Gaza since 2008. With this and similar conflicts in mind, the discussion of *in bello* proportionality considers the effect that contemporary battleground conditions —fighting terrorists in the midst of civilians—may have on our judgments about disproportionality and the use of excessive force.

The proportionality requirement *in bello* places military organizations and their soldiers under a duty to minimize harm to civilians.[5] Discharging this duty will invariably involve incurring some costs. Do these costs include placing soldiers at risk of life and limb in order to spare civilian lives on the enemy side? Walzer tells us that they do.[6] The penultimate section of this chapter considers whether soldiers are required to assume avoidable risks in order to minimize harm to civilians, and the publicized debates which surrounded it following the 2008–2009 Gaza conflict. The final section concludes these various issues and discusses the difficulties in reducing civilian casualties within "the war on terror."

Ad bellum proportionality

Just war theory—ad bellum restraints

War must have a just cause. It must also be necessary and a "last resort," in relation to other acceptable means towards achieving its benefits, such as diplomacy. Once other options have been reasonably exhausted, war must be declared by a legitimate authority and fought for the right intentions (those embedded in the war's just cause). And it must not be futile—it must have some chance of achieving its goals, or else its losses would be senseless and unjustifiable. Finally, the various just war traditions include an *ad bellum* proportionality condition requiring that the destructiveness of war must not be excessive in relation to the relevant good the war will achieve.[7]

As Thomas Hurka explains, *ad bellum* proportionality requires balancing the good that the war is designed to bring about, as against the harms it is intended to avert.[8] This was Francisco de Vitoria's understanding and it is echoed in countless contemporary discussions of proportionality.[9] It involves weighing the costs and benefits of war as a whole, though how exactly these are to be estimated or compared remains very vague.[10]

What seems clear is that proportionality *ad bellum* is inevitably tied to just cause: an aggressive war cannot have any relevant benefits to balance against the harms it inflicts. Only a war fought for a good reason, namely wars of self-defense, can pass the *ad bellum* proportionality test.[11] Whether this is also true of *in bello* proportionality presents a further controversy, considered in the following section.

When wars are fought for the right reasons, the benefits side of the proportionality calculus includes their initial just cause—typically resisting aggression. Just war theory also acknowledges several legitimate "conditional" goals that the military is entitled to pursue, such as disarming a threatening enemy and deterring further aggression. These goals are conditional in that they would not in themselves justify the resort to war. Nonetheless, Hurka asserts that when they accompany an initially sufficient just cause for war, specifically self-defense, these additional goals also count as potential benefits that weigh against the harms of the war and contribute to its proportionality.[12]

The ills of war, on the other side of the balance, are not difficult to comprehend —death and destruction, usually on a devastating scale. Determining all the relevant evils and their precise weighting in the overall proportionality calculus is, however, no simple matter. As for the balance between the goods and evils of any given war, Hurka concludes simply that "a conventional war fought to defend a nation's sovereignty against aggression is normally proportional . . . the relevant goods clearly outweigh the relevant evils."[13] This limited conclusion appears widely accepted, as wars undertaken sincerely in national self-defense rarely face charges of *ad bellum* disproportion.

Nevertheless, even this commonplace assumption has recently been contested from the perspective of revisionist just war theory, further obscuring the *ad bellum* proportionality requirement. Revisionist just war theorists question whether national self-defense necessary implies that one's war is proportionate. Arguing against national partiality, McMahan suggests that "just combatants may not defend the lives of just civilians by action that would kill an equal or even a slightly lesser number of innocent bystanders, such as neutral civilians or unjust civilians."[14] Relying on the distinction between doing and allowing, he argues controversially that an army may only prevent its own people from dying at the hands of the enemy if it can do so without actively, albeit unintentionally, killing more innocent people on the enemy side.[15]

Whatever the appropriate balance, it is clear that all these proportionality calculations are forward-looking, contributing even further to the indeterminacies of this criterion.[16] With regard to projected benefits, Stephen Lee points out that the criterion is not only vague, but also "easily manipulated to produce the desired results and it is subject to self-deceptive assessments."[17] States tend to overestimate the likelihood of their success, thus enhancing the projected benefits side of the proportionality calculus beyond the good they are sincerely likely to achieve. For one thing, "Usually, both sides to an armed conflict believe that they will win. But they cannot both be right."[18] Consequently, Lee argues, "the [*jus ad bellum*] proportionality criterion is not in practice a very useful rule."[19]

At the other end of the balance, calculating the harms that the war is intended to avert is also entirely future oriented, and therefore equally subject to manipulation and uncertainty. The destructiveness of a defensive war is not balanced against the level of aggression which has already occurred and to which the war is responding. Instead, prior acts of aggression are enlisted in proportionality arguments, when they are, primarily as indication of the enemy's further intent and potential capabilities. As Hurka points out, the appropriate balance is *not* between the anticipated destruction on the enemy side weighed against previous casualties; those lives are already lost. Instead we must consider the estimated number of lives that would have been lost had the war not been fought.[20] The relevant comparison at the *ad bellum* level is between the anticipated destruction on the enemy side as opposed to the number of civilians on our side who would be saved by the military strategy under consideration. "Proportionality is not measured by the number of civilians actually killed, but rather by the risk posed."[21]

Consider Israel's Second Lebanon war, as well as its recent incursions into Gaza, in terms of the just war requirement to balance the harm inflicted with the harms that the action is intended to avert. How would we measure these and what do we have to go on? As Walzer pointed out back in 2006: "Proportionality must be measured not only against what Hamas and Hezbollah have already done, but also against what they are (and what they say they are) trying to do."[22] At the start of Israel's Operation Cast Lead Walzer commented:

> Before the six months of cease fire (when the fire never ceased), Hamas had only primitive and home-made rockets that could hit nearby small towns in Israel. By the end of the six months, they had far more advanced rockets, no longer home-made, that can hit cities 30–40 kilometers away. Another six months of the same kind of cease fire, which is what many nations at the UN demanded, and Hamas would have rockets capable of hitting Tel-Aviv. And this is an organization explicitly committed to the destruction of Israel. How many civilian casualties are "not disproportionate to" the value of avoiding the rocketing of Tel-Aviv? How many civilian casualties would America's leaders think were "not disproportionate to" the value of avoiding the rocketing of New-York?[23]

As Walzer explains, put this way, the answer is likely to be too many.[24] Proportionality always requires an essentially inaccurate prediction of prospective scenarios and foreseeable (or unforeseeable) danger, and states are likely to err in their own favor and tolerate too much devastation on the enemy's side. The resort to war, and particularly its conduct, is limited by weightier restrictions, other than proportionality. *Ad bellum* proportionality is theoretically significant within the just war tradition, but it is largely inapplicable in practice to concrete cases,[25] and Walzer describes it as a relatively minor restriction on war.[26]

Ad bellum proportionality as a legal restraint

International law, like contemporary just war theory, recognizes self-defense and the resistance of armed aggression as the primary justification for war; it does not contain any precise *ad bellum* proportionality restriction. Article 51 of the UN Charter affirms the inherent right of any member state of the United Nations to defend itself against armed attacks.[27] There is no reference to proportionality as a limitation on the right to self-defense in either the UN Charter or in UN Security Council Resolutions, though it may be assumed that some very minor incidents fall beneath a reasonable understanding of "armed attack."[28]

Nonetheless, it is widely accepted as part of customary international law that self-defense must be not only necessary, but also proportionate.[29] As opposed to the terms of engagement which are the subject of International Humanitarian Law, *ad bellum* proportionality applies to the legitimacy of the forceful action as a whole, rather than its specific tactics.[30] It throws a wide net, rather than focusing narrowly on collateral damage to civilians, applying instead to the general overall level of devastation anticipated as a result of the proposed military action. This would include the harm of violating territorial integrity, damage to infrastructure, effects on third parties, and so on.[31]

Legally, the requirements of both necessity and *ad bellum* proportionality owe their genesis to the diplomatic correspondence between the USA and the UK in relation to *The Caroline incident* (1837) involving a preemptive attack by the British forces in Canada on a ship manned by Canadian rebels, planning an attack from the USA.[32] This exchange is not unanimously accepted as authoritative, and in any event applies largely to the requirement of necessity, more than it does to proportionality, and was articulated specifically in the context of preemptive action.[33] Since that time, however, the International Court of Justice (ICJ) has reaffirmed the requirements of necessity and proportionality as limitations on self-defense.[34]

The specific content of any legal *ad bellum* proportionality test nonetheless remains extremely vague and controversial, as it does within just war theory. The conventional legal understanding of the *ad bellum* proportionality requirement is that an attacked party is justified in halting and repelling the attack, restoring the *status quo* that prevailed prior to the attacks, rather than achieving any far reaching military goals beyond that. Self-defense should not be retaliatory or punitive and reprisals are generally agreed to be unlawful.[35]

The indeterminacies of this requirement far exceed its discernable limits. Clearly, proportionality does not require equivalence between the force of the attack, or attacks, and the force employed defensively in response. It "does not mean that the defending state is restricted to the same weapons or the same number of armed forces as the attacking state; nor is it necessarily limited to action on its own territory."[36] Proportionality neither requires the parties to a conflict to be equally matched in strength, nor that the military might they employ remain proportionate to their adversary's capabilities. There is nothing disproportionate in a strong power fighting against a smaller entity, or with a superpower combating terrorists. Proportionality is not a rule of "fair play" in the sense of leveling the playing field, or giving one's opponent a sporting chance. Proportionality is a measure in relation to the goal of halting or repelling attacks; but it is not a simple comparison between the extent of force employed by the defender and the attacker.[37]

International law does not require members of the United Nations to balance their survival, or that of their citizens, as against the evils of war.[38] It remains doubtful whether a legal charge of *ad bellum* disproportion could ever be leveled against a state engaged in defending itself. As Judith Gardam points out, in the "war on terror," states have assumed wide reaching strategies—both geographically and as regards the extent of devastation—claiming the right to strike out wherever the presence of their terrorist enemies are established or suspected. Faced with international terrorism that knows no boundaries, it is even more difficult to gauge the role of any *ad bellum* proportionality rule.[39]

To sum up: the relevant international legal documents do not contain any positive reference to proportionality as a limitation on self-defense in response to an armed attack. Nevertheless, such a restriction is recognized as part of customary international law. It is derived from the 1837 *Caroline Incident*, and reinforced more recently by several ICJ opinions. It is widely acknowledged that a military operation should not exceed the goal of restoring the *status quo* that predated the armed attack to which it is responding, though this does not tell us much about the legitimate extent of the response and leaves many indeterminacies regarding the lengths states may resort to in order to achieve their defensive goal.[40] In fact, judging proportionality in relation to successfully repelling attacks implies, perhaps problematically, that greater force that is more likely to achieve the war's ends in terms of thwarting aggression, is more proportionate than a milder alternative that is unlikely to succeed in securing the war's objective.

In bello proportionality

Just war theory

The most fundamental distinction governing conduct in war separates soldiers from civilians. More precisely, it distinguishes those who actively partake in combat from those who are not directly engaged in it. As we saw in Part I, traditional just war theory and international law regard all combatants as legitimate military targets, while civilians are not. Nonetheless, many civilians are inevitably killed in legitimate military operations.

The standard justification for incidental civilian fatalities appeals to the Doctrine of Double Effect according to which the stringency of the prohibition on killing non-combatants in wartime does not apply to unintended effects.[41] On this account, indirect consequences of war are tolerated, in so far as they are necessary and incurred only as a sincerely unintended by-product of an assault on a military target, and this target was aimed at narrowly in an attempt to avoid bad consequences. Finally, proportionality requires the selection of military tactics that do not cause excessive incidental harm to civilians in relation to the benefits they achieve.[42]

The proportionality standard in war limits collateral damage in relation to the military advantages of the operation that causes that harm. Thus, proportionality adds significantly to the requirement of distinction that applies to direct targeting, by further addressing and restricting incidental harm to civilians as well. It also tightens the requirement of necessity, by insisting that the price of any possible tactic in terms of civilian casualties must be not only necessary (the minimal force required) for achieving a given military target, but also non-excessive in relation to the advantage of achieving the target in question.

Consequently, proportionality may require forgoing a military target or tactic which passes the test of "necessity," if the cost to civilians is estimated to be disproportionate to the value of the military advantage anticipated from the action. In such cases in which the costs to civilians would be excessive in relation to the advantage of securing a particular military target, proportionality requires forgoing the specific target and taking a different route towards achieving the war aims and bringing the fighting to its conclusion.

This wartime restriction is significant, but also extremely specific. It is part and parcel of the *in bello* protection of civilian immunity, and as such applies only to the extent of civilian casualties. Necessity precludes wanton, unnecessary, killing of combatants as well as civilians. Neither necessity nor proportionality restricts the extent of military casualties as long as these are conducive to self-defense. Once the war has begun, there is no restriction on the number of enemy combatants one is allowed to attack, so long as there is any military advantage to doing so.[43]

To this limited extent, Hurka points out, just war theory parallels individual self-defense: if I am attacked by a gang of a hundred, I am permitted to kill any number of them in order to defend myself or save another. Proportionality does not require that I kill just one attacker in order to retain a 1:1 proportion, and then spare the remaining 99 aggressors who may proceed to kill me.[44] (In fact it would be entirely futile to kill only one of the attackers). Proportionality does not require the parties to a conflict to maintain a roughly equal casualty count. It does not mean symmetry, and applies only to civilians unengaged in hostilities.[45]

Finally, within traditional just war theory, the legitimate degree of civilian casualties, the proportionality of harm, is measured only in relation to estimated military advantage and not in relation to the war's overall justness. "Military advantage" is a term of comparison which applies neutrally to combatants on both the just and unjust side alike.[46] In keeping with its independence thesis—separating *jus ad bellum* from *jus in bello*—traditional just war theory does not judge the extent of collateral damage to civilians in relation to the overall justness of the war, or the moral significance of achieving its goals.

Neutrality and equal application reflect the difficulties in determining just cause as well as further considerations for *jus in bello* independence, discussed throughout the first part of this book. Contemporary criticisms of this traditional independence thesis naturally result in conflicting interpretations of the proportionality standard as well. Revisionist just war theorists argue that unjust wars, by definition, can never fulfill the *jus in bello* requirements of necessity and proportionality—any killing for an unjust cause will always be disproportionate. Unjust combatants cannot uphold standards of necessity and proportionality because their aggressive killing in war (of combatants as well as civilians) is entirely futile and detrimental.[47]

Hurka shares this moral view that (as a rule) only just combatants can carry out proportionate attacks. Like McMahan, he questions the moral validity of judging the bad consequence of harm to civilians as against military objectives without any reference to justness of cause.[48]

> The level of destruction permitted in a war against a genocidal enemy such as Nazi Germany is surely greater than in the Falklands war. But this claim contradicts the dominant view in the just war tradition, which treats the *ius in bello* as entirely independent of the *ius ad bellum*.[49]

Hurka continues:

> If "military advantage" justifies killing civilians, it does so only because of the further good such advantage will lead to, and how much it justifies depends

on what those good are . . . if we consider the morality of war rather than its legality, the independence of its two branches cannot be maintained.[50]

While this may be true at a deep moral level, on a more practical note both Hurka and McMahan concede some useful reasons for maintaining the traditional separation between just cause and *in bello* rules within the laws of armed conflict.[51] As Judith Gardam notes, "Any retreat from that position will result in the application of lower standards by states in pursuit of their objectives."[52] "The alternative approach might even lead to more destructive wars since, notoriously, often both sides in a conflict believe their cause is just."[53]

Traditional just war theory aims to supply a set of workable action guiding moral rules restraining the conduct of war. Consequently, despite its critics, mainstream just war theory as well as international law, maintains the separation between proportionality *in bello* and our judgment of the war itself: each side typically believes their cause to be just and of paramount importance, but this cannot excuse them from causing more incidental harm to civilians than absolutely necessary.[54] While the direct targeting of non-combatants is ruled out by the principle of discrimination, the twin requirements of necessity and proportionality further rule out reckless or excessive harm.

Necessity rules out purposeless or wanton violence. This, Walzer points out, is no small achievement, as negligent and unnecessary harm to civilians is a frequent occurrence in war even where civilians are not directly targeted.[55] Proportionality further precludes not only utterly useless, gratuitous harm to civilians, but also some unintended killing within a military advantageous tactic, if it is to incur civilian losses on a scale that would be grossly out of step with the military advantage anticipated. While this requirement is clearly non-negligible, it is again extremely indeterminate and context dependant.

For all these restrictions, civilians in wartime remain in grave danger. This is true even in the most conventional wars. So much more so within contemporary wars against irregulars, who deliberately place civilians in the front line, engage them as human shields and conduct fighting in their midst. Unconventional tactics do not in any way free the other side from its obligation to respect civilian immunity. Immoral and illegal conduct on the part of one's adversary cannot excuse adopting their tactics. However, while the requirement to spare civilians remains intact regardless of the enemy's violations, the battlefield conditions in which these principles operate may change dramatically.

When an army is forced to fight among civilians, attaining any military objectives will carry higher costs in terms of collateral damage. This change in battle conditions means, inevitably, that many more civilians will be harmed. Reducing civilian casualties will be far less feasible under these conditions, and a high death toll may be regrettably unavoidable in order to secure any military goals whatsoever. Judging proportionality in relation to military objectives suggests that this change in circumstances makes a difference to proportionality judgments. A given degree of harm to civilians that might be deemed excessive in one context—conventional warfare—might be regarded as permissible in a setting in which there is no feasible way of avoiding it while fighting to secure the military ends. At the same time, the requirement of proportionality also suggests, plausibly, that a higher degree of care and caution is required when fighting in civilian surroundings.

In bello proportionality as a legal restraint

As opposed to any *ad bellum* proportionality requirement, *in bello* proportionality is clearly a legal, as well as a moral, limitation. Protocol 1, added to the Geneva Conventions (1977), reaffirms and strengthens the traditional *jus in bello* requirements. Article 51 (5) (b) regards an attack as indiscriminate, and therefore prohibited, if, among other possibilities, it is "an attack which may be expected to cause incidental loss of civilian life, injury to civilians, damage to civilian objects, or a combination thereof, which would be excessive in relation to the concrete and direct military advantage anticipated."[56]

The same terminology, prohibiting measures "which would be excessive in relation to the concrete and direct military advantage anticipated" is reiterated in Article 57 of Protocol 1. Article 57 requires military planners and decision makers to refrain from attacks that would result in such excesses, and "to take all feasible precautions in the choice of means and methods of attack with a view to avoiding, and in any event to minimizing, incidental loss to civilian life, injury to civilians and damage to civilian objects."[57]

The legal restriction on excessive force and limitation of proportionality in war adopts the traditional separation between *jus ad bellum* and *jus in bello* and applies regardless of the justness of cause.[58] It prohibits extensive harm to civilians, including damage to civilian objects and their environment, in the course of operations that could be expected to accomplish only comparatively trivial military goals.[59] In this vein, Article 8 (2) (b) (iv) of the Rome Statute of the International Criminal Court brands as a war crime:

> . . . intentionally launching an attack in the knowledge that such attack will cause incidental loss of life or injury to civilians or damage to civilian objects or widespread, long-term and severe damage to the natural environment which would be clearly excessive in relation to the concrete and direct overall military advantage anticipated.[60]

With regard to the legal criteria, both Yoram Dinstein and David Luban note that the proportionality standard of the Rome Statute is manifestly weaker than the one required in Additional Protocol 1.[61] In order to be prosecutable as a war crime, an attack must be not only excessive, as in the Protocol 1 prohibition, but also "clearly excessive," and this is judged in relation to the "overall" military advantage anticipated, rather than in relation to the "concrete and direct" military advantage, as stipulated in protocol 1. This lowers the protection for civilians because the wider the category of benefits that may be weighed against the cost of harming civilians, the lower the protection for civilian interests.[62]

Nevertheless, Luban continues, these discrepancies between Protocol 1 and the Rome Statute should not be read as a lowering of the standard of rightful conduct required of military organizations under the laws of war. Instead, they represent the difference between defining the rightful standard as opposed to a criminal offence: "The drafters apparently thought that fairness to the accused requires a less stringent standard. It follows, however, that the Rome Statute's standard should not be taken to represent the standard of rightful conduct."[63]

The criteria in both documents remain forward looking, referring to *expected* injury to civilians, and *anticipated* military advantage.[64] The Rome Statute prohibits launching an attack in *the knowledge* that such attack *will* cause clearly excessive harm.[65] Moreover, as in traditional just war theory, the legal requirement refers only to the extent of civilian casualties; not to the relation between the numbers of combatants killed on each side.[66] "Under the laws of war, any number of combatants can be killed to prevent the killing of even one innocent civilian."[67] As Walzer put this recently, proportionality is not the idea of "tit for tat."[68]

Risk-taking

What precautions are armies required to take in order to avoid excessive civilian casualties? Most notably, do these include placing soldiers at greater risks in order to minimize harm to enemy civilians, and, if so, to what extent? International humanitarian law does not address, let alone settle, this issue directly.[69] It has been debated by political theorists in the abstract, as well as with reference to various historical examples and concrete scenarios.[70]

Walzer first raised this question in *Just and Unjust Wars* with examples from World War I and the Korean War. He states there that armies must not only attempt to spare civilians, but they also must take "due care" in order to minimize the dangers they impose on civilians and avoid extensive collateral damage. "And if saving civilians' lives means risking soldiers' lives, the risk must be accepted."[71]

Later discussions shifted to the Gulf, Kosovo, and Iraq wars. In some cases, placing soldiers at risk to spare civilians involves a choice between alternative flight altitudes; in others it concerns carefully pursuing combatants among civilians. The wider issue at stake here, as Luban describes it, is the choice between close versus distant engagement, or between force-protection versus the protection of enemy civilians.[72] Dilemmas of this kind are obviously most pronounced when fighting takes place in residential areas, and have been most recently debated worldwide in connection with the conduct of the IDF in the Gaza Strip.

Not everyone accepts Walzer's view, particularly within the military, arguing instead that a state's priority is to protect its own citizens—soldiers and civilians alike—and have no call to require their soldiers to risk their lives further in order to protect an enemy population.[73] Such arguments, however intuitive, are none-theless off the mark as they entirely misconstrue the issue at hand. No one calls for soldiers to risk their lives in order to protect enemy civilians from external violence, as they are required to do for their own population. "Due care," as Walzer describes it, requires soldiers to minimize the dangers they themselves impose.[74] Luban explains this in terms of special versus universal obligations. Soldiers have a special obligation to protect their own people from enemy violence, while the issue in hand is the responsibility to protect the innocent from violence of one's own making, which is a universal obligation.[75]

A stronger way of putting this, as McMahan has recently, rephrases the requirements in terms of the distinction between killing and letting die, or, more generally, between doing and allowing. Soldiers have a special positive obligation to protect their own civilians from enemy fire. They are under a negative duty to refrain from killing enemy civilians. Properly understood, taking "due care" requires soldiers to assume some risk rather than actively (albeit unintentionally) killing more enemy civilians. This negative obligation to refrain from killing, McMahan continues, is stronger than the positive obligation to protect from harm, even when this harm is described, as it is by Walzer, as harm of our own making.[76]

Prioritizing the welfare of civilians, requiring soldiers to take some risks on their behalf, is consistent with just war theory on both its central accounts, traditional and revisionist. Traditionalists prioritize the wellbeing of civilians regardless of their collective's cause for war or individual responsibility. Revisionists cannot accept this, but they do agree on some further reasons for requiring soldiers to take risks in order to spare civilians. Risk taking is part of a soldier's professional role, part of the vocational core of soldiering, just as it is for policemen, bodyguards, firefighters or lifeguards.[77]

Hurka holds the middle ground between prioritizing soldiers and prioritizing the well-being of civilians. On the one hand, he acknowledges, the soldiers in questions are *our* soldiers. On the other, they are legitimate military targets and their deaths are to be expected, as civilians' deaths are not. Neither national partiality nor civilian immunity, he argues, clearly tips the balance, concluding intuitively that we ought to consider the lives of our soldiers and enemy civilians as carrying approximately equal weight.

This balance would require maintaining a roughly 1:1 proportion between the number of enemy-civilians killed collaterally and the estimated number of soldiers *who would have been killed* had an alternative, more risky, tactic been adopted. It suggests that a civilian should not be required to lose his life "collaterally" in order to save less than one of our soldiers. Hurka's standard is not intended to be mathematically precise, but it does "imply that any act that kills significantly more civilians than it saves soldiers is morally impermissible," and that a tactic that kills many enemy civilians rather than sacrifice a few soldiers would normally count as disproportionate.[78]

How much extra risk, to themselves and their mission, are soldiers actually required to assume on these accounts in order to minimize harm to civilians? None of the theorists debating this issue supplies a precise answer. According to Lee, "The answer depends on the importance of the military objective, the urgency of the attack, the military costs of the alternatives, and the degree to which the alternative would lessen civilian risk."[79] While neither national partiality nor operational considerations can excuse negligence towards enemy civilians, an army's responsibility towards its own soldiers must also be recognized alongside its military goals.

Walzer readily acknowledges that "there is a limit to the risks that we require. There are, after all, unintended deaths and legitimate military operations, and the absolute rule against attacking civilians does not apply."[80] While commanders must value the lives of civilians and may not protect their soldiers at the wholesale expense of the enemy population, "No one would want to be commanded in wartime by an officer who did not value the lives of his soldiers."[81] More recently he concedes: "They don't have to take suicidal risks, certainly."[82]

In an article co-authored with Avishai Margalit, following the 2009 Gaza conflict, Walzer reaffirms his requirement of "due care" for civilians on all sides and the priority he attributes to their welfare. Any alternative doctrine, the authors pointed out, would totally erode the most basic *jus in bello* distinction between combatants and civilians. We must require *our* soldiers to take risks in order to spare *their* civilians.[83] Restating Walzer's earlier account, they emphasize that not intending civilian deaths, while knowing they will occur, is not enough. Soldiers "must *intend not* to kill civilians, and that active intention can be made manifest only through the risks the soldiers themselves accept in order to reduce the risks to civilians."[84]

While Walzer and Margalit admit they cannot delineate the extent of required risk taking with any precision, they do supply a very helpful set of analogies as an instructive guideline, particularly for the benefit of Walzer's Israeli critics: assume counterfactually that Hezbollah had captured kibbutz Manara in northern Israel, taking effective control of the area and holding all kibbutz members hostage as Hezbollah fought Israel from within the kibbutz, using its members as human shields. The authors then argue that "Whatever Israel deems acceptable as 'collateral damage' when its own captured citizens are at risk—that should be the moral limit in the other cases too."[85] And they conclude with a slightly, though significantly, different formulation: "Conduct your war in the presence of non-combatants on the other side with the same care as *if* your citizens were the non-combatants."[86]

Taken literally, this second formulation is over demanding if it is understood as requiring soldiers to assume heroic risks for the sake of enemy civilians, as they might do if the surrounding civilians were their own.[87] Luban explains more plausibly that the requirement of due care excludes any supererogatory risks soldiers may take in order to save their own civilians. Instead, it requires only that soldiers assume the degree of risk for the protection of enemy civilians that they would consider adequately up to standard if the endangered civilians were their own compatriots.[88]

Luban goes further than anyone in fleshing out the implications of the Walzer-Margalit requirement.[89] While they do not require heroic risks, Luban explains, Walzer and Margalit indicate that soldiers should not offload large risks onto civilians in order to spare themselves far smaller risks. So, for example, Luban concedes that running a fifty-fifty chance of death or injury is too much to ask of a soldier. "A five percent chance of death or injury, while surely significant, may not be too much to ask of a soldier if it saves innocent civilians whose peril under Distant Engagement is dire."[90] This, he suggests, will almost always preclude entirely distant engagement, or zero-tolerance warfare: "A state's army, dedicated to the protection of its own civilians, would not obliterate entire 'friendly' buildings containing co-nationals from a distance in order to safeguard its soldiers," and so it should not do so when enemy-civilians are in the buildings either.[91] This standard is not overly onerous and mostly affirms and applies the basic requirement of distinction.[92]

It is however noteworthy that the practical implications of Walzer and Margalit's instructive scenario are somewhat obscured by their further observation that the risks imposed on soldiers are neither suicidal, nor do they have to take risks that render their mission impossibly difficult.[93] Armies are not required to forgo their cause, or surrender their military objectives on the grounds that the fighting will cause harm to civilians. On the contrary, the latter stands in relation to the mission's anticipated success and its military significance.

In their example, once Walzer and Margalit concede that Israeli soldiers "don't have to take risks that make the recapture of Manara impossibly difficult," it is entirely predictable that the collateral damage to civilians is going to be staggeringly high, even if they are our own civilians. Most military operations which involve civilian hostages and shields are not "Entebbe-like" in their outcome, not even when carried out by the legendary IDF. If Manara is to be recaptured, as Walzer and Margalit's example assumes that it must be, only a miracle would prevent large scale civilian casualties, no matter how high the degree of risk assumed by our soldiers, and regardless of the nationality of the surrounding hostages.

Concluding remarks: proportionality in combating terror

Assessing proportionality is one of the most difficult exercises of modern warfare. Its calculations—*ad bellum* and *in bello*—are vague and abstract, lending themselves to considerable uncertainties in concrete situations. Thinking about any of these issues mathematically is hard and harsh. There is always the sense in which one burned child is an unspeakable tragedy, disproportionate in relation to any objective whatsoever. But this is not the understanding of "disproportion" employed within just war theory or adopted by international law.

As a moral standard, *proportionality ad bellum* requires very generally that a war, on the whole, should not cause more harm than good. As a legal principle, it precludes overstepping ones legitimate war aims. In both cases, proportionality *ad bellum* is inevitably tied to just cause. As such, it is plagued with all the indeterminacies surrounding *jus ad bellum* more generally.

Revisionist just war theorists insist that proportionality *in bello* is also dependent on just cause. No harm in war can be morally proportionate unless it is outweighed by morally good results, and the extent of legitimate harm depends on the urgency of attaining these good results. This is clearly inapplicable as an action guiding principle in war, in which just cause is the very issue of contention with each party claiming justice on their side.

Traditional just war theory and international law adopt a practical approach, symmetrically applicable to all parties: the *jus in bello* principle of proportionality compares civilian casualties to the military benefits one expects to gain by launching an attack. Whatever the cause, however just or urgent it is perceived to be, the military must not be negligent with the lives of civilians. Distinction prohibits the direct targeting of non-combatants. Necessity precludes wanton, gratuitous, harm. Proportionality tightens the protection of civilians by specifying that any collateral damage must be not only necessary, but also non-excessive in relation to the military goal to which it contributes. Some targets must be forgone altogether if securing them would inflict disproportionate collateral harm in relation to the military advantage anticipated.

This restraint applies only to civilians. The deaths of combatants do not count negatively in proportionality calculations. Combatants are legitimate targets and, subject to necessity, any number of them may be killed in war. Moreover, killing combatants is a military advantage and weighs on the positive side of the balance. Even where civilians are concerned, proportionality does not compare the number of casualties on each side.[94] This is a common mistake. Equal numbers of casualties are not necessarily more proportionate than a lopsided outcome. Relative casualties are often a function of war-fighting capability, technology, and troop numbers.

When is harm to civilians clearly disproportionate or excessive? Except in the most obvious cases (wiping out a village to kill a soldier on leave is the exemplar the Red Cross uses),[95] this question is difficult to answer absent any neat algorithm to weigh innocent lives against military gains. One may therefore try to compare the number of enemy civilians killed to the number of compatriots saved by a military action. Or, one may try to quantify military benefits in terms of reducing enemy capabilities or establishing deterrence. Regardless, proportionality is an extremely elastic concept that allows field commanders almost unlimited leeway when determining whether civilian casualties are excessive.[96]

Proportionality requires military planners to balance benefits and harms that have not yet occurred and are ultimately subject to the fortunes of war. This is an entirely prospective project, based on imprecise and uncertain predictions and estimates, leaving ample room for human error, self-deception and manipulation. For all these reasons, Walzer tells us, there are far more important questions to ask:

> [W]ho is responsible for putting civilians in the line of fire? . . . Is the attacking army acting in concrete ways to minimize the risks they impose on civilians? Are they taking risks themselves for that purpose? Armies choose tactics that are more or less protective of the civilian population, and we judge them by their choices?[97]

These judgments cannot be made in the abstract. Civilian casualties have risen dramatically within "the war on terror" in which irregular combatants habitually position themselves among civilians. Terrorists create intolerable battle situations intentionally designed to render the separation between non-combatants and military targets excruciatingly difficult to maintain. Considering allegations of disproportion against Israel in Gaza, Moshe Halbertal helpfully suggests that "One way to think about this is to compare it with what other civilized armies achieve in the same type of warfare."[98] No matter the level of adherence on the part of the army, the extent of collateral damage is far greater worldwide when combating irregular militants, who fight among civilians, defy the principle of distinction, masquerade as non-combatants, and hide behind human shields, than it was in the trenches of WWI.[99]

Where combatants fight without uniform and civilians engage in hostilities, even counting casualties is fraught with ambiguity.[100] Police, for example, are an interesting category within the Laws of Armed Conflict. Whether members of law-enforcement agencies may be subsumed in the course of war under the heading of members of armed forces, and therefore be considered legitimate targets for attack, depends on whether the armed law enforcement agency has been officially incorporated into the armed forces, or is otherwise involved in hostilities.[101]

During the 2008–2009 Gaza conflict, Israel argued that Hamas police served as an auxiliary army unit and consequently that its members were legitimate military objectives.[102] Critics regarded Israel's attack on Hamas policemen as indiscriminate, counting these casualties as civilian and adding their deaths to the negative side of the proportionality equation. If Israel's claims were accurate, targeting Hamas policemen was not only permissible but also counts on the benefits side of the proportionality calculus as the achievement of a legitimate military goal. As Michael Gross points out, "Obviously, this makes a huge difference when assessing proportionality . . . the dispute turns on *affiliation*. Who, exactly, counts as a civilian or combatant?"[103]

Armies launching attacks must take all feasible measures to distinguish between militants and civilians, and minimize harm to the latter. Soldiers must actively intend not to kill civilians and are both legally and morally required to take active measures to this effect. But armies must also look out for their soldiers, and they must employ measures sufficiently powerful to secure their military goals, or else they render their war futile and all its casualties redundant.

The feasibility of preventing civilian casualties is considerably reduced when confronting irregular militants who blur the combatant–civilian distinction. This is not to say that terrorists shoulder the sole responsibility for the welfare of their civilians.[104] Regardless of any violations on the part of the enemy, armies, and their soldiers, must still actively try, and preferably be seen to try, to minimize civilian casualties, even at the cost of assuming additional risks to themselves. Some armies try harder than others. Perhaps no army tries hard enough. In the realities of modern warfare, however, try as they may they are often destined to fail.

The following chapters offer further opportunity to consider both collateral and direct harm to civilians caught up in international conflicts. They also revisit the wartime requirements of necessity and proportionality outlined in this chapter, in several concrete cases: besieged cities, nuclear threats, and direct targeting.

Notes

1. The Preamble to Additional Protocol I states that its provision apply "without any adverse distinction based on the nature or origin of the causes espoused or attributed to the Parties to the conflict." Protocol Additional to the Geneva Conventions of 12 August 1949, and relating to the Protection of Victims of International Armed Conflicts (Protocol 1) 1977. www.icrc.org/ihl.nsf/full/470?opendocument
2. Michael Walzer, *Just and Unjust Wars* (New York: Basic Books, 1977), 21. See also, 127.
3. Thomas Hurke, "Proportionality in the Morality of War," 33 (1) *Philosophy & Public Affairs* (2005), 34–66, 35.
4. Hurka, "Proportionality in the Morality of War," ibid, 34–66, 36–38.
5. Protocol 1, Article 57 (2) (ii).
6. Walzer, *Just and Unjust Wars*, 151–6. Michael Walzer and Avishai Margalit: "Israel: Civilians & Combatants," 56 (8) *The New York Review of Books*, May 14, 2009. Michael Walzer, "On Proportionality," *Dissent*, January 8, 2009. www.dissentmagazine.org/online.php?id=191
7. Hurka, "Proportionality in the Morality of War," 35.
8. Hurka, ibid, 38–66, 38.
9. Stephen P. Lee, *Ethics and War an Introduction* (New York: Cambridge University Press, 2012), 85–86, cites Vitoria's understanding of *(in bello)* proportionality as "the obligation to see that greater evils do not arise out of the war than the war would avert." Francisco de Vitoria, "On the Law of War," in Anthony Pagden and Jeremy Lawrence (eds.), *Political Writings* (Cambridge: Cambridge University Press), esp. 303–8; 315. See also, Jeff McMahan, *Killing in War* (Oxford: Oxford University Press, 2008, 18. And: Asa Kasher, "Operation Cast Lead and the Ethics of Just War," *AZURE*, No. 37 (Summer 5769/2009), 43–75, 53 who describes the balance in very similar terms, referring to it as "Macro-Proportionality." www.azure.org.il/article.php?id=502&page=all. David Rodin, *War and Self-Defense* (Oxford: Oxford University Press, 2003), 114.
10. John Forge, "Proportionality, Just War Theory and Weapons Innovation," 15 *Sci Eng. Ethics* (2009): 25–38, 26, 28. Lee, 214, 85–93.
11. Lee, 214.
12. The distinction between "sufficient" and "contributing" just causes is drawn by: Jeff McMahan and Robert Mckin, "The Just War and the Gulf War," 23 *Canadian Journal of Philosophy* (1993): 501–41, 512–3. Cited in Hurka: "Proportionality in the Morality of War," 41. On indirect intentions and legitimate side effects such as deterrence, see also Kasher, "Operation Cast Lead and the Ethics of Just War," pp. 43–75, 50–51.
13. Hurka, 51–66, 66.
14. Jeff McMahan, "The Just Distribution of Harm between Combatants and Noncombatants," 38 (4) *Philosophy and Public Affairs* (2010), 342–379, 377.
15. Ibid.
16. Michael Walzer, "On Proportionality," *Dissent*, January 8, 2009.
17. Lee, 92.
18. Lee, 92.
19. Ibid.
20. Hurka, "Proportionality in the Morality of War," 59; See also Kasher, "Operation Cast Lead and the Ethics of Just War," 52–53 (his discussion of "Macro-Proportionality").
21. Alan Dershowitz, "Israel's Policy is Perfectly Proportionate," in the Wall Street Journal, January 2, 2009. http://online.wsj.com/article/SB123085925621747981.html
22. Michael Walzer, "How Aggressive Should Israel Be?" *The New republic*, July 2006, 2.
23. Michael Walzer, "On Proportionality," *Dissent*, January 8, 2009.
24. Walzer, ibid.
25. Forge, "Proportionality, Just War Theory and Weapons Innovation." Lee, 92.
26. Walzer, "On Proportionality." See also Lee, 92.
27. See: Charter of the United Nations, Chapter VII, Article 51. www.un.org/en/documents/charter/chapter7.shtml

28. For example: Did the four rockets fired from Lebanon in the course of Israel's operation in Gaza constitute and armed attack justifying war on Lebanon? Or would opening a second front in that instance have constituted a disproportionate response? Certainly it would have been imprudent.

29. Christine Grey, *International Law and the Use of Force* (Third edition) (Oxford: Oxford University Press, 2008), 148–150, and his accompanying footnotes 147 and 150. Judith Gardam, "Proportionality and Force in International Law," 87 *American Journal of International Law* (1993), 391–413, 391; Judith Gardam, *Necessity, Proportionality, and the Use of Force by States* (New York: Cambridge University Press, 2004), 11–12. Judith Gardam, "A Role for Proportionality in the War on Terror," 74 *Nordic Journal of International Law* (2005), 3–25, 3–6. Alan Dershowitz, "Israel's Policy is Perfectly Proportionate." http://online.wsj.com/article/SB123085925621747981.html

30. Lee, 214.

31. Gardam, "A Role for Proportionality in the War on Terror," 5.

32. Grey, *International Law and the Use of Force*, 148–149. Gardam, "A Role for Proportionality," 3.

33. Grey, 149.

34. Grey, 149–150, with reference to: *Military and Para-Military Activities in and Against Nicaragua*, ICJ Reps. (1986), p. 14, Para 194; *Oil platforms Case* (Iran v. United States) ICJ Reps. (2003), p. 161, Para. 43; *Armed Activities on the Territory of the Congo* (Democratic Republic of Congo v. Uganda), ICJ Reps. (2005), p.168, Para. 147; *ICJ: The Legality of the Threat or Use of Nuclear Weapons*: ICJ Reps. (1996), p. 226. Para. 141, 143.

35. Gardam, "A Role for Proportionality," 7. Grey, 150–151.

36. Grey, 150.

37. Gardam, "A Role for Proportionality," 12–13.

38. Referring to a Hamas rocket which incurred no casualties as it directly hit an empty Israeli kindergarten in Beer-Sheba in December 2008, Alan Dershowitz commented that: "Under international law, Israel is not required to allow Hamas to play Russian roulette with its children's lives." (Dershowitz, "Israel's Policy is Perfectly Proportionate."). Proportionality does not require states to take wild chances with the lives of their citizens.

39. Gardam, "A Role for Proportionality," 16–17, 25.

40. Gardam, ibid, 13–24.

41. On Double Effect, see: Walzer, *Just and Unjust Wars*, 151–9; 257, 277, 280, 283, 317, 321.

42. Walzer, *Just and Unjust Wars*, 153–5.

43. Walzer, *Just and Unjust Wars*, 138–147; Hurka, "Proportionality in the Morality of War," 58; That this is the unanimous view within traditional JWT is conceded even by Jeff McMahan, *Killing in War*, pp. 18, 22–23, 29–30, who criticizes this view.

44. Hurka, "Proportionality in the Morality of War," 58.

45. Walzer, "On Proportionality."

46. Lee, 214.

47. Jeff McMahan, "The Ethics of Killing in War" 114 *Ethics* (2004), 693–733, at sec. V, 708–718. More recently: McMahan, *Killing in War*, pp. 18–32, esp. on pp. 24–32; McMahan, "The Just Distribution of Harm," 342–379, esp. 350–558, 351, 358. McMahan's extremely nuanced discussion of this issue allows for highly anomalous conditions in which unjust combatants might act proportionately: On McMahan's account, the only justified acts that unjust combatants can perform in the course of their unjust war are acts which respond to wrongful acts committed by the just side (e.g., if just combatants kill the innocent on the unjust side, then the unjust combatants are justified in responding, and their counter attacks in these rare cases can be proportionate).

48. Hurka, "Proportionality in the Morality of War," 44–45; Lee, 214.

49. Hurka, 44.

50. Hurka, 45 and his accompanying footnote 15.

51. McMahan, *Killing in War*, 30–31. Hurka, 45; Lee, 214–215. See also David Rodin, "The Moral Inequality of Soldiers: Why *jus in bello* Asymmetry is Half Right" in David Rodin and Henry Shue (eds.) *Just and Unjust Warriors The Moral and Legal Status of Soldiers* (Oxford: Oxford University Press, 2008), 44–68, 53.
52. Gardam, "Proportionality and Force in International Law," 394.
53. Hurka, 45, in agreement with Gardam, ibid, 392–394. McMahan, "The Just Distribution of Harm," 357–358.
54. See Walzer and Margalit: "Israel: Civilians & Combatants," *NYRB*, 3–4.
55. Walzer, *Just and Unjust Wars*, 129.
56. Protocol Additional to the Geneva Conventions of August 12, 1949, and relating to the Protection of Victims of International Armed Conflicts (Protocol 1) 1977. Article 51 (5) B). www.icrc.org/ihl.nsf/full/470?opendocument
57. Ibid, Article 57 (2) (a) (iii).
58. Preamble to Protocol 1, ibid.
59. McMahan, *Killing in War*, 30.
60. Rome Statute of the International Criminal Court, Article 8 (2) b (iv). http://untreaty.un.org/cod/icc/statute/romefra.htm
61. Yoram Dinstein, *The Conduct of Hostilities Under the Law of International Armed Conflict* (Cambridge: Cambridge University Press 2004), 120, on the addition of the adverb "clearly." David Luban, "Risk Taking and Force Protection," *Reading Walzer* (Routledge: Yitzhak Benbaji and Naomi Sussman eds.), 277–301, 296.
62. Luban, "Risk Taking and Force Protec–tion," ibid.
63. Luban, ibid, 297.
64. Dinstein, *The Conduct of Hostilities*, 120, referring to Article 51 (5) (b) of Additional Protocol 1.
65. Rome Statute of the International Criminal Court, Article 8 (2) b (iv).
66. Cf. Hurka, 53. Michael L. Gross, *Moral Dilemmas of Modern War* (New York: Cambridge University Press, 2010), 163.
67. Dershowitz, "Israel's Policy is Perfectly Proportionate." See also Kasher, "Operation Cast Lead and the Ethics of War," 6. Hurka, 58.
68. Walzer, "On Proportionality."
69. Luban, 279.
70. Walzer, *Just and Unjust Wars*, 151–156.
71. Walzer, ibid, 151–156, at 156.
72. Luban, esp. 280–81.
73. Asa Kasher and Amos Yadlin, "Assassination and Preventive Killing," *SAIS Review*, Vol. 25, No. 1 (Winter-Spring 2005), 47–57, esp. 50–51: "A combatant is a citizen in uniform. In Israel, quite often, he is a conscript or on reserve duty. His state ought to have a compelling reason for jeopardizing his life. The fact that persons involved in terror are depicted as noncombatants and that they reside and act in the vicinity of persons not involved in terror is not a reason for jeopardizing the combatant's life in their pursuit. He has to fight against terrorist because they are involved in terror, and he has to defend the citizens of his state. The terrorists shoulder the responsibility for their encounter with the combatant and should therefore bear the consequences." See also, Lee, 219, who cites a similar argument by Canadian Forces Colonel J.G. Fleury.
74. Walzer, *Just and Unjust Wars*, 156.
75. Luban, 284, 289.
76. McMahan, "The Just Distribution," 369–372.
77. McMahan, "The Just Distribution of Harm," 354, 366–370, esp. 366–367. See also 372–3. Luban, 285–287. Hurka, 63.
78. Hurka, 63–66.
79. Lee, 220.
80. Walzer, *Just and Unjust Wars*, 156.
81. Ibid, 155.
82. Walzer and Margalit: "Israel: Civilians & Combatants," *NYRB*, 5.

83. Walzer and Margalit, 2. See also the follow-up on this exchange in: Asa Kasher and Major General Amos Yadlin, with a reply by Margalit and Walzer, "Israel & the Rules of War: An Exchange," *New York Review of Books*, June 11, 2009. www.nybooks.com/articles/archives/2009/jun/11/israel-the-rules-of-war-an-exchange/
84. Walzer and Avishai Margalit: "Israel: Civilians & Combatants," 6.
85. Walzer and Margalit, 5.
86. Walzer and Margalit, 7.
87. Luban, 283.
88. Luban, 283, and his footnote 21, 290.
89. Luban, 280–290.
90. Luban, 282.
91. Luban, 287.
92. Despite Kasher, other co-authors of the IDF code of ethics clearly endorse Walzer's view. See: Moshe Halbertal, "The Goldstone Illusion—What the UN report gets wrong about Gaza—and war," *The New Republic* (November 2009), esp. Sec. II. p. 3. www.tnr.com/article/world/the-goldstone-illusion?page=0,3 See also "Israel: Civilians and Combatants: An Exchange, Shlomo Avineri and Zeev Shternhell, Reply by Avishai Margalit and Michael Walzer," *NYRB* (August 13, 2009), in Margalit and Walzer's reply: "Judging from the IDF spokesman's reaction to the exchange between Kasher and Yadlin and Moshe Halbertal and Avi Sagi in the *Yediot Ahronot* of April 10, the official IDF position is closer to our position than that of Kasher and Yadlin."
93. Walzer and Margalit: "Israel, Civilians and Combatants," 5.
94. Walzer, "On Proportionality;" Kasher, "Operation Cast Lead and the Ethics of War," 53.
95. API commentary, 1977, Article 57, Par. 2213. www.icrc.org/applic/ihl/ihl.nsf/Comment.xsp?viewComments=LookUpCOMART&articleUNID=50FB5579FB098FAAC12563CD0051DD7C
96. Michael L. Gross and Tamar Meisels, "Just War Theory and the 2008–09 Gaza Invasion" (A Response to Jerome Slater). 38 (1) *International Security* (Summer 2013), 164–167, 167.
97. Walzer, "On Proportionality."
98. Moshe Halbertal, "The Goldstone Illusion—What the UN report gets wrong about Gaza—and war." *The New Republic* (November 2009), 8.
99. See: Gross, *Moral Dilemmas of Modern War* 171, discussion of changed battled conditions in the age of asymmetrical warfare and its effect on the proportionality requirement. On the increase in civilian casualties over the past 100 years, see also Walzer and Margalit, "Israel: Civilians and Combatants" NYRB, 56 (8) May 2009, 2. For a recent study, see: "A Secure Europe in a Better World—*European Security Strategy"* Document Proposed by Javier Solana and adopted by the heads of States and Government at the European Council in Brussels December 12, 2003. On p. 3: "over the last decade . . . most of the victims have been civilians." And page 5: "Since 1990, almost 4 million people have died in wars, 90 percent of them civilians."
100. Gross, *Moral Dilemmas of Modern War*, 255–256.
101. See Protocol 1 to the Geneva Conventions, Article 43 (3). And Dinstein, 95.
102. Halbertal, "The Goldstone Illusion" 2, addresses the accusation that Israel's targeting of Hamas police constitutes an attack on noncombatants: "It is also clear that applying the international law of war to this new battlefield is fraught with problems. . . . There is no question that, in an ordinary war, a police force that is dedicated to keeping the civilian peace is not a military target. . . . What happens in semi-states that do not have an institutionalized army, whose armed forces are a militia loyal to the movement or party that seized power? In such situations, the police force might be just a way of putting combatants on the payroll of the state, which basically assigns them clear military roles." See also Gross, *Moral Dilemmas of Modern War*, 256.
103. Gross, ibid., 255–6.
104. Cf. Kasher and Yadlin, "Assassination and Preventive Killing," 51.

5

ECONOMIC WARFARE

The case of Gaza

Kinetic warfare is not the only source of harm to civilians during conflict. Since ancient times, civilians have suffered shortages and deprivation, even starvation, during wartime. Siege, Michael Walzer tells us, "is the oldest form of total war," and he dubs this "war against civilians."[1] In recent years, international critical attention has focused the discussion of economic warfare largely on Israel's restrictive policies toward the Gaza Strip, referred to popularly as "the Gaza Siege." In view of unfolding events, alongside the ethical questions they raise, it is worth taking a second look at Israel's policy of restrictions on Gaza from its onset.

In June 2010, Israel's Netanyahu government announced a significant loosening of restrictions on the entrance of goods into Gaza, allowing practically all non-military goods to enter the strip. Essentially, any ban on purely civilian goods, as well as many dual-usage goods, appears to be largely behind us. Most other issues surrounding the Gaza Strip lie ahead. The controversy, critique, and condemnation surrounding Israel's unraveling policy persist.

Many issues of principle remain as they were, and concern Israel's security alongside the extent of its obligation toward the civilian population of the Strip. The interest in resolving them has only heightened. The various Israeli High Court opinions on Gaza, particularly on the energy cuts implemented shortly after Israel's disengagement, raise several noteworthy issues that have not gone away. All would become increasingly relevant in the unlikely event that Israel were to proceed with any unilateral disengagement. Some issues that arise out of Gaza may also have a bearing on other postwar occupations and their aftermath.

The unresolved issues of principle are many, and present themselves as follows:

1. First and foremost stand the ongoing legal debates over Gaza's post-disengagement status and relationship to Israel, and Israel's subsequent

obligations. Is Gaza an independent hostile entity inhabited by enemy civilians, or is it *de facto* still under Israeli occupation?

2. Either way, has the Strip ever been literally "besieged" by Israel, or does Israel continuously impose various economic sanctions on Gaza that it tightens and loosens as need be? While the latter rings more pleasantly in Israeli ears, it is doubtful whether terminology has any bearing on the situation.

3. Whatever the current state of consignments into Gaza, the principled question remains that of Israel's responsibility for the plight of civilians under the rule of Hamas. Throughout the various phases post-disengagement, Israel has continuously insisted that the responsibility for civilian suffering falls almost entirely on Hamas. This is an old argument of besieging forces, and it points us toward enduring issues about the distribution of responsibility for civilian suffering under siege or sanctions. It also raises questions about the legitimacy of economic warfare in general, not merely in Gaza. How can sieges, blockades and sanctions comply with the requirement of distinction and respect civilian immunity when they directly cause harm to civilians by restricting their every-day supplies?

4. Refraining from prohibiting sieges, blockades and economic sanctions, humanitarian law permits this type of harm to civilians, perhaps under the auspices of the Doctrine of Double Effect. Sieges and economic sanctions are also left unrestricted by the legal provisions which protect civilians from excessive harm. The proportionality requirements emanating from Additional Protocol 1, discussed in the previous chapter, concern the lawfulness of a military attack, and do not impose any such restrictions on sieges or sanctions. From a moral perspective and in keeping with the just war tradition, however, it was specifically the twin requirements of necessity and proportionality, rather than any illegitimacy of the measures themselves, that came into play at some point down the road as Israel endlessly pursued its ineffective restrictions on Gaza.

5. Finally, I shall have something to say about the rights Israel still retains, and ought to retain, over Gaza's borders and imports.

The territory

In October 2000, a second Intifada erupted in Gaza and the West Bank. By the end of that year, Gaza had become a source of terror not only by means of rockets shot at nearby Israeli towns and settlements, but also by means of suicide bombers entering Israel, exploding themselves together with dozens of civilians. In order to prevent these actions Israel built an electronic fence surrounding Gaza. The fence proved most effective in preventing people from infiltrating Israel, but obviously could not prevent firing high trajectory weapons. The firing of rockets on nearby Israeli towns and settlements continued.

In summer 2005, Israel withdrew its military forces and civilian settlers from the Gaza Strip, thus formally ending its 38-year military occupation of that area.

The disengagement was followed by elections in the West Bank and Gaza, and subsequently by the violent takeover of Gaza by Hamas. The result was an increase in rocket attacks against civilian targets in Israel. At that time, Israel explicitly expressed its interest in throwing Hamas out of power without using military power. Economic sanctions were put into effect.

Pursuant to its withdrawal, followed by Hamas' takeover of Gaza and the rise in terror attacks, Israel declared the Gaza Strip a "hostile entity," controlled by a terrorist organization that is in a state of war with Israel. Consequently, Israel regards itself as bound primarily by minimal humanitarian obligations toward a civilian population in wartime, under the international laws of war, rather than bearing general responsibility for the welfare of Gaza's inhabitants, as it did during the occupation. On this understanding, Israel held that it was not obliged to supply unlimited quantities of goods to that territory, and that it was within its rights to place limitations on consignments, especially when some supplies were being used for the purposes of terror attacks against Israel.[2]

Crucially, Israel asserted the right to prevent certain goods from reaching Gaza, even when supplied by foreign sources. Following the kidnapping of Israeli soldier Gilad Shalit by Hamas militants in June 2006, economic sanctions were hardened, allowing only basic supplies and humanitarian aid into Gaza.

Under the traditional law of occupation, it is difficult to continue regarding Israel straightforwardly as the occupying power in Gaza. According to Article 42 of The Hague Regulations, "Territory is considered occupied when it is actually placed under the control of the hostile army; the occupation extends only to the territory where such authority has been established and can be exercised."[3] This sets the legal requirements for the commencement of occupation and is considered to reflect customary international law.[4]

In the case at hand, since 2005 Israel has had no physical presence in the Gaza Strip itself, and there can be little doubt that Hamas, and not Israel, exercises effective authority over the territory.[5] In this sense, certainly, the occupation has been terminated. On the other hand, despite Israel's withdrawal from Gaza, some legal theorists downplay the significance of a lack of physical presence on the ground,[6] and no one denies the continued Israeli influence on the goings-on within the Gaza Strip.

In January 2008, Israel's High Court of Justice rejected a petition by human rights organizations for an injunction against Israel's Prime Minister and Defense Minister regarding their government decision to reduce electricity and fuel supplies to the Gaza Strip.[7] These reductions represented a small part of the wider policy of restrictions on the entry of goods into Gaza. The Israeli High Court acknowledged that Israel continues to control the border crossings between Israel and the Gaza Strip and noted the long and recent history of occupation resulting in Gaza's heavy reliance on Israel for its everyday supplies and livelihood.[8] Nevertheless, the court essentially accepted the respondents' argument whereby the only obligation Israel has toward the civilian population of Gaza derives from the state of warfare that currently obtains between Israel and the Hamas government. Such humanitarian obligations toward enemy civilians in wartime are minimal, requiring the unlimited passage of foodstuffs, clothing and medical supplies for children and pregnant women, as well as the rapid and unimpeded passage of vital goods to the civilian population, preventing their starvation.[9]

There is no doubt that Israel is legally obligated under these requirements, and Israel itself has assumed this responsibility. The legal dispute regarding energy cuts surrounded the respondents' claim that Israel is not obligated to supply *non-vital* goods, that is, supplies that are beyond what is required to meet the most basic humanitarian needs.[10] This applied equally to other civilian goods that Israel refused to supply. Israel further denies that it is legally obligated to ensure an unconditional flow of aid to Gaza from the outside world. Israel has since reaffirmed its position that it no longer occupies Gaza—terminating such occupation was the purpose of its unilateral withdrawal—and that it therefore does not bear the legal responsibilities of an occupying power.[11] At the same time, Israel continues to control many of Gaza's surroundings—by air, land, and sea.

If Israel were to be regarded unequivocally as the continuing occupier of Gaza, Article 59 of the Geneva Convention (IV) would then apply.[12] Construed as a belligerent occupier, Israel would be obligated to permit *all* humanitarian relief so far as this is necessary to supplement inadequate supplies.[13] In particular, as an occupying power Israel would be obligated to facilitate the provision of all consignments of foodstuffs, medical supplies, and clothing, whether by human-itarian organizations or by foreign states, to the population of Gaza at large. Crucially, if Israel were regarded unambiguously as the occupying power, and if Gaza is inadequately supplied (as the UN asserts, and Israel denies), then its obligation to accept any relief scheme on Gaza's behalf is entirely unconditional.[14] Israel would then retain only the right to search and regulate the passage of the relief supplies.[15]

While Israel has good grounds to argue that it no longer occupies Gaza which is under the effective control of Hamas, the current law on belligerent occupation does not neatly resolve the complexity of the Gaza situation. Perhaps in view of these uncertainties about the legal status of the Strip, as well as the factual controversy over whether Gaza is adequately (though minimally) supplied, the Israeli court required Israel not only to ensure the safe passage of essential goods but also to supply them to at least a minimal degree and to monitor the situation in the region.[16] It is, however, noteworthy that these further obligations do not derive from Israel's part in the hostilities but rather from its special relationship with Gaza, the long history of occupation, and the lingering possibility that Gaza is in a sense still occupied by Israel. Since that time, Israel has in fact removed virtually all restrictions on purely civilian supplies.

What is the subsequent status of this newly formed territory, particularly with relation to its former occupier, and what are the enduring obligations of the latter? Discussing unilaterally terminated occupations, international law scholar Eyal Benvenisti looks at these underdeveloped issues concerning the obligations of an occupier in the period leading up to unilateral withdrawal and in its immediate aftermath, observing that such obligations remain largely indeterminate within the international law of occupation, which is designed to apply while occupation lasts.[17]

In the Gaza case, most likely, neither the category of occupation nor that of entirely terminated occupation fully succeeds in capturing the complex situation in the strip. Article 42 of the 1907 Hague Regulations supplies a legal basis for the Israeli court opinion requiring the fulfillment of only minimal obligations toward enemy civilians in wartime. There are, on the other hand, reasons stemming from both recent history and ongoing events for supporting the court's further requirement, largely unexplained but willingly assumed by Israel, whereby it supply vital resources to all segments of the population and monitor humanitarian conditions, as well as for supporting Israel's recent removal of most restrictions on non-vital supplies. In a later decision, the Israeli court noted that, though Gaza ought not to be regarded from the viewpoint of international law as a territory subject to a belligerent occupation, still, "because of the unique situation that prevails there, the State of Israel has certain duties to the inhabitants of the Strip."[18]

This unique situation combines several specific factors: an unusually long history of military occupation; geographical proximity to the former occupier combined with lack of viability and lingering economic dependence; Gaza's ongoing non-state status and its relation to the West Bank, which is under Israeli control, as well as the current state of belligerency. All this could have been, and ought to have been, foreseen when unilateral withdrawal was contemplated.

Determining the boundaries of responsibility for formally occupied regions is an increasingly pressing task in general. In relation to Gaza in particular, it seems that Israel was within its legal rights in withholding some *non-vital* goods from reaching the Strip, whether or not it is regarded as an occupier. Israel asserts plausibly that Gaza is no longer under its occupation, and that it is in any case adequately, though at times minimally, supplied. In assuming additional responsibilities of its own accord—supplying goods and monitoring the humanitarian situation—Israel essentially claimed to be acting within its legal rights whether or not regarded as an occupying power.

Siege warfare

In its various opinions on Gaza, the Israeli court neither addressed, nor was it required to address the question posed frequently in the media: is Gaza literally besieged? Facts about everyday life in Gaza and the extent of civilian suffering are contested between the warring parties, but the situation is no doubt grave on all accounts. Recalling historical cases of siege warfare, on the other hand, indicates that Israel's economic restrictions on Gaza, however objectionable, have remained a far cry from total war or collective starvation, such as characterized historical cases like the siege of Jerusalem by the Romans or the German siege of Leningrad in WWII.

Clearly, as indicated by even the most critical televised reports from Gaza, its civilians are not starving, malnourished, or lacking in basic clothing, footwear and the like; no one walks barefoot or is emaciated. As we witness during Israel's military incursions, the population at large monitors CNN and Al.-Jazeera on television; many possess cell phones, cameras, and personal computers with which to report their grievances to the outside world. Gazans also have access, via human rights organizations, to appeal their cases to the Israeli High Court. In emergency situations, at least, they have access to the Israeli health care system. This in itself is a feeble defense of Israel's actions, but it goes a long way toward refuting the charge that those actions have created a humanitarian crisis.

Though Palestinian activists and supporters often use the terminology of "siege" in their condemnations, bringing deplorable historical examples to mind, this is largely a matter of political polemic. Equally, any Israeli insistence on referring to its actions as mere sanctions does not vindicate Israel's position. The use of the terms "siege" or "blockade" as opposed to "economic sanctions" does not in itself settle any interesting questions in this case or any other.

Sieges and blockades are well within the legal arsenal of military tactics. The Hague Regulations (1907) recognizes the use of siege warfare as a legally legitimate measure.[19] Siege warfare, blockades, and sanctions are not prohibited by international law, and are in principle within any military's "tool box," though with some significant qualifications. Since 1977, Article 54 of Protocol 1 prohibits the starvation of the civilian population as a means of warfare, as well as the destruction or removal of installations that are vital to the civilian population. This does not preclude any form of blockade, closure, siege, or economic sanctions.

The Israeli court was quite right, then, neither to examine the issue of siege warfare, nor was it called upon to do so. Nowhere in its various decisions, not even in the appellants' argument, was the term "siege" ever even mentioned. Pointing out that Gaza is "besieged" does not get us anywhere in evaluating Israel's past or recent actions.

From a political–moral perspective as well, classification in itself is not crucial; but related issues might be. Michael Walzer argues that even outright sieges may be morally permissible in the face of necessity, though on his account this is so only when civilians are ensured at least the right to exit the besieged city, if they wish to do so: "People have a right to be refugees," he argues.[20] Walzer takes his cue from Talmudic law, cited by Maimonides, placing a moral restriction on this practice, and sanctioning the siege of a city from only three sides, not all four, thus guaranteeing the inhabitants' right to escape starvation and death.[21] Needless to say, Israel's blockade of Gaza literally neither be carried out from all sides, as the Gaza Strip borders Egypt, nor do Gaza's inhabitants face starvation and death at the hands of Israel. In effect, however, the bulk of the civilian population of Gaza does not have an escape route. Israel's restrictions over recent years, such as the closing of border crossings, are largely coordinated with Egypt, so that the two external powers together control the entrances and exits from all sides.[22]

A further cause for concern is that some instances of economic sanctions may, under certain circumstances, have more serious consequences for the civilian population than outright sieges do. Oliver O'Donovan makes this point in *The Just War Revisited* in a way that appears particularly apt to Israel's problematic involvement in Gaza.[23]

O'Donovan construes war as an act of armed judgment,[24] and defines both economic sanctions and sieges as acts of war (as opposed to a means of avoiding war), though both are taken to be intermediate hostile measures as they do not involve the direct use of force.[25] One of the reasons for resorting to such measures, as opposed to full-scale war, O'Donovan tells us, is "to provide a first, mild stage in the hostilities, to bring moderate pressure to bear to achieve a settlement, if possible, before the resort to arms becomes necessary."[26] Another instance in which sanctions appear especially appropriate is where direct military action faces logistic impediments.[27] Most likely, both types of rationale were present in Israel's original decision to impose restrictions on Gaza, but neither could seriously be invoked after Israel undertook full-scale military action in Gaza in December 2008, and in view of its more recent military operations in the Strip.

As for the first of these motivations for resorting to economic measures—using sanctions tactically as a form of pressure, a first step in hope of a settlement before resorting to harsher measures—O'Donovan points to the necessity of having clearly in mind what is to be done if sanctions fail to achieve their purpose within tolerable limits of damage to the community.[28] This has been a particularly troubling concern in the case of Gaza, and a shortcoming of Israeli tactics in the Strip. Despite Israel's various military incursions into Gaza alongside its loosening of restrictions, it is entirely unclear whether anyone has any idea what to do next. Outright sieges of a city or a garrison eventually end, albeit brutally, when the besieging army storms it and the stronghold falls.[29] Economic sanctions of whatever degree may be entirely open-ended. Even if originally justifiable as a pressure tactic, as a mild first step in hostilities and a hopeful alternative to war, they could no longer be justified on this basis.

Furthermore, as O'Donovan points out with regard to the economic sanctions that preceded the 1991 Gulf War, economic sanctions are particularly problematic when directed against an economy that is not developed enough independently to produce adequate supplies of food and other essential provisions.[30] This has certainly been the case with Gaza.

In some cases, of which Gaza may be one, economic sanctions can be worse than traditional sieges. For O'Donovan, this observation derives partly from his general theological framework whereby a just war is understood as an act of armed judgment whose aim is to achieve peace and normality.[31] In keeping with conventional just war theory, the aim of waging war is to achieve a just peace. If sanctions are open-ended, while sieges are not, they may have graver consequences, not only in terms of immediate civilian suffering but also in terms of the prospects for peace, understood as reinstating normality for the community.[32] War—whether it is indeed an act of judgment or not—must come to an end. Certainly, old-fashioned wars have clear beginnings and endings.[33] But economic sanctions may be as open-ended as the terrorist campaigns they purport to combat.

Israel's loosening of the restrictions on Gaza, along with the continuing unrestricted supply of vital needs, goes a long way toward alleviating immediate civilian suffering. But the long-term concerns regarding peace and normality remain, as no overall end to the conflict is clearly in sight. This, however, has little to do with the economic restrictions on Gaza in particular.

Responsibility for civilians

Siege or no siege, how is responsibility for the deprivation of civilians to be distributed between the civilians' own government and the external restricting power?

In 70 AD the Romans besieged the city of Jerusalem. The success of their military campaign in Judea is notoriously depicted on Rome's Arch of Titus. In *Just and Unjust Wars*, Walzer discusses Josephus's account of this siege. One interesting defense of siege warfare, Walzer observes, attempts to shift responsibility for civilian suffering and death to the leaders of the besieged city, or even to the inhabitants thereof, for failing to surrender. He quotes Josephus on this point:

> Titus, he tells us, lamented the deaths of so many Jerusalemites, "and, lifting up his hands to heaven. . .called God to witness, that it was not his doing." Whose doing was it? After Titus himself there are only two candidates: the political or military leaders of the city, who have refused to surrender on terms, and forced the inhabitants to fight; or the inhabitants themselves who have acquiesced in that refusal and agreed, as it were, to run the risks of war. Titus implicitly, and Josephus explicitly, opt for the first of these possibilities. Jerusalem, they argue, has been seized by the fanatical zealots, who have imposed the war on the mass of moderate Jews, ready otherwise to surrender.[34]

Walzer does not accept this argument as a justification of siege warfare; nor should we. He notes that such an easy shift in responsibility would render the commander of the attacking army "an impersonal agent of destruction, set off by the obstinacy of others, but with no plans and purposes of his own."[35] Nevertheless, as Walzer comments, "the attribution of responsibility in siege warfare is a complex business."[36]

In its decision on Israel's cutting of electricity supplies to Gaza, the Israeli court declared that the Gaza Strip is "controlled by a murderous terrorist group that operates incessantly to cause injury to the state of Israel and its citizens."[37] Such terror, the court said, has escalated and intensified since Hamas consolidated its control over Gaza, and includes the continuous firing of missiles and mortar shells at civilian communities within the state of Israel.[38] The city, in short, has been seized by fanatic militants who subject the moderate majority to the consequences of conflict.

In an interim decision regarding fuel supplies, the court had already ruled that proposed energy cuts were permissible, noting that militants in Gaza actually employed a considerable amount of energy in fueling their terror machine and that it was possible for the Hamas government to set priorities in distribution by directing energy to meet civilian needs—supplying energy to hospitals, water pumps, etc., so as to avoid a humanitarian crisis—while at the same time reducing terror activity against Israel.[39]

The court, not unlike Titus, attempted to shift responsibility for any deprivation of the civilian population from the shoulders of the Israeli government and onto those of Hamas. It affirmed the Israeli government's assertion that restrictions on energy are intended, and deemed likely, to harm the terror infrastructure in Gaza, and that the Hamas government could control distribution, if it chose to do so, so as to ensure that the vital needs of its people were met. Thus, the court implied that, if the population is severely harmed by an energy crisis, this is the fault of its own government and belligerents, who inflict the suffering on their own civilians rather than reducing the amount of fuel used for terror attacks against Israel.[40] Such arguments, which are popular among Israelis generally, are problematic and do not supply a conclusive defense of Israel's various restrictions.

As Walzer notes, siege warfare poses a most puzzling exception to the basic rule of *ius in bello* prohibiting the deliberate assault on civilians.[41] Civilians are not legitimate targets; they are not to be aimed at. In the case of siege warfare, Walzer suggests that the proposed shift in responsibility from the besieging forces to the leadership of the besieged city enables the former to claim that he is not aiming at civilians at all. The besieging army aims only to reduce its opponent to surrender, not to reduce a population to starvation. If the city's leadership and army, often backed up by the city's inhabitants themselves, insist on holding out, the civilians' suffering is merely incidental to the attack.[42] On this account of responsibility, such casualties in Gaza as are attributed to Israel, and form the grounds of international condemnation, might nonetheless be justified with reference to the Doctrine of Double Effect.

The Israeli court has repeatedly referred to the "the terrorist infrastructure" in Gaza,[43] and to Gaza as an area "controlled by a murderous terrorist group that . . . violates every possible precept of international law with its violent actions, and makes no distinction toward civilians—men, women, and Children."[44] The court noted this as an indication both of the future harm that might be prevented by resorting to economic warfare and of the magnitude of the risks presented by the situation. With regard to fuel supplies specifically, aside from Hamas's direct neglect of civilian needs, Palestinian militants habitually raid the entry points through which vital humanitarian supplies pass from Israel into Gaza, and seize the fuel supplies for their militant purposes.[45]

All this, however, is a relatively small victory for proponents of siege warfare in general and of restrictions on Gaza in particular. It is true that the besieged government is in charge of distributing scarce supplies. It is, however, Walzer notes, entirely predictable that it will supply the military before it cares for civilians. So although civilian casualties may not be the main intention of the aggressor, placing the civilian population in the front line of the conflict is a direct and entirely foreseeable result of the aggression. As Walzer explains, if the besieged army is to hold out at all, it will have to be fed (or fueled, as the case may be) ahead of civilians. If the army, or in this case the terrorists, are to be reduced, civilians must suffer first: "Civilians suffer long before soldiers feel the pinch."[46]

The notion of intervening agency may be more useful here than the Doctrine of Double Effect, both in vindicating Israel's position and in understanding the legality of siege warfare, with which Walzer struggles. On this alternative account, the actions of Hamas cut the causal connection between Israel's sanctions—legitimately directed toward the terrorists—and the harm to civilians. Civilian casualties in Gaza would not count then as a secondary effect of Israel's actions. It is indeed most difficult, as Walzer notes, to construe harm to besieged civilians as a merely incidental effect when civilians are in the front line of the conflict. On this alternative account, Hamas—its government priorities and its militants' actions—disconnect Israel's restrictions from any harm to Gaza's civilians. Hamas, then, not Israel, is the direct cause of civilian suffering in recent years.

All this assumes that responsibility in such cases is a fixed commodity lending itself to distribution or disconnection. This assumption implies that the fault lies either with the besieging army or with the leadership of the city, or else that the sum total of responsibility is distributed between the two—in equal or unequal shares. In such cases, however, responsibility may not appear in fixed amounts at all. It is quite possible that both Israel and Hamas are each *fully* responsible for the suffering in Gaza. Egypt and/or other actors within the international community may also carry some substantial portion of the blame.

Either way, direct harm to civilians, and the case of Gaza in particular, clearly require to be confronted more directly than with theoretical arguments over shifts and shares of responsibility. As Walzer observes, sieges and economic sanctions are inherently difficult to apply without violating civilian immunity. In *The Just War Revisited*, O'Donovan points out that: economic sanctions "are always likely to be indiscriminate. They strike directly at the ordinary, life-sustaining functions of the community . . . They attack the life of society as such, not the threat posed by the activities of the state to other societies."[47] Often, economic sanctions

> . . . aim to affect the political will of the hostile government through the economic straits into which the population at large is thrown. If the population is unaffected, the whole strategy has failed, since there is no other way in which they were going to persuade the government to change its mind.[48]

This may or may not be the case with all past restrictions on Gaza. Cuts in energy, like cuts in fuel supplies, are more directly aimed at Hamas militants than are restrictions on purely civilian goods, such as specific types of food provision. Attaining the desired effects in the case of fuel restrictions—directly depriving the militants from fueling their terror machinery—does not require ordinary residents of Gaza to put pressure on Hamas. It aims more directly at depriving Hamas militants of access to fuel. On the other hand, even in such cases of goods with both military and civilian usages it is easily predictable that civilians will suffer from embargoes and cutbacks.

Furthermore, most of the restrictions placed on Gaza in recent years were more directly aimed at civilians. This is precisely O'Donovan's point in the passage quoted above about economic sanctions being worse, in some respects, than traditional sieges:

> It is important here to understand the structural difference between economic boycott and traditional siege. A siege used to be undertaken in order to inhibit troops from free movement. Civilians in a besieged city might starve; but that was not the point of the operation, and you would always prefer, other things being equal, to pin your enemy's forces down in a city which had been deserted by its civilian inhabitants.[49]

In the case of sanctions, by contrast, the presence of civilians and their suffering is integral to the military tactic, and cannot possibly be construed as a double effect. In the Israeli case, if there has been any logic at all to Israel's policy of restricting the supply of purely civilian goods to Gaza, it was the hope of the Israeli government that disgruntled civilians would eventually pressure Hamas into reducing terrorist activity and releasing the kidnapped Israeli soldier held by its militants until October 2011. More ambitiously, at various points Israel may have hoped to remove Hamas from power altogether without resorting to military measures.

Regarding responsibility for this inevitable harm to civilians, Walzer concludes that, at least from a moral perspective, and in keeping with other parts of the war convention, sieges and blockades can be justified only if the besieging army takes responsibility for the needs of the besieged civilian population and sees to their provisions.[50] In the case of Israel, the state willingly and fully accepted this responsibility all along, at least to the extent of supplying basic humanitarian needs, securing the passage of minimal goods and monitoring the humanitarian situation in the Strip.[51] It has been this commitment throughout, reinforced at various points by the Israeli court, that has rendered Israel's restrictions possibly legitimate, not the argument whereby Hamas, rather than Israel, is responsible for the plight in Gaza. No doubt Hamas carries that responsibility. But Hamas's unquestionable blame for the suffering of its people cannot free Israel from the responsibility to protect civilians from its own limitations on their everyday supplies.

Necessity and proportionality

Toward the end of its opinion on electricity cuts, the Israeli court stated that it

> . . . will not intervene with regard to the security means adopted by the security officials—neither with respect to their effectiveness nor with respect

to their wisdom—except with regard to the legality of such. Our role is limited to the judicial review of compliance with Israeli law and international law that binds the state of Israel, to which—as the Respondents declared before us—the State is bound to adhere.[52]

The Israeli court describes itself as applying only the test of "reasonableness" to any given security measure.[53] In its decision in the Gaza case, the court did not even directly confront the question of whether denying electricity to a civilian population could *reasonably* be expected to reduce hostilities.

On the political front, Israel has been accused of inflicting collective punishment, carrying out acts of pure vengeance on a civilian population rather than implementing a preventive strategy. Were Israel's restrictions a necessary and appropriate measure for addressing the security crisis in the Israeli South? Was the harm Israel was inflicting on the inhabitants of Gaza likely to be effective in achieving Israel's legitimate security aim, namely, increasing its own security by reducing the rockets? Or was the suffering Israel inflicted on civilians largely superfluous?

The first set of questions that arises is whether the measures undertaken were necessary and appropriate for attaining Israel's military objective. As for necessity: needless to say, Israel is responsible for the safety of its citizens in the south of the country, who had been under rocket and mortar attack for several years. Clearly, this was not a tolerable situation for any sovereign state or for its citizens to endure. Between June 2006 and October 2011, Israel also had the additional responsibility for the welfare of its abducted soldier Gilad Shalit held by Hamas for over 5 years in unknown conditions and with total disregard and utter contempt on the part of Hamas for international law.

Necessity, however, implies not only the need to do something but also the appropriateness of the measures in question for achieving the security goal. Unlike in the traditional case of sieges, Israel was obviously uninterested in recapturing the territory that it had just recently withdrawn from voluntarily. If military reoccupation had at any point been the aim, this could certainly have been achieved. Israel, however, could not have been expected to abandon its citizens in Southern Israel to their fate. At the time of the initial implementation of sanctions, Israel was still hoping to avoid large-scale military conflict with Hamas in Gaza, though it had not refrained from limited military incursions.

Discussing *Moral Dilemmas of Modern Warfare*, Michael Gross points out that, in an age when low-intensity warfare is increasingly replacing conventional armed conflict, nations fighting terrorists who intentionally target non-combatants are faced with very difficult questions of appropriate response. Policy-makers are naturally fearful of extensive civilian casualties and eager to avoid the widespread devastation associated with conventional war.[54] Within this problematic context, the appeal of economic warfare is apparent, and Israel's sanctions were implemented as its best first shot.

It was, however, a shot in the dark, as sanctions often are. It was questionable from the start whether reductions in supplies of electricity and fuel to Gaza, alongside restrictions on supplies such as pasta, halva, chocolate, pumpkin, sewing machines, children's toys, and the like were likely to affect a terrorist organization aiming at Israeli civilians and intent on the destruction of the Jewish state. If economic sanctions were entirely insufficient for meeting the security threat, they could not possibly have been regarded as necessary. If doomed to fail, they could not justify any degree of harm to civilians, and any resultant suffering would be entirely unnecessary and therefore excessive. Notwithstanding this observation, if there was any serious prospect of securing military advantage via sanctions rather than war, it is not clear that Israel should be faulted for initially resorting to economic warfare as milder than the military option, with full-scale conflict as the last resort.

As for proportionality, international humanitarian law does not impose any criteria of proportionality upon the lawfulness of siege warfare specifically.[55] From an ethical standpoint, it remains an open question whether the measures undertaken by Israel were excessively harmful to civilians in relation to the security goal they were designed to achieve.

Describing this idea of proportionality as a requirement of the war convention, Walzer (citing Henry Sidgwick) explains that: "We are to weigh the 'mischief done' against the contribution that mischief makes to the end of victory."[56] As we saw in the previous chapter, proportionality, strictly speaking, precludes not only utterly useless, gratuitous harm to civilians (already precluded by the requirement of necessity) but also some unintended harm arising from successful military operations that might incur civilian suffering on a scale that would be seriously out of step with the military advantage anticipated.[57] Even if they passed the test of necessity, did Israel's sanctions comply with the notion of proportionality limiting even military necessity and advantageous operations only to those that do not cause "disproportionate" unintended suffering to civilians?

It is obviously difficult to determine precisely how much harm to civilians constitutes a "disproportionate" cost in relation to the gains of any military measure. Given reasonable hope of success, however, it is not implausible or unusual to regard the suffering associated with economic sanctions as proportionate harm in relation to the advantage of reducing missile attacks on civilian centers.

Time, however, is of the essence. As events unfolded and the sanctions progressed and intensified, doubts about the proportionality of these measures became increasingly acute. O'Donovan discusses proportionality as a requirement of the just war, applying it to economic warfare. With sanctions in particular, O'Donovan notes the troubling likelihood of disproportion, alongside the dangers of lack of discrimination discussed above, ". . . it is clear that general economic sanctions can be disproportionate. They take longer than military action to have effect, and they expose societies to various consequential ills with long term implications, including the breakdown of civil order."[58] In relation to Gaza, I think it is superfluous to elaborate on this eventuality.

Both Walzer and O'Donovan take up a second long-term consequential consideration regarding proportionality, concerned "not only with reducing the total amount of suffering, but also with holding open the possibility of peace and the resumption of pre-war activities . . . ."[59] Indeed, much criticism of Israel turned on precisely this point, whereby Israel's mode of combat appeared to be destroying both the prospect of attaining peace and the possibility of Gazans building their society and eventually returning to a normal life. At worst, it was suggested that Israel's strategy was designed deliberately to hamper this possibility of eventual normalization and peace.

Worse still, Israel's strategy was not working: civilians were suffering on both sides—Gazans were deprived and the rockets kept flying into Israel. If not entirely predictable from the start, it soon became apparent that Hamas was not going to help the civilian population at the expense of its terror machinery. What was the logic of maintaining sanctions on civilian goods at this point?

When sanctions are unsuccessful, they are most difficult to abandon. Revoking sanctions, like military retreat, may signal weakness and encourage the enemy. At these points, continuing the sanctions carries its own military advantage, or at least lack of disadvantage. This is a further shortcoming of the tactic—it is very difficult to terminate.

The rest is history. Israel continued to impose its ineffective economic sanctions on Gaza; Hamas continued and intensified its policy of launching rockets at Israeli civilians, until Israel decided that "enough is enough."[60] Israel's subsequent "Operation Cast Lead" considerably reduced the rocket attacks, albeit somewhat temporarily, after 8 long years. It also brought allegations of "disproportion" and the use of "excessive force" to the forefront of accusations against Israel, as both a legal and a moral charge, as discussed in the previous chapter. Whatever the legal assessment of the degree of force employed during this military incursion in 2008–2009, as well as subsequent military action, Israel has certainly not exhibited weakness. From this point on, Israel ran out of any possible excuses for restrictions on the supply of purely civilian goods to Gaza. The continued implementation of the sanctions, even if justifiable at the start, became entirely unnecessary after this point, and any continued suffering they caused to civilians was then superfluous.

Concluding remarks

Whether an Occupied Territory inhabited by terrorists or under the outright and effective control of Hamas, Gaza is legitimately prevented by Israel from acquiring military supplies to hurl at Israeli civilians and from kidnapping Israelis. Israel is well within its legal rights in continuing to monitor and supervise consignments to Gaza, so as to prevent any military, or potentially military, goods from reaching Hamas.[61]

The wholesale condemnation of Israel for "besieging" Gaza and causing a humanitarian crisis has been unwarranted from the start. The terminology is at one and the same time both exaggerated and unnecessary. Economic sanctions are bad enough.

On the assumption that Hamas, and not Israel, effectively controls Gaza, restrictions on civilian goods were conceivably justifiable at the onset as a pressure tactic designed to halt terrorism while avoiding larger-scale military conflict. It is also noteworthy that the various measures resorted to have all along been shared and coordinated with Egypt, as well as, for the most part, with the Palestinian Authority in Ramallah.[62]

Once they were clearly failing to achieve their goals, however, the sanctions quickly ran afoul of the twin requirements of necessity and proportionality. While the Israeli court had no legal cause or grounds to consider these requirements, viewed from the perspective of the ethics of war the suffering inflicted on civilians could no longer qualify as necessary and proportionate, on any account. In the wake of Operation Cast Lead in particular, there remained little justification for restricting the supply of purely civilian goods into the Gaza Strip. Israel's loosening of these sanctions over a year later may best be described as a "better late than never" remedy to this situation.

Nonetheless, under any set of assumptions regarding the legal status of the Gaza Strip, Israel has the right under international law to search and regulate the passage of all relief supplies into Gaza, whether by sea or by land, in order to safeguard its own security and the safety of its citizens. Naturally, Israel retains the right to secure its borders so as to defend its soldiers and civilians against possible abduction into Gaza.

Restraint and economy of harm is required and warranted only in the case of *bona fide* civilians, and not in the case of terrorists or their sponsors. It is to the threat posed by the latter, specifically Iran, and the ethical and legal challenges involved in responding to such threats in a timely manner, that I turn now.

Notes

1. Michael Walzer, *Just and Unjust Wars: A Moral Argument with Historical Illustrations* (New York: Basic Books, 1977), 160.
2. HCJ 9132/07. January 30, 2008. http://mfa.gov.il/MFA/ForeignPolicy/Issues/Pages/Court%20upholds%20Israeli%20limitations%20of%20the%20supply%20of%20fuel%20and%20electricity%20to%20Gaza%203-Feb-2008.aspx. Accessed June 24, 2014.
3. Regulations Concerning the Laws and Customs of War on Land. The Hague, October 18, 1907, Article 42. www.icrc.org/ihl.nsf/385ec082b509e76c41256739003e636d/1d1726425f6955aec125641e0038bfd6
4. There has admittedly been some legal controversy with regard to the second part of this Article and the stipulation that occupation extends only where the authority of the occupying army "has been established and can be exercised," which raises the question whether an occupying army must hold effective control or merely the potential for effective control in order to be regarded as the occupier and obligated to assume responsibilities as such. See: Eyal Benvenisti, "The Law on the Unilateral Termination of Occupation," in A. Zimmermann and T. Geigerich (eds.) *Verofentlichungen des Walter-Schucking-Instituts fur Internationalis Recht an der Universitat Keil* (2009) Available at: http://papers.ssrn.com/sol3/papers.cfm?abstract_id=1254523. "The dispute relates to the question whether . . . the foreign army must actually substitute its own authority for that of the ousted government . . . or whether it is sufficient that the foreign government is actually controlling the area and therefore in a position to substitute its own authority for that of the former government. If actual control was required, an army that controls an area, but refrained from actually exercising it vis-à-vis the civilian population, would not be considered an occupant and thereby would be absolved from assuming

responsibilities towards the civilian population. Similarly, if actual substitution was required, an occupant who decided to terminate its direct relation with the local population could claim that it was no longer an occupant." (Benvenisti, 2009, Section B). In the Case Concerning Armed Activities on the Territory of the Congo (Democratic Republic of the Congo V. Uganda), I.C.J. Reports, 2005 (Paragraphs 173, 177), the International Court of Justice opted for a requirement of actual control, but this interpretation is still disputed.

5. Eyal Benvenisti, "The Law on the Unilateral Termination of Occupation," ibid. Mustafa Mari, "The Israeli Disengagement from the Gaza Strip: An End of The Occupation?" in 8 *Yearbook of International Humanitarian Law* (2005), 356–268, 359.
6. Yuval Shani, "Faraway, So Close: The Legal Status of Gaza after Israel's Disengagement," 8 *Yearbook of International Humanitarian Law* (2005), 369–383.
7. HCJ 9132/07. January 30, 2008.
8. HCJ 9132/07, 2008, ibid, §12.
9. Geneva Convention IV (1949) Relative to the Protection of Civilian Persons in Time of War, Article 23; Protocol Additional to the Geneva Conventions of August 12, 1949, and relating to the Protection of Victims of International Armed Conflicts (Protocol 1) 1977, Article 54; Yoram Dinstein, *The Conduct of Hostilities under the Law of International Armed Conflict* (Cambridge: Cambridge University Press, 2004), 139; and: HCJ 9132/07, 2008, ibid, §13.
10. HCJ 9132/07, 2008, ibid, §15
11. HCJ 6659/06 *Anonymous V. The State of Israel* (Judgment June 11, 2008), Para 11: "The State of Israel has no permanent physical presence in the Strip, and it doesn't even have any real potential to fulfill the obligations . . . no real potential for effective control in what transpires in the Gaza Strip." This case on "unlawful combatants" is available via www.asil.org/ilib080717.cfm#j4
12. Geneva Convention IV (1949) Relative to the Protection of Civilian Persons in Time of War, Article 59.
13. Akande Dapo, "Legal Issues Raised by Israel's Blockade of Gaza," EJIL *Analysis* (2010) www.ejiltalk.org/legal-issues-raised-by-israels-blockade-of-gaza/
14. The ICRC commentary to Article 59 states that: "The obligation on the Occupying Power to accept such relief is unconditional. In all cases where the occupied territory is inadequately supplied the Occupying Power is bound to accept relief supplies destined for the population." See: www.icrc.org/ihl.nsf/COM/380-600066?Open Document
15. Geneva Convention IV (1949) Relative to the Protection of Civilian Persons in Time of War, Article 59; Yoram Dinstein, *The Conduct of Hostilities under the Law of International Armed Conflict*, 138.
16. HCJ 9132/07 § 4& 19.
17. Benvenisti, 2009, Sec. C.
18. HCJ 6659/06, §11.
19. The Hague Regulations (IV): Laws and Customs of War on Land, October 18, 1907, Section II Chapter I, Article 27: "Means of Injuring the Enemy," explicitly refers to sieges and bombardments.
20. Walzer, Just and Unjust Wars, 168.
21. Walzer, ibid.
22. It is entirely clear that any closure on Gaza from the Israeli side, as well as the sea, would still be relatively ineffective without Egyptian cooperation.
23. Oliver O'Donovan, *The Just War Revisited* (Cambridge University Press, 2003), 101–108.
24. O'Donovan understands just war as an extraordinary extension of ordinary acts of judgment, that is, the extraordinary extension of the ordinary function of government as judgment, where such ordinary means of judgment are unavailable. (O'Donovan, *The Just War Revisited*, 6–7).

25. O'Donovan, ibid, 101: Both are modes of war as they "employ the power of the state . . . in a way that would constitute an offence against the opposing state, were it not for that state's prior offence which has given just cause for war."
26. O'Donovan, ibid, 106–107.
27. Ibid.
28. Ibid, 107.
29. Ibid, 107–108.
30. Ibid.
31. O'Donovan, ibid, 59.
32. Ibid.
33. Paul Gilbert, *New Terror, New Wars* (Edinburgh: Edinburgh University Press, 2003), 4.
34. Walzer, *Just and Unjust Wars*, 162.
35. Walzer, ibid, 162.
36. Walzer, ibid.
37. HCJ 9132/07, §22.
38. HCJ 9132/07, 2008, §2.
39. HCJ 9132/07, interim decision, November 29, 2007. www.gisha.org/UserFiles/File/LegalDocuments/fueloct07/english/EnglishTranslationofHCJ9132decision_2_.pdf. Accessed June 24, 2014.
40. HCJ 9132/07, interim decision, ibid, 2007 §4, 5.
41. Walzer, Just and Unjust Wars, 162.
42. Ibid, 162–163.
43. HCJ 9132/07, 2008, e.g. §4,
44. HCJ 9132/07 2008, §22.
45. See, for example, The Los Angeles Times, April 20, 2008. http://articles.latimes.com/2008/apr/20/world/fg-gaza20
46. Walzer, *Just and Unjust Wars*, 171–172.
47. O'Donovan, *The Just War Revisited*, 102.
48. Ibid.
49. Ibid.
50. Walzer, *Just and Unjust Wars*, 174–175.
51. HCJ 9132/07, 2008, §4, §19.
52. HCJ 9132/07, 2008, §20.
53. E.g. when considering Israel's security wall in what is probably the leading case on court's policy concerning proportionality, see HCJ 2056/04 *Beit Surik*, §36, §42 §46, §59, §61, §80. See also the opinion of Justice Barak in HCJ 399/06 Susia V. Government of Israel, esp. §9.
54. Michael L. Gross, *Moral Dilemmas of Modern War* (New York: Cambridge University Press, 2010), 101.
55. The provisions contained in the 1907 Hague Regulations relevant to the requirement proportionality deal specifically with weapons (e.g., Art. 23(e) Hague Regulations) and do not impose any criteria of necessity or proportionality on economic tactics. Nor does Article 54 of Additional Protocol I impose such criteria on siege warfare. The proportionality requirements emanating from Additional Protocol I concern the lawfulness of an "attack," which in international humanitarian law has a very specific meaning relating to the conduct of hostilities (see, e.g., Article 49 Additional Protocol I).
56. Walzer, *Just and Unjust Wars*, 129.
57. Cf. Aharon Barak, "Proportional Effect: the Israeli Experience," University of Toronto Law Journal, 57 (2) (2007), 369–382, 374–380.
58. O'Donovan 105, and he notes the British experience of imposing sanctions on Rhodesia in 1965 as a case in point.
59. Walzer, *Just and Unjust Wars*, 132. See also, O'Donovan, *The Just War Revisited*, 59.
60. As stated repeatedly in the media by Israeli MK and former minister Ms. Tzipi Livni, serving as Israel's Foreign Minister at that time.

61. Geneva Convention IV (1949), Article 59; Dinstein, *The Conduct of Hostilities under the Law of International Armed Conflict*, 138.
62. This point has been noted by Walzer, most recently in an interview with *Haaretz*, but it is sadly downplayed by the rest of the world: "this is not an Israeli siege but a joint Israeli–Egyptian siege and it has Palestinian support in Ramallah and any changes in the siege have to be negotiated with the Egyptians and the Palestinian Authority," see: www.haaretz.com/print-edition/features/it-might-have-been-wise-to-look-the-other-way-1.295795.

6

PREEMPTIVE STRIKES

Israel and Iran

In the wake of the US invasion of Iraq, considerable academic attention has been focused on preventive war.[1] Classic accounts of "anticipation" had been offered before.[2] Recent sanctions on Iran and the debate over its nuclear program now suggest the usefulness of an *ex ante* perspective rather than the *ex post* analysis offered thus far primarily with reference to Iraq. Many of the crucial concrete questions regarding the feasible success and extent of an early military attack on Iran, its costs and its benefits, need to be settled in practice rather than in the realm of political theory. These questions remain subject to considerable dispute even among military experts. I focus instead on contemporary literature on just war theory, much of which opposes early strikes, and suggest that it may actually contain the resources for supporting an early attack in this case. I suggest that Iran may be a legitimate candidate for early military action designed to prevent it from developing nuclear weapons. Under certain restrictive conditions, this chapter suggests, a unilateral Israeli strike against Iran would be justifiable, both morally and legally, as self-defense.

Terminology

Preemptive war aims to avert an imminent harm; preventive war aims to avert a harm that is more temporally distant.[3] Unilateral preventive war—unilaterally averting a remote threat—is widely condemned morally, and legally prohibited. By contrast, most contemporary just war theorists regard a unilateral response to an imminent attack as justifiable self-defense, though the precise meaning of imminence, as well as individual cases, remain contested.

Legal scholars ask the same questions about the legitimate onset of war and the meaning of "imminence." Legal disagreements are phrased in terms of the license granted to states (or their "inherent right" recognized) in the UN Charter to act in self-defense "if an armed attack occurs." While the UN Charter system aims to avoid war, Chapter VII of the Charter recognizes two exceptions to its prohibition on the threat or use of force: self-defense if "an armed attack occurs" and military action undertaken with Security Council authorization.[4] For the lawyers, the question is whether any early act of belligerency in question can be assimilated to "self-defense" provided for under Article 51 of the Charter. Otherwise, it can be legal only when undertaken with authorization from the United Nations Security Council. At what early stage might we regard an armed attack as having "occurred," or begun to occur, legally and morally, justifying an unauthorized unilateral response?

George Fletcher offers an interesting conceptual point regarding the various commentaries on Article 51. On the plausible assumption that an imminent attack is one which is already "actually present," "in progress" and in that sense has begun to "occur," there is absolutely nothing preemptive about responding to it. If one views imminent danger as the first part of an armed attack which is already occurring, one does not then require a separate theory of preemption. "You do not need a broad notion of what constitutes an attack and a theory of preemptive war; one or the other will do."[5]

Why wait?

Striking early may prove less costly in human life than waiting for the threat to mature. Jeff McMahan points out the following regarding Israel's attack on Iraq's nuclear facility in 1981:

> Israel reasonably believed that if it did not attack immediately, it would have lost its only realistic chance to eliminate this threat to its own continued existence. It attacked the reactor on a Sunday, when French engineers who were building the plant were absent, thereby destroying it without causing casualties. It is, indeed, an important feature of this example that there were no illegitimate human targets and thus no attacks, whether intended or unintended, on the innocent. Although this preventive attack was clearly illegal and was universally condemned at the time, a very strong case can be made that it was an instance of legitimate prevention.[6]

Walter Sinnot-Armstrong makes a similar point about the Israeli attack on Osirak from a consequentialist perspective:

> If they had waited to bomb it when it was active, then very many people in Iraq would have been killed by the explosion and nuclear fallout, whereas only a few people were killed when they bombed the reactor before it was active.[7]

Israel's attack on Osirak was widely criticized at the time as illegal, for responding to a less than imminent threat. It was condemned by the UN Security Council without a US veto. But the limited casualties it incurred as opposed to the harm it prevented suggest that striking early, at least in some cases, is morally advantageous both from any consequentialist moral perspective and from the perspective of respecting the rights of the innocent. From the sixteenth to the nineteenth centuries European thinkers argued straightforwardly for the legitimacy of preventive war aimed to forestall even the most remote threats, particularly any alteration in the European balance of power.[8] This was their logic: (a) war is inevitable; (b) fighting later rather than sooner will be far more costly, if possible at all.[9] So why wait?

Consequences

The answer (as usual) comes from Walzer and has been restated many times since: reinstating a permissive doctrine of prevention would lower the threshold for war and again make war too frequent and routine, this time with devastating modern weapons.[10] It would make war too frequent because the doctrine of preventive war would justify too many wars: calculating far in advance whether war is in fact inevitable, and estimating the costs of fighting sooner rather than later, is extremely uncertain and would sanction military action too often and too soon based on biased and imprecise calculations.[11] This would be open to bad-faith abuse.[12] It would make war too routine because such a doctrine treats war casually, as an instrument of policy rather than a last resort in the face of actual aggression.[13] Furthermore, the preventive war doctrine generates conflict. If states expect to be attacked at any time by others who perceive them as threatening, they would then each have a strong reason to strike first at their potential adversaries: a permissive doctrine of prevention actually *makes* rival states into potential threats.[14]

Alan Buchanan points out that these consequentialist objections contain two separate arguments that can be overcome. First, they raise the dangers associated with accepting a general rule permitting prevention. These "bad practice" objections do not in themselves rule out any possibility of justified prevention in exceptional circumstances.[15] In some rare cases, the benefits of a particular preventive war, and the costs of refraining from it, may be so overwhelming as to outweigh the bad consequences of harm to the general rule. As for arguments concerning potential error and abuse, Buchanan believes these defects can be remedied by subjecting preventive war to review by improved international institutions, though these do not (yet) exist.[16] Others, like Henry Shue and David Luban, call for more reliable intelligence information than was gathered and supplied prior to the US invasion of Iraq.[17]

Admittedly, there remains a consequentialist presumption against any benefits of war and in favor of refraining from it, as David Rodin is quick to point out. Assessing the overall results of any proposed war is a most indeterminate task, with the one available certainty that it will cause large-scale death and devastation.[18] As a rule, then, consequentialist cost–benefit analysis will work against taking military action (preventive or otherwise) and in favor of restrictive doctrines. This presumption, however, applies to wars generally, rather than to preventive action specifically, and it does not rule out war entirely.

All these consequentialist concerns have one further failing, as David Luban notes: arguing that a doctrine of prevention is likely to license too many wars begs the central question by assuming that more preventive wars are necessarily too many. If particular preventive wars are justified in terms of self-defense and preserving innocent life and basic rights, then more preventive wars may at times be preferable to fewer preventive wars. Moreover, sometimes, as in the 1930s, abstaining from preventive war may result in more war rather than less war. Appeasement, as opposed to prevention, may actually lead to war. Luban does not wholeheartedly endorse such arguments, but he concedes they are not without merit in the specific case of rogue regimes.[19] The term "rogue regime," commonly refers to authoritarian states that severely violate human rights, sponsor terrorism, and seek to acquire weapons of mass destruction. Following the experience of Hitler's Germany, Luban defines a "rogue state" (for the purpose of preventive war doctrine) as a "threat state"—a state fostering a militaristic and violent ideology, backed up by a track record of violence, "and a build-up in capacity to pose a genuine threat."[20]

Liability to harm

Apart from consequentialist reasons for avoiding escalation in conflict and the aspiration to minimize human suffering caused by too many wars, there are also principled right-based objections to preventive war. As long it has not engaged in acts of aggression, a sovereign state and its members have a legal and moral right not to be attacked.[21] McMahan raises this problem and, following Walzer, also supplies the answer. He describes the type of threat that could justify preventive action as analogous to the domestic crime of conspiracy. McMahan argues that putting an adversary at risk by committing a crime of aggression that falls short of attack—such as violating a ceasefire agreement; preparing, or conspiring, to commit an attack; or even just forming certain mental states of harmful intention—can, in principle, generate moral liability to attack.[22] Considering the grave consequences of war, however, the burden of proving such conspiracies would be very high.[23] Adopting this analogy with conspiracy, David Luban also suggests that in some cases active preparation for war, planning purposefully to use WMD, is analogous to conspiracy to commit a crime.[24] Forming the wrongful intentions—intending to launch a large-scale assault on basic human rights—backed up by persistent and overt action to further this plan is comparable to the domestic crime of conspiracy and is sufficiently criminal to deprive a sovereign state and its soldiers of their immunity from military attack.[25]

On the individual level, McMahan and Rodin raise a further objection to preventive war, which is in keeping with their more general critique of traditional just war theory. Both object to the traditional assumption that soldiers may be targeted purely by virtue of their military status regardless of whether they are themselves guilty of any aggressive crime.[26] In this context of preventive war,

McMahan questions which individuals, if any, within the target state, could possibly be liable to preventive attack. Any conspiracy or harmful intention will usually be forged in the minds of politicians, who are legally immune from attack, while attacking the non-conspiring military is tantamount to targeting the innocent.[27] Rodin concurs: only the ruling executive, a small cabal of military and political elite, is likely to be party to any secret plan of wrongful aggression. Plain soldiers will know nothing of the "conspiracy" and therefore remain innocent of aggression and non-liable to preventive attack.[28] Attacking them would be targeting the innocent.

McMahan and Rodin's worry about covert conspiracies unbeknown to the ordinary soldier cannot, however, apply to states which overtly and repeatedly threaten other states with large-scale violence.[29] As we saw in Chapters 1 and 3, McMahan generally aspires to place greater responsibility on the individual soldier for participating in unjust aggression.[30] This ought to apply to conspiracies as well. Even under McMahan's individualist approach to war, it would be something of a stretch to regard uniformed combatants in such cases as totally innocent, and their targeting as indiscriminate. At least in cases of openly threatening states whose aggressive intentions are discernable, McMahan, of all people, ought to acknowledge soldiers' responsibility to be knowledgeable, or at least suspicious, of their country's intentions. If they ignore this responsibility, or the aggressive conspiracy underway, they are thereby, in McMahan's own terms, morally liable to attack if they continue to participate in any military activity.

Both the consequentialist objections and the liability-based opposition to early military action can be overcome. As for consequences, it is quite conceivable that the benefits of a particular early strike will outweigh the bad consequences, including the harm the action will cause to the general practice of refraining from preventive wars. As for liability, a state and its military are liable to preventive force if it acts in ways that are analogous to conspiring to commit a crime of aggression.

Perhaps partly for these reasons, preventive war is not necessarily illegal; it can be perfectly legal, but only when authorized by the United Nations. A domestic analogy illustrates this point: one may not use preventive force against one's enemy; one has rather to report to the police. If there are cases in which preventive war might indeed be justified, then they should be taken before the UN.[31] The question remains whether any unilateral early strike might be regarded as justifiable "preemption," rather than "prevention," by virtue of responding to an imminent threat. If something like a conspiracy is underway, at what point might the danger posed satisfy the legal requirement of imminence, legitimizing a resort to unauthorized unilateral force in response?

Imminence and WMD

Ordinarily, under the UN Charter system the unilateral use of force absent the prior occurrence of an armed attack is illegal. It is, however, generally (though admittedly not unanimously) accepted that Article 51 permits member states not only to engage in armed self-defense after they have been attacked but also to preempt an armed attack that is "imminent."[32] As Fletcher puts this, "no one would reasonably propose a doctrine of self-defense that was limited to striking back only after being struck by a phalanx of bombers or guided nuclear missiles," pointing out that such a requirement would in fact turn self-defense into reprisal.[33] While it is clear, Fletcher continues, in customary international law that the right of self-defense includes the response to an *imminent* attack, there is no treaty explicitly defining "imminence," and it is consequently legally unclear what this actually means in terms of triggering the right to self-defense.[34]

Discussing early military action, Walzer describes a continuum of "anticipation," rather than a stark dichotomy between imminent and non-imminent threats. At the most restrictive end of this continuum he quotes former US Secretary of State Daniel Webster (1842) regarding the Caroline case: "In order to justify pre-emptive violence, Webster wrote, there must be shown 'a necessity of defense. . .instant, overwhelming, leaving no choice of means, and no moment for deliberation'."[35] Walzer argues that this doctrine of preemption, popular among legal scholars, is too restrictive, as it permits no more than the obvious instinctive last-minute response to an attack which is already underway, and does not address itself usefully to the real-world experience of imminent war. Walzer charts a middle course, more permissive than Webster's "reflex action" at the point of imminent attack, but falling short of permissive prevention prompted by vague and remote dangers. Drawing the line between justified and unjustified first strikes at the point of "sufficient threat," Walzer argues that preemptive action is justified where the following three conditions obtain: "A manifest intent to injure, a degree of active preparation that makes that intent a positive danger, and a general situation in which waiting, or doing anything other than fighting, greatly magnifies the risk."[36]

The imminence requirement is usually described as a requirement of evidence. The closer the attack is temporally, the more certain we can be of its actual occurrence and the necessity of defensive force.[37] In principle then, if the evidence of future harm were to be entirely sound, "mere temporal distance is not sufficient to cancel the right of self-defense," as Alan Buchanan points out.[38] This used to be David Rodin's view as well.[39] More recently, Rodin argues that imminence is not merely an epistemic requirement, subsidiary to the condition of necessity, but actually more fundamental to the right of self-defense. Violent self-defense is either excused under conditions analogous to individual duress in the face of imminent danger, or else it is justified as a right, reacting to one's adversary's wrongful aggression. In either case, Rodin argues, it is an absolutely fundamental requirement for self-defense that our potential target has taken action that is imminently threatening us.

If self-defense is an excuse for violence in psychologically compelling situations of great fear and pressure, then the danger must be, in the language of the Caroline doctrine, literally: "Instant, overwhelming, leaving no choice of means, and no moment for deliberation."[40] Even if such psychological excuses can be invoked by states, "When the attack is remote and merely potential there is no psychological necessity of this form."[41] If, on the other hand, self-defense is understood as a rights-based *justification*, then it is applicable only when the target of defensive force has at least begun to commit an act of wrongful aggression against us, rendering him liable to our violent response. Absent his active aggression, our target is innocent and non-liable to our attack. Either way, Rodin maintains that, even under hypothetically assumed certainty regarding an adversary's future plans, violence can be neither justified nor excused as self-defense unless wrongful aggression against us is imminent in the sense that it has already begun to occur.[42]

Rodin's rights-based challenge, whereby the targets of prevention are not liable to attack because they have not yet acted aggressively, has already been met by McMahan and Luban's analogy between aggressive plans and the crime of conspiracy.[43] If, contra Rodin and McMahan, one assumes the traditional liability of soldiers, they are liable to attack because the state they represent has already taken aggressive steps analogous to conspiracy. Furthermore, even if Rodin is right that the imminence of the danger we face from their conspiracy is an indispensable requirement for justified self-defense, this does not settle all interpretive questions concerning the meaning of "imminence," however fundamental it may be. Rodin argues persuasively that the Bush doctrine of preventive war attempted to supplant, rather than interpret, the requirement of imminence.[44] It remains an open question whether non-literal interpretations of imminence are plausible when they come from sources other than the Bush administration.

It has been noted more than once that imminence may no longer be comprehensible solely in the straightforward temporal sense, especially in the age of WMD. The requirement of imminence may be fundamental to justifications of self-defense, but this requirement is not necessarily a simple countdown of weeks or days before the impending attack, but rather the notion that a first strike is justifiable when it is undertaken at something like the last moment for successfully preventing the harm it is intended to forestall.[45] This understanding essentially adapts the just war requirement of "last resort" to the sphere of anticipation.[46] Fletcher supplies the following example:

> Suppose a terrorist threatens to implant an undetectable nuclear device that is set to explode in a year. He can be stopped now, but once the device is implanted, it will be too late. . . . In these cases, the attack is not imminent, but the threat is real and ineluctable, and recognizing a right of legitimate defense would seem sensible and appropriate.[47]

Certainly, the future attack in the example is not imminent in any temporal sense, and yet recognizing a right to self-defense does seem sensible and appropriate.

To be sure, the construction of an atomic energy plant, or even the possession of nuclear weapons, does not automatically constitute an impending threat justifying preventive war. Even with regard to military capability, Walzer cautions that standard military preparations that characterize the classic arms race do not necessarily count as a sufficiently serious threat to justify war "unless it violates some formally or tacitly agreed upon limit."[48] In the Iranian case, for instance, enrichment of uranium violates international limits set by UN Security Council and International Atomic Energy Agency resolutions.[49] Furthermore, Fletcher's terrorist example and Luban's reference to rogue states suggest the urgency of limiting nuclear capability specifically in the hands of regimes that actively support terrorism. This would not apply to nuclear power in the hands of stable democracies with a provable no-first-use policy for their nuclear arsenal.

Arguing for a restricted doctrine of prevention which would justify first strikes against rogue states constructing WMD, Luban interprets imminence in probabilistic rather than temporal terms. In the traditional legal understanding of imminence a first strike can be assimilated to self-defense when the wrongful aggression is temporally imminent. Luban argues that, on the same logic, an attack that is imminent in terms of probability, being all but certain, justifies preventive war as self-defense.

This understanding of imminence, in terms of probability rather than timing, is persuasive because "responding" to a temporally imminent nuclear attack is entirely meaningless as self-defense. Continuing to regard imminence in purely temporal terms renders the inherent right to self-defense totally void when facing WMD. One simply cannot defend oneself against a nuclear strike that is literally on its way. While a permissive free-for-all doctrine of prevention is both unjustifiable and highly undesirable, permitting military action only once an armed attack has literally begun to occur is a hollow license in the nuclear age. When suffering from the aggression of a "rogue state" is imminent in the probabilistic sense, Luban argues, when it is virtually a sure thing, preventive war is assimilated to self-defense in just the same way as preemptive war against temporally imminent attacks is justifiable as defensive.[50]

Nuclear deterrence

One obvious objection to this argument that preventive war is sometimes necessary and a last resort in order to prevent nuclear war is that it discounts the possibility of future mutual deterrence as protection against genocidal attacks. Even if a "rogue" succeeds in constructing WMD, mutually assured destruction would render any nuclear attack irrational for either party, thus eliminating the need for force entirely. Such a strike, it might be argued, is neither necessary, nor is it a last resort since nuclear deterrence will achieve the same goal. In this vein, it is sometimes pointed out in response to concerns over Iran's atomic energy project that a resort to nuclear warfare on the part of Iran would be totally irrational. It would be utterly suicidal for Iran to use atomic weaponry on Israel, and so, it is unlikely to occur. This suggests that "the only thing we have to fear is fear itself."[51]

It is apparently unclear to the international community that Iran would in fact refrain from using nuclear weapons for fear of a counter-attack. Crucially, even if Iran were to refrain, at least for the time being, from resorting to WMD (both directly and by possible terrorist proxy), the infliction of perpetual terror by way of threat in itself constitutes an attack against Israel and the rights of individual Israelis to live safely and freely. This type of attack on the basic rights of individual Israelis is virtually certain, with the significant prospect of an actual genocidal attack backing it up. It would be neither irrational nor farfetched on the part of Iran to hope that the threat of a nuclear attack might sufficiently frighten many Israeli citizens into early evacuation, leaving their state considerably weekend, perhaps open to be overrun. Given the Jewish experience of persecution and genocide, "fear itself" might very well do the trick of dismantling the Jewish state.

Walzer captures this type of terrorizing fear when he considers that a threat may be sufficient to justify defensive war against states and nations that are in a sense already ". . . *engaged in harming us* (and who have already harmed us, by their threats, even if they have not yet inflicted any physical injury)."[52] Furthermore Iran has already inflicted material harm with its complicity in terrorism against Israelis, as in funding Hamas, and in this sense many Iranian armed attacks against Israel have already occurred. Certainly, support for such attacks indicates a manifest intent to injure. Much more active preparation in the nuclear direction and Iran's intent becomes a positive danger. An early military strike against Iran might then be justified as defensive, in Walzer's terms, when a general situation emerges in which waiting, or doing anything other than fighting, greatly magnifies the risk.[53]

More generally, it is important to keep in mind that mutual assured destruction is always unreliable and poses a constant danger of collapsing into nuclear war. The experience of the Cold War is not entirely telling. In retrospect, with the collapse of the Soviet Union, it is easy to declare the success of this strategy. It is more difficult, and at the same time also necessary, to recall that matters might not have turned out as well as they did. Needless to say, nuclear deterrence is also a morally problematic strategy, if not altogether morally impermissible.[54] It involves the terrorizing threat of killing millions of civilians in response to an attack that will have already occurred, so that the counter action would be largely gratuitous mass violence. From a more practical perspective, it is not clear that a state is required to place itself and its citizens at such risk if it has the military capacity to avoid it. Certainly, a Cold War type scenario is not something to aspire to. In more contemporary cases of mutual nuclear threats, their eventual conclusion remains an open question.

In an article titled "Optimal War and Jus Ad Bellum" Eric Posner and Alan Sykes argue that deterrence might be ineffective against leaders who are not particularly concerned for their people. Leaders themselves might have reasonable hope of escaping the consequences of retaliation, or they might be religious fanatics, or ideologues, prepared to launch an attack regardless of possible retaliation and the threat to their own safety. "Consider the religious zealots who believe that death during war against enemies will bring them to a blissful existence."[55] With regard to Iran, Posner and Sykes argue that "Iran's public and government have strong religious motivations . . . It is not obvious that threats of retaliation following an actual attack will dissuade aggression by such governments."[56]

Be that as it may, far more significantly they question whether nuclear deterrence is going to be terribly effective against terrorists and their supplier states. If the fear is of a state dispensing some form of nuclear weapons to terrorist groups, there may be little possibility of deterring either culprit with a threat of retaliation. International terrorists without much of a permanent base are very difficult to deter. States are unlikely to suffer the brunt of nuclear retaliation for a terrorist attack. In the Iranian case, given Iran's track record of aiding terrorist organizations, it could eventually supply its terrorist clients with WMD with the hope of avoiding retaliation on its soil. A nuclear attack on their entire populations in response to an assault, however massive, launched by a handful of terrorists would be ruled out as excessive and disproportionate.[57] In cases in which the concern is partly about terrorists obtaining WMD, it is at least questionable whether deterrence is always a feasible option. From a moral perspective, it is generally a dubious measure of mutual self-defense. Nuclear deterrence and mutually assured destruction are not part of the arsenal which must be exhausted before last resort can be said to have been reached.

Probability and risk

How likely exactly does a future nuclear attack have to be in order to qualify as imminent in the probabilistic sense outlined above?

Luban's explanation of "probable imminence" is particularly noteworthy. He insists, plausibly, that the future attack must be extremely likely (say an 80 percent imminence threshold) *in the present*:

> ... it would be a mistake to calculate the likelihood by computing the cumulative likelihood over time, for even relatively improbable attacks can attain a high cumulative likelihood within a few years. A back of the napkin calculation illustrates the problem. . .at an annual probability of 10 percent, the likelihood is more than 80 percent that an attack will occur within fifteen years and a few months.[58]

This, Luban observes, cannot be right: "Otherwise, small probabilities that may represent nothing more than the possibility of something unexpected and weird happening will quickly mount up."[59]

Calculating "imminence" in the probabilistic rather than purely temporal sense, Luban focuses on the likelihood of the risk maturing into an actual attack. Luban reasonably insists that the probability of a future attack must be provably high in the present rather than representing some possible fluke, though the anticipated attack need not actually occur anytime soon. And he adds that any considerations of likelihood must be based on intelligence information rather than guesswork. But he does not say much at these points about how we should calculate the overall risk factor, which cannot be simply a matter of probabilities. In his later "Preventive War and Human Rights," however, he concludes his discussion on WMD with the following indispensable observation: "The higher the stakes in a single attack by the enemy, the lower the threshold for preventive action."[60]

Borrowing Luban's figurative napkin for a moment, it might be worth scribbling another calculation onto the back of it, based on this last comment. Risk equals magnitude of harm times the probability of its occurrence.[61] Once we exchange Webster's purely temporal requirement that the pending attack is "instant, overwhelming, leaving no choice of means, and no moment for deliberation" for a probabilistic interpretation, then the magnitude of harm, and not merely its likelihood of maturing, ought to form part of our calculations as well. When we substitute "instant" for "probable," the enormity of a looming attack explains part of its "overwhelming" nature. Considering probabilities in this context cannot be solely a matter of mathematical likelihood of *something* occurring, without serious consideration of what it is that is likely to occur.

Precise probability of an Iranian nuclear attack on Israel—either directly or by terrorist proxy—and its possible timing remain very hard to gauge, but the scale of the harm to be averted is not. This is where magnitude of harm fits into the risk factor. Any quantitative, rather than straightforwardly temporal, inter- pretation of the imminence requirement has to account not only for the likelihood of an attack at any particular time but also for the extent of harm in question. On anything but the most antiquated understanding of imminence, relevant only to attacks with conventional weapons, the sheer vastness of the potential atrocity has to fit into calculations of imminence and urgent necessity, as part of the overwhelming nature of the threat.[62] Hence Luban's conclusion that, "the higher the stakes in a single attack by the enemy, the lower the threshold for preventive action."[63]

Clearly, even when the stakes are high enough, the probability of actual attack has to be significant in order to justify the use of force under the auspices of self- defense. It cannot be merely a national psychosis about pending Holocausts. The point remains, however, that "probabilistic imminence" must be worked out in relation to the magnitude of harm and not merely likelihood of attack. If high probability can replace temporal imminence as a sufficient condition for justified preemption, this is because we perceive the "overwhelming" nature of a pending attack in terms of its extent and not merely in terms of its temporal proximity. Such overwhelming risk is a matter not only of probability percentage-wise, but also of the scale of harm that is likely to ensue. It is the extent of the projected harm (the prospect of the mushroom cloud hovering above) multiplied by the likelihood of its overtaking us that renders the threat overwhelming, though it may still take some time to mature.

Last resort and proportionality

Recognizing that the magnitude of risk lowers the threshold for preventive warfare clearly does not in itself automatically justify any specific attack. Optimally, any early strike would be an international endeavor, authorized in advance by the UN Security Council. Failing that, a unilateral attack intended to prevent a threatening state from developing nuclear weapons could only be justified at the point of last resort, as the last chance of averting a catastrophic harm. Moreover, the larger the costs that are likely to ensue, the greater caution required.

As for halting Iran's nuclear program, four rounds of international sanctions have been implemented, and the UN has asserted its authority to oversee Iran's nuclear plant. More stringent sanctions have been implemented by the US and some of its allies. More recently, the international community has reached an agreement with Iran to lessen sanctions against the country in exchange for curbing its nuclear program. These alternatives to war, such as increased international pressure alongside renewed diplomatic efforts, and perhaps even some unorthodox acts of war such as cyber warfare, would have to be exhausted before any large-scale early military strike could be morally, let alone legally, justifiable, or even worth the risks from a prudential perspective.

To be sure, however, as Thomas Hurka points out relying on Walzer, "last resort" cannot be understood literally.[64] If it were, it would rule out war entirely. "For we can never reach lastness, or we can never know that we have reached it. There is always something else to do: another diplomatic note, another United Nations resolution, another meeting."[65] Furthermore, any alternatives to military action must achieve roughly the same just goal as the war aims to secure. Surrender is not required. In that sense, too, "lastness" cannot be taken literally.[66] Last resort implies exhausting a reasonable range of alternatives before resorting to military measures.

Beyond last resort, satisfying the just war requirement of proportionality *ad bellum* will depend on the extent of military action required and its costs—both direct and collateral—as against its projected benefits. In the Iranian case, it is obvious that any Israeli military action would be limited, falling far short of conquest. It is wildly optimistic, on the other hand, to expect the threat of a nuclear Iran to be halted by a single in-and-out Israeli air strike. On all accounts, the situation is extremely complicated. Such a strike is likely to cause widespread collateral damage. It might result in enhanced terrorism against Israel as well as Jewish communities abroad; it might conceivably result in war with other neighboring countries.

As for the benefits, the optimal aim of any military action against Iran would be forestalling a developing harm and postponing the threat as far as possible into the unforeseeable future. Short of conquest, it is doubtful whether any nation can be prevented indefinitely from attaining nuclear power if it remains determined to do so. Halting a terrorizing genocidal threat and significantly postponing its recurrence, with the hope of future improvement in the overall situation, is nonetheless no small achievement. If and when halting a nuclear threat against Israel and its neighbors emerges as necessary and achievable (and these are admittedly two big "ifs") such an objective could potentially justify rather massive damage to the Iranian side.

Nothing succeeds like success, and its estimated likelihood is a crucial issue for proportionality calculations. As Hurka explains, "The *jus ad bellum* insists that the war must have a *reasonable hope of success* in achieving its just cause and other relevant benefits; if it does not, its destructiveness is to no purpose and the war is wrong."[67]

This goes for war in general. In the case at hand, the high stakes and the preemptive nature of the potential operation suggest a relatively high burden of proof regarding feasibility. Whether or not disarming Iran, even temporarily, is an attainable goal remains an open question which needs to be settled by military experts, or else only in hindsight. Iran's nuclear potential is not located at one nuclear facility, as was the case with Iraq's Osirak, but rather widely spread out throughout Iran's vast territory. Nonetheless, Israel's Netanyahu government believes that, at least with considerable American involvement, the military enterprise of denuclearizing Iran is realizable. They had better be right if they are to justify military action, particularly action undertaken in advance and on the scale and scope that would be required in this case.

Concluding remarks

Back in *Just and Unjust Wars* Walzer warns that "The boastful ranting to which political leaders are often prone isn't in itself threatening; injury must be 'offered' in some material sense as well."[68] Nor are provocations the same as threats.[69] What then should we make of former Iranian President Ahmadinejad's repeated threats to wipe Israel off the map,[70] or of the ongoing anti-Israeli rhetoric by Iranian Supreme Leader Ayatollah Khamenei and his fellow ayatollahs?

Clearly, empty threats do not constitute just cause for war. Current Iranian President Rouhani is more soft-spoken than his predecessor, and widely described in the west as a moderate. Rouhani has referred to Israel only mildly as "an old wound on the body of the Islamic world."[71] As for derogatory references to "the fake Zionist regime," "the occupying regime of Jerusalem" and even holocaust denial, we should recall Walzer's comment that "Insults are not occasions for wars, any more than they are (these days) occasions for duels."[72] But while offensive remarks are surely no cause for war, diplomatic retractions, mild rephrasing and verbal assurances are no guarantee of peace for our time. Ultimately, "sufficient threat" is largely a matter of context and material injury.

Considering this wider context in the Iranian case would include enhanced uranium enrichment as well as long-standing support for terrorism. Rendering aid to terrorist organizations such as Hezbollah in Lebanon, Islamic Jihad and Hamas, responsible for the murder of countless Israelis, suggests not only a manifest intent to injure but also that injury has in fact already been "offered" in a material sense as well. Sometimes the boastful ranting of political leaders turns out to be sufficiently threatening when threats are expressed against a background of a considerable build-up of arms alongside active support for, and complicity in, the murder of civilians.[73]

Talk of an Iranian threat and means of contending with it requires considering the various complex issues raised by this contemporary case in its political, moral and legal contexts. The stickiest questions require military expertise and concern the assessment of future events. There is no hope of conclusively settling the controversial debate over an early attack on Iran from a purely theoretical perspective. Perfect knowledge is only attainable in retrospect and the most we can hope for in advance is the clearest and most careful analysis of the situation from every possible perspective.

In thinking about the specifics of this case, we should resist easy answers from those who would entirely disregard international constraints in favor of renewing an overall permissive doctrine of prevention.[74] Routine and predictable opposition to any early military action is however equally dangerous and simplistic. There is no call for automatic rejection of the military option from the perspective of the just war tradition or international law. Both contain the resources for supporting such action in certain circumstances, and there are sound reasons for suggesting that Iran may be just the right type of case. Possibly, the language of preemption and imminence may not even be necessary when we recognize Iranian sponsored terrorism as armed attacks which have already occurred. Certainly, funding and supporting these attacks offer material injury and constitute manifest intent to injure on the part of Iran. Ultimately, the appropriate response hinges at least in part on military calculations of risk, cost and benefits and estimated chance of success. Political and military opinions are destined to differ. In the end, whichever course of action is undertaken, or refrained from, will be judged by history.

As for the appropriate timing of early military action (if there is to be any): American assessments indicate, as I have suggested, that the threat to be averted, in relation to which "imminence" is to be judged, is not an actual Iranian attack but rather the point at which Iran could obtain nuclear capacity. The official American position whereby a nuclear Iran would be unacceptable implies that this eventuality in itself would constitute a harm to be averted whenever it emerges as imminent. Certainly, it cannot be averted after it matures. Preemption in such cases, once a threatening nation is armed with nuclear weapons and poised to attack, is clearly not a feasible option.

If this is so, then, *if and when all else fails*, and subject to reliable intelligence, reasonable hope of success and proportionality, the right time to strike would not be when an actual nuclear attack is imminent, but rather when Iran is on the brink of acquiring nuclear weapons. Any later than that and the response is too late, useless and probably suicidal; any sooner, and the threat is non-imminent in any sense of the word. However, if there is to be any margin for error, the magnitude of the risk implies that it would be preferable and justifiable to err on the side of striking somewhat too early rather than striking too late.

Notes

1. For example, David Luban, "Preventive War" 32 *Philosophy and Public Affairs* (2004), 207–248, 207. Allen Buchanan and Robert O. Keohane, "The Preventive Use of Force: A Cosmopolitan Institutional Proposal" 18 *Ethics and International Affairs* (2004), 1–22. Allen Buchanan, "Institutionalizing the Just War" 34 *Philosophy and Public Affairs* (2006), 2–38. Henry Shue and David Rodin (eds.) *Preemption—Military Action and Moral Justification* (Oxford: Oxford University Press, 2007). George Fletcher and Jens David Ohlin, *Defending Humanity—When Force is Justified and Why* (Oxford: Oxford University Press, 2008) Chapter 7, 155–176: "Preemptive and Preventive Wars." Jeff McMahan, "Preventive War and the Killing of the Innocent," in Richard Sorabji and David Rodin

(eds.) *The Ethics of War: Shared problems in Different Traditions* (Aldershot UK: Ashgate, 2006), Chapter 9, 169–190. Whitley Kaufman, "What's Wrong with Preventive War? The Moral and Legal Basis for the Preventive Use of Force" 19 *Ethics and International Affairs* (2005), 23–28. And (just before the invasion of Iraq): Michael Byers, "Preemptive Self-Defense, Hegemony, Equality and Strategies of Legal Change" 11 *The Journal of Political Philosophy* (2003), 171–190 (primarily on US "exceptionalism").

2. Most notably, Michael Walzer, *Just and Unjust Wars: A Moral Argument with Historical Illustration* (New York: Basic Books, 1977), 74–85. Chapter 5: "Anticipation." For a prominent (pre-Iraq) account of anticipation in international relations, see: Randall L. Schweller, "Domestic Structure and Preventive War—Are Democracies more Pacific?" 44 *World Politics* (1992), 235–269.

3. See the discussion in Shue and Rodin, *Preemption*, 2–6. On terminology, see also Kaufman, "What's Wrong with Preventive War?" 23, n. 1. For this distinction between prevention and preemption, see: Walzer, *Just and Unjust Wars*, ibid, 75; Shue and Rodin, 2–6; Buchanan, "Justifying Preventive War" in Shue and Rodin (eds.) *Preemption*, Chapter 5, 126–142, 126; Rodin, "The Problem with Prevention," in Shue and Rodin (eds.) *Preemption*, Chapter 6, 143–170, 144; Luban, "Preventive War," 213; Luban, "Preventive War and Human Rights" in Shue and Rodin (eds.) *Preemption*, Chapter 7, 171–201, 171. Neta Crawford, "The False Promise of Preventive War," in Shue and Rodin (eds.), *Preemption*, Chapter 4, 89–125, 105–106. Walter Sinnot-Armstrong, "Preventive War— What is it Good For?" in Shue and Rodin (eds.), *Preemption*, Chapter 8, 202–221, 215. Kaufman, "What's Wrong with Preventive War?," 37. Fletcher and Ohlin, *Defending Humanity*, 161–162. McMahan, "Preventive War and the Killing of the Innocent," 170.

4. See: Charter of the United Nations, Chapter VII www.un.org/en/documents/charter/chapter7.shtml

5. Fletcher and Ohlin, *Defending Humanity*, 158.

6. McMahan, "Preventive War and the Killing of the Innocent," 183.

7. Sinnot-Armstrong, "Preventive War—What is it Good for?," 217.

8. Kaufman, "What's Wrong with Preventive War?, 25, 29, 31, cites Vattel, Grotius, Pufendorf, Vitoria and Gentili. Walzer, 76–77 and Luban, P.W., 219, cite Bacon, Vattel and Burke. See also: Rodin, "The Problem with Prevention," 149, and Buchanan, "Institutionalizing the Just War," 6. Suzanne Uniacke, "On Getting One's Retaliation in First," in Shue and Rodin (eds.), *Preemption*, Chapter 3, 69–88, 74, cites Grotius. Fletcher and Ohlin, *Defending Humanity*, 156, 174, cite Kant. Crawford, "The False Promise of Preventive War," 116–117, cites Gentili and Bacon, as well as pointing to the prevalence of preventive war in ancient Greece and Rome.

9. Walzer, 81; Luban, "Preventive War," 223. McMahan, "Preventive War and the Killing of the Innocent," 171. Rodin, "The Problem with Prevention," 150. Buchanan, "Institutionalizing the Just War," 6.

10. Walzer, 76–80; Luban, "Preventive War and Human Rights," 172; McMahan, "Preventive War and the Killing of the Innocent," 171; Rodin, "The Problem with Prevention," 150, who cites Luban on this point, as does Buchanan, "Institutionalizing the Just War," 7.

11. Rodin, "The Problem with Prevention," 145–148.

12. Luban, "Preventive War and Human Rights," 172, 200; Luban, P.W., 228. McMahan, "Preventive War and the Killing of the Innocent," 175; Eric A. Posner and Alan O. Sykes, "Optimal War and Jus Ad Bellum" *University of Chicago Law and Economics Working Paper Series* (2004), Olin Working Paper no. 211; U. of Chicago Public Law Working Paper no. 63. 1–41, at 8, 22, 27. Accessible at http://papers.ssrn.com/sol3/papers.cfm?abstract_id=546104. Last accessed June 8, 2014.

13. Luban, P.W., 209–10, 224–5. Rodin, "The Problem with Prevention," 150–155.

14. Luban, P.W., ibid, 228; Luban, "Preventive War and Human Rights," 172. Crawford, "The False Promise of Preventive War," 120–124. Henry Shue, "What Would a Justified Preventive Military Attack Look like?," in Shue and Rodin (eds.), *Preemption*, Chapter 9, 222–246, 232–3. Fletcher and Ohlin, 157.

15. Buchanan, "Justifying Preventive War," 128–131. Sinnot-Armstrong describes this in terms of the distinction between act consequentialism and rule consequentialism, attributing the latter to Luban. He argues that specific cases of prevention are justifiable on act-utilitarian grounds, which he (Sinnot-Armstrong) endorses. Even with rule utilitarianism, however, the rules need not be absolute, as their ultimate justification is greater utility. Sinnot-Armstrong, "Preventive War—What is it Good For?," 202–221.

16. Buchanan, "Justifying Preventive War," 128–135, esp. at 131–135. See also Luban's response to Buchanan's arguments in "Preventive War and Human Rights," 199–201, Appendix 2.

17. Shue, "What Would a Justified Preventive Military Attack Look like?," 230–232; Luban, P.W., 233–234; Luban, "Preventive War and Human Rights," 190.

18. Rodin, "The Problem with Prevention," 146–148, esp. 147–148.

19. Luban, P.W., 228–230.

20. Luban, P.W., ibid, 230–231; "Preventive War and Human Rights," 190.

21. Rodin, "The Problem with Prevention," 164–165. McMahan, "Preventive War and the Killing of the Innocent," 175.

22. McMahan, ibid, at 179–85. See also Kaufman, "What's Wrong with Preventive War?," 31.

23. McMahan, Ibid.

24. Luban, "Preventive War and Human Rights," 191. Cf: McMahan, "Preventive War and the Killing of the Innocent," 182–185.

25. Luban, "Preventive War and Human Rights," 191–192, 195.

26. See Chapter 1 of this book, along with its references to: Jeff McMahan, *Killing in War* (Oxford: Oxford University Press, 2009); Jeff McMahan, "The Ethics of Killing in War" 114 *Ethics* (2004), 693–733. David Rodin, *War and Self-Defense* (Oxford: Oxford University Press, 2003), Chapter 4, 70–99.

27. McMahan, "Preventive War and the Killing of the Innocent," 185–188. See also Rodin, "The Problem with Prevention," 164–166.

28. Rodin, ibid, 169.

29. See Buchanan, "Justifying Preventive War," 137–138.

30. McMahan, "The Ethics of Killing in War," 702–708 and 722–725; Jeff McMahan, "Just Cause for War" 19 *Ethics & International Affairs* (2005), 1. McMahan, *Killing in War*, 182–188.

31. This is the central argument in: Kaufman, "What's Wrong with Preventive War?," esp. 23, 31, 32–38.

32. Fletcher and Ohlin, 156, 158; Luban, P.W., 212–214. Both regard it as entirely uncontroversial that customary international law recognizes preemptive self-defense in the face of imminent danger as covered by Article 51. This is occasionally disputed, see: Rodin, "The Problem with Prevention," 144; Byers, "Preemptive Self-Defense," 172.

33. Fletcher and Ohlin, *Defending Humanity*, 155, see also p. 90. George Fletcher, *Basic Concepts of Criminal Law* (Oxford: Oxford University Press, 1998), 133: "A pre-emptive strike against a feared aggressor is illegal force used too soon; and retaliation against a successful aggressor is illegal force used too late."

34. Fletcher and Ohlin, ibid, 156.

35. Walzer, *Just and Unjust Wars*, 74. The Caroline incident (1837) involved a preemptive attack by the British forces in Canada on a civilian US steamboat (on American territory) that was used to smuggle and sell arms to Canadian rebels. The incident gave rise to an exchange of letters between Webster and British Special Minister Lord Ashburton, leading up to the Webster–Ashburton Treaty (1842). The quote is from a letter dated July 27, 1842 in which Webster states that it was for the British Government to justify the incursion of its forces by showing "a necessity of self-defense, instant, overwhelming, leaving no choice of means, and no moment for deliberation." See (among many other accounts): Christine Grey, *International Law and the Use of Force* (Oxford: Oxford University Press, Third edition, 2008), 148–149. Rodin, *War and Self-Defense*, Chapter 5 on "International Law," 103–121, 111–114. Yoram Dinstein, *War, Aggression and Self*

Defense (Cambridge: Grotius Publications, 1988), 227–228. Crawford, "The False Promise of Preventive War," 118–119.

36. Walzer, ibid, 81.
37. McMahan, "Preventive War and the Killing of the Innocent," 172–174. Buchanan, "Justifying Preventive War," 126–128. Buchanan & Keohane, "The Preventive Use of Force," 4. Sinnot-Armstrong, "Preventive War—What is it Good For?," 215–217, where he argues that the temporal imminence of the attack is significant primarily as an epistemic indication of the probability of its occurrence. For discussion and partial rejection of this argument on the grounds that it does not always apply, see Kaufman, "What's Wrong with Preventive War?," 29.
38. Buchanan, "Justifying Preventive War," ibid, 126.
39. Rodin, *War and Self-Defense*, 41. Rodin, "The Problem with Prevention," 151.
40. Rodin, "The Problem with Prevention," ibid, 162–164, 163.
41. Rodin, ibid, 163.
42. Rodin, ibid, 161–166.
43. For the debate between Rodin and Luban on the conspiracy analogy, see Rodin, ibid, 166–170, and Luban, "Preventive War and Human Rights," 192–196.
44. Rodin, ibid, 163, cites The National Security Strategy of the United States of America (September 2002). http://georgewbushwhitehouse.archives.gov/nsc/nss/2002/ See also: See: John Yoo "Using Force" (2004) 71 University of Chicago Law Review, http://papers.ssrn.com/sol3/papers.cfm?abstract_id=530022 Last accessed March 8, 2012.
45. Walzer, *Just and Unjust* Wars, 75, Luban, "Preventive War and Human Rights," 172; and the hypothetical examples, in McMahan, "Preventive War and the Killing of the Innocent," 180–185. On the other hand, Crawford, "The False Promise of Preventive War," 119, insists that an attack is only imminent if it "can be made manifest within hours or weeks."
46. See: Luban, "Preventive War and Human Rights," ibid, 173; Shue, "What Would a Justified preventive Military Attack Look Like?," 228.
47. Fletcher and Ohlin, 163.
48. Walzer, *Just and Unjust Wars*, 80.
49. See UN Security Council Resolution 1737, December 23, 2006 www.acronym.org.uk/official-and-govt-documents/un-security-council-resolution-1737-2006-non-proliferation. Accessed June 8, 2014.
50. Luban, P.W., 230–1, 233; "Preventive War and Human Rights," 171.
51. Franklin Delano Roosevelt, *First Inaugural Address* (1933), "declaring war" on the great depression: www.bartleby.com/124/pres49.html. See also Jeremy Waldron's discussion of the impact of "fear itself" on terrorized societies, with the example of the US economy after 9/11, in Jeremy Waldron, *Torture, Terror and Tradeoffs—Philosophy for the White House* (Oxford: Oxford University Press, 2010): Chapter 5: "Safety and Security," 111–165, 154.
52. Walzer, 81. Emphasis is in the original.
53. Walzer, ibid.
54. Walzer, ibid, 269–283.
55. Posner and Sykes, 9.
56. Posner and Sykes, ibid, 16.
57. Posner and Sykes, ibid, 9.
58. Luban, "Preventive War and Human Rights," 173.
59. Luban, ibid, 190.
60. Ibid.
61. McMahan, "Preventive War and the Killing of the Innocent," 173: "expected harm" = "the magnitude of harm times the probability." Waldron, *Torture, Terror and Tradeoffs*, Chapter 2: "Security and Liberty: The Image of Balance," 20–47, 24: "R = magnitude of harm times the probability of its occurrence."
62. On "urgent necessity" as a condition for justified preemptive action, see Shue, "What Would a Justified Preventive Military Attack Look Like?," 227–230.

63. Luban, "Preventive War and Human Rights," 190.
64. Thomas Hurka, "Proportionality in the Morality of War," 33 *Philosophy & Public Affairs* (2005), 34–66, 37. On "last resort" see also Walzer, 84 (in connection with preemption) and 213.
65. Michael Walzer, *Arguing About War* (New Haven and London: Yale University press, 2004), at 88.
66. Hurka, "Proportionality and the Morality of War," 37. "Last-resort" does not imply surrender. Needless to say, it was not incumbent on Great Britain to make a separate peace with Nazi Germany before resorting to war as a last option. Nor would it have been wrong to resort to war earlier than it did.
67. Tomas Hurka, "Proportionality and Necessity" in: Larry May, ed., *Essays in Political Philosophy* (Cambridge: Cambridge University Press, 2008), 127. Emphasis appears in the original. www.chass.utoronto.ca/~thurka/docs/propandnec.pdf
68. Walzer, *Just and Unjust Wars*, 80.
69. Walzer, ibid, 81.
70. For some of this controversy over Ahmadinejad's statements about Israel, see for example: Julian Borger and Robert Booths, "Britain walks out of conference as Ahmadinejad calls Israel 'racist'," *The Guardian*, April 20, 2009. www.guardian.co.uk/world/2009/apr/20/un-conference-boycott-ahmadinejad. Accessed June 8, 2014. Ethan Bronner, "Just How Far Did They Go, Those Words Against Israel?" *The New York Times*, June 11, 2006. www.nytimes.com/2006/06/11/weekinreview/11bronner.html?_r=1. Accessed June 8, 2014. Toby Harnden, "The New York Times Explains Away Mahmud Ahmadinejad's threat to destroy Israel," *The Telegraph*, May 15, 2009. http://blogs.telegraph.co.uk/news/tobyharnden/9804928/New_York_Times_explains_away_Mahmoud_Ahmadinejads_threat_to_destroy_Israel/. Accessed June 8, 2014.
71. BBC News, Middle East: "Iran's Rouhani calls Israel 'old wound' on Islamic world," August 2, 2013. www.bbc.com/news/world-middle-east-23548906. Accessed June 8, 2014.
72. Walzer, *Just and Unjust Wars*, 81.
73. In this connection, I highly recommend Paul Berman, *Terror and Liberalism* (New York & London: Norton, 2003), Chapter VI: "Wishful Thinking," esp. at 123–128, Berman's description of the French anti-war socialists in the 1930's.
74. E.g., see again The National Security Strategy of the United States of America (September 2002). http://georgewbushwhitehouse.archives.gov/nsc/nss/2002/ and John Yoo, "Using Force:" http://papers.ssrn.com/sol3/papers.cfm?abstract_id=530022 Accessed March 8, 2012. See also the description of "The Bush Doctrine" in Kaufman, "What's Wrong with Preventive War?," 23.

7

ASSASSINATION

Targeting nuclear scientists

Introduction

Historically, airstrikes on nuclear facilities (Osirak in 1981 and the attack on Syria's nuclear reactor in 2007) have not been the only measure Israel has resorted to in order to impede its enemies' nuclear programs. In the early 1950s, Israeli Mossad agents carried out a series of assassination operations against prominent Arab scientists. Most notably, Israel was assumed to be responsible for the death of Egyptian theoretical physicist Dr Ali Mustafa Mosharafa. More recently, five Iranian nuclear scientists have been furtively killed over the past decade, most with motorcycle-borne assailants attaching small magnetic bombs to the exterior of the victims' cars.

Various issues of principle arise in these cases, some of which were covered by discussion in the previous chapter. These concern the preemptive nature of attacks on citizens of states that are not officially engaged in war, as well as the violation of state sovereignty. Recent assassinations were carried out outside the framework of any internationally recognized state of hostility. At best, they were preemptive hostile acts perpetrated on foreign soil. As noted in Chapter 6, there also remain considerable practical disagreements about the authenticity, gravity, and immediacy of any Iranian threat to which these assassinations are allegedly responding, as well as about the feasible and appropriate means of contending with it.

This chapter sets aside these surrounding *jus ad bellum* issues, such as whether any military action against Iran can be justified at the present time. Instead, this final part of the book focuses exclusively on the civilian status of the selected targets, questioning the legitimacy of selecting scientists as direct targets of attack. Are scientists who partake in their nations' armament program ever liable to attack, even in wartime or in the course of preemptive self-defense?

The traditional answer given by just war theory, as well as by international law, has always been that they are not. Men and women of science, even nuclear science, are clearly civilians. *Jus in bello* rules—both legal and moral—prohibit the targeting of civilians in wartime, while peacetime rules prohibit murder. Even where combatants are concerned, assassination may fall under the Geneva conventions' prohibition on killing by perfidious means if it involves "... acts inviting the confidence of an adversary to lead him to believe that he is entitled to, or is obliged to accord, protection under the rules of international law applicable in armed conflict, with intent to betray that confidence."[1] Such acts include the assailant's feigning of civilian status, as assassins commonly do.[2]

While there are good moral reasons for upholding all these rules, as I shall indicate throughout, they may not exhaust our moral thinking on assassination, or settle all controversy over the status of its potential targets. In contrast to an absolute prohibition of indiscriminate terrorism or the use of torture, an absolute moral ban on assassination is difficult to justify. For example, few, if any, would argue that the assassination of Nazi leaders, officials or key weapons manufacturers would have been undesirable during World War II, or in the years leading up to it. I doubt there is anyone who does not support some (non-hypothetical) instance of assassination or political murder throughout human history. (How many of us would have opposed the assassination of Heydrich?).

The next section distinguishes assassination from typical cases of targeted killing, as well as from terrorism, and considers the compelling moral arguments against assassination specifically. While these forceful arguments support the legal ban on perfidious killing, I argue that they are ultimately inconclusive in determining the right course of action in every specific case, and cannot prescribe an absolute moral prohibition on assassination.

The following section discusses the violation of civilian immunity involved in the targeting of scientists and the suggestion that targeted killing involves an unraveling of the norm against homicide.[3] Civilians retain their legal immunity from attack unless (and for such time as) they participate directly in hostilities.[4] Notwithstanding civilian immunity, however, both reigning theories of the just war discussed throughout this book, suggest that civilians may lose their natural immunity from attack when they contribute directly to the business of fighting, and not only when actively participating in combat. From a consequential perspective, this section points to the advantage of pinpointed attacks in attaining military goals with a minimum of casualties.

The final discussion in this chapter pursues the analogy between nuclear scientists and munitions workers. Weapons manufacturers, their factories and employees, are accorded less than absolute protection within just war theory, and even by international law. Both the traditional account of just war theory and its contemporary revisionist versions allow for the partial extension of combatant status to civilians who are either threatening or responsible for an unjust threat. Considering these arguments helps to illuminate our thinking on contemporary cases, suggesting that scientists involved in weapons manufacturing may in some cases be morally liable to attack.

Recent dramatic events compel us to think through this issue of political violence against arms producers in a principled manner, whatever our particular views on the Iranian case may be. Political judgments concerning the particular targets recently selected for assassination will remain an open question.[5] In the Iranian case, the assassination of scientists may well form part of a combined, and as yet unfolding, strategy. If an Israeli attack on Iran's nuclear facilities is forthcoming, these preceding assassinations will have deprived Iran of some of the individuals who could contribute to the rehabilitation of its nuclear capacity, rendering a military strike more effective and its results more durable. All this remains unknown and arguable. Surrounding issues concerning preemption, state sovereignty, necessity and the utility of anticipatory attacks will not be revisited in this chapter.

Several further caveats: the succeeding discussion does not take place at any "deep moral level" of the type notably suggested by Jeff McMahan for reflecting on the rules of war.[6] All the following moral arguments are intended to guide action, not merely to appraise it, and hence apply at every level of morality, if there is in fact more than one. I will not argue for any incongruence between the laws of war—prohibiting the direct targeting of non-combatants—and a deep morality of war which recognizes civilian liability to attack. Morality rightly prohibits the targeting of civilians, as is well reflected in the Laws of Armed Conflict, and this prohibition ought to be sustained for reasons of deep morality and not merely out of practical considerations. The discussion considers the possibility of rare exceptions to the existing, and morally justified, legal rules. I will not propose a change in the contemporary laws of armed conflict or adjustment of our morality of war in view of modern realities such as the emergence of nuclear power or the prevalence of asymmetric warfare.[7] Instead, I apply existing moral theories and legislation to new cases.

Finally, the discussion does not concern the paradox, suggested by Michael Walzer, whereby a political leader may at times be right, even required, to "dirty his hands" in doing what it is morally wrong for him to do.[8] The issue at hand concerns possible moral justifications for particular assassinations, rather than excuses. Are there exceptional cases in which we ought to be sympathetic toward assassins—morally justifying them and cheering them on—even as we recognize their breach of morally worthy legal rules?[9]

Assassination

The assassinations of key civilians are not typical cases of what is called "targeted killing," which usually refers to a state targeting members of irregular belligerent organizations.[10] The standard justification for targeted killing of "terrorists" points to the controversial assignment of combatant status to the targets in question.[11] In Israel, the High Court of Justice defined the targets of Israel's assassination policy in the West Bank and Gaza during the Second Intifada as "civilians who are unlawful combatants."[12] Justice Aharon Barak stated that civilians who illegally participate directly in hostilities lose the protections accorded to civilians in wartime, though they remain civilians who do not acquire the war rights of soldiers.[13]

None of this can be said of Iranian scientists, who are unquestionably non-combatants. Partly for this reason, no one takes responsibility for their assassination.[14] Scientists are civilians, and the assassination of civilians is illegal. As Michael Walzer maintains regarding political assassination, "Characteristically (and not foolishly) lawyers have frowned on assassination."[15] Not foolishly, because assassins target non-military personnel who stand clearly under the protection of the war convention and positive international law.[16] The requirement to distinguish between soldiers and civilians is the central principle of *jus in bello*, restricting warfare and preventing it from deteriorating into wholesale slaughter.

Whatever the arguments for war, there is obvious moral merit in narrowing the cycle of violence by limiting the scope of legitimate targets, most notably by upholding the legal protection of civilians.[17] If not always entirely innocent or non-threatening, civilians are almost always entirely defenseless, supplying an additional, non-consequencialist, moral reason for their comprehensive immunity.[18] Notwithstanding this, following Walzer, the assignment of particular categories of people to the class of protected non-combatants may only partially represent our common moral judgments about their assassination.[19]

While assassinations target civilians they are not, strictly speaking, incidents of terrorism, though they are sometimes described in these terms. According to Walzer, "terrorism" (as distinct from political assassination) is the intentional random murder of defenseless non-combatants with the intent of spreading fear of mortal danger amidst a civilian population as a strategy designed to advance political ends. "Randomness is the crucial feature of terrorist activity," because it is precisely the fear of arbitrary death, by pure chance, that terrorizes civilians at large and induces political surrender to the terrorists' cause.[20]

The assassination of scientists may spread fear within a small subset of the scientific community but it is not random, nor can it serve as a terrorizing deterrent. Scientists in totalitarian states cannot be terrorized out of participating in their nation's nuclear project because they are unlikely to have much choice in the matter. Assassinations aim at particular people whose direct contribution to a nuclear threat is deemed significant, and their removal believed beneficial to impeding it. This, for example, was the case when the United States considered assassinating German physicist Werner Heisenberg, believed to be working on an atomic bomb for Adolf Hitler in the early 1940s.[21]

Assassination has in its favor that it does not kill randomly or indiscriminately. Assassination, Walzer maintains, necessarily involves the drawing of a line "between people who can and people who cannot be killed."[22] The former consist exclusively "of officials, the political agents of regimes, thought to be oppressive."[23] Not unlike the laws of war, the assassin's "political code" *aims* narrowly at its victim and refrains from targeting large categories of people whom the assassin regards as immune from attack.[24] At times, avoiding all-out war and/or large-scale collateral damage is the very purpose of resorting to this limited tactic. The assassin aims narrowly at a civilian representative, or operative, of a regime regarded as oppressive or dangerous. Ultimately, Walzer tells us, "we judge the assassin by his victim, and when the victim is Hitler-like in character, we are likely to praise the assassin's work, though we still do not call him a soldier."[25]

Such praise, however, will depend entirely on our political assessment of the target in question. Most victims of assassination are not Hitler-like cases, and judgment of the victim and his assassin are likely to be controversial. Unlike the neutral *in bello* laws of war that apply regardless of justice of cause on either side, our moral assessment of any particular assassination requires taking a substantive stand on the political struggle engaged in by the assassin as well as of the threat to be averted.[26] Jeremy Waldron argues against assassination precisely on the grounds that a norm permitting such killings cannot work as a neutral principle. When contemplating the incorporation of a norm permitting targeted killing within the international laws of armed conflict, Waldron cautions us to consider whether we would be comfortable with such a norm in the hands of our adversaries, as well as the potential abuse such a norm might generate in the hands of our own governments.[27]

Understood as a pragmatic warning, this argument certainly has much merit. When instituting a new norm—either by legislation or even by international practice —we have to worry about the ways in which our enemies (perhaps even our own leaders) might act on it, possibly interpreting it in ways anathema to us and to our disadvantage. Recent attempts to assassinate Israeli diplomats, probably in retaliation for the killing of Iranian scientists, are cases in point.[28] This practical consideration, however, cannot in itself yield an absolute prohibition on assassination, or offer a decisive consideration regarding the introduction of a new, permissive, norm into the international arena.[29] It is in the nature of practical consequential considerations that they can pull in various directions. As in the case of the rule against preventive war, here too, it is certainly not inconceivable that the benefits of a particular act of assassination, or set of assassinations, and the drawbacks of refraining from them, will be so overwhelming as to outweigh even the bad consequences of harm to the general rule.

Beyond any practical warning, there is obviously also the related deontological requirement of universalizability. Taken as a normative warning in this case, testing the universalizability of assassination does not require us to consider practical obstacles such as "the bad guys" taking hold of our permissive rule and abusing its license. It is an intellectual exercise, which requires us to consider the application of the norm we select, interpreted accurately and in good faith, by our adversaries. In concrete terms, it might require us to put a different face on the targets we are considering.

Applied to the issue at hand, endorsing a permissive norm allowing the assassination of nuclear scientists would commit us to regard our own scientists, professors of physics and weapons manufacturers, as liable to personal attack by foreign forces in comparable circumstances. Would Israel, for example, be comfortable with the application of such a norm to the 6,000 or so employees of Rafael (Authority for the Development of Armaments) or Israel's Aerospace Industries (IAI)? What if Palestinian militants, unable to attack a munitions facility, were to target one of the buses collecting these employees for work every morning, thus (let us suppose) setting back the latest stage of Israel's drone program which they regard as threatening? As in the actual cases of atomic scientists, we can assume little if any collateral damage, while key personnel are killed by those who regard them as a significant threat and their killings as a form of self-defense. The guerillas may have no other recourse for halting the weapons program. In that sense the hypothetical attack is necessary and proportionate (for attaining the military goal), and it is effective. In both the hypothetical and the actual cases, the targets carry with them significant replicable knowledge which they can recreate if their facility is destroyed.[30] Nevertheless, we do not usually view our own scientists as threatening and liable to assassination.

A further argument against assassination points to *post-bellum* considerations. Assassination, Michael Gross points out, particularly as a subset of perfidy, deepens hostility and mistrust, which jeopardizes the chances of attaining peace between the warring parties, thus not only enhancing but also prolonging the conflict.[31] Gross's *post-bellum* concerns are raised exclusively in the context of national liberation struggles, such as the Israeli–Palestinian conflict, rather than as a conclusive argument against all forms of targeted killing within interstate warfare. Nonetheless, at least in local national liberation movements, Gross argues, the antagonism and mistrust caused by assassination undermine efforts at post-war peace and reconstruction.[32]

In a similar vein, more conclusively condemning the practice in general, Waldron cites *The Metaphysics of Morals* (1797), where Kant wrote:

> A state against which war is being waged is permitted to use any means of defense except those that would make its subjects unfit to be citizens. . . . Means of defense that are not permitted include using its own subjects as . . . assassins or poisoners (among whom so-called snipers, who lie in wait to ambush individuals, might well be classed). . .[33]

Waldron goes on to explain that

> Some of the reasons Kant adduced for his position have to do with the longer term prospects for peace. In his earlier essay on "Perpetual Peace" . . . Kant said: "No nation at war with another shall permit such acts of war as shall make mutual trust impossible during some future time of peace" and he cites "the use of Assassins (*percussores*) [and] poisoners (*venefici*)" as examples.[34]

Waldron argues that we should take what Kant says seriously because

> Such stratagems make murderers of our citizens, and . . . being a murderer in this sense is not just a fact about killing someone (like being a soldier on active service). It is something vicious one becomes, a dishonorable character one takes on, one that cannot then be sloughed off just as soon as the circumstances that call for targeted killing have ended.[35]

Kant's primary example for this argument, however, in both *The Metaphysics of Morals* and "Perpetual Peace," is the use of spies.[36] In "Perpetual Peace" Kant cautions against the perfidious nature of spying (just as he argues in *The Metaphysics of Morals* against the use of sharpshooters lying in wait to ambush individuals), and he takes this to be a prime example of dishonor. Moreover, Kant cautions that, once used, any of "these malicious practices would be carried over into peacetime and thus destroy its purpose altogether."[37] Spying is also Kant's first example in the relevant section of *The Metaphysics of Morals* of methods that are to be wholly excluded: "Using one's own subjects as spies. . . ."[38]

Perhaps Kant was right, as he certainly was in "Perpetual Peace," about espionage spilling over into peacetime. Nevertheless, the international community has not suspended its use of spies on the basis of this argument, and it is therefore unclear how conclusive it is, in and of itself, with regard to any of the other dishonorable measures to which Kant refers. In spite of Kant's compelling argument, few nations refrain from spying, either in war or in peacetime, and there is no crime of spying under international law.[39] It is not clear that we should treat assassination any differently, at least on the basis of this argument alone.

Admittedly, spying contributes less directly to killing than assassination does, but this was not Kant's objection to assassination. In the case of both espionage and assassination alike, Kant's concern was for maintaining mutual trust with a view to future peace, as well as the honor of combatants. These are weighty, but not exclusive, considerations, and have not tipped the balance in the case of espionage, though Kant was concerned primarily with this practice. In some cases, attaining mutual trust, reducing hostilities and negotiating peaceful solutions may not even be feasible, regardless of any assassination or spying.[40] It remains indeterminate how conclusive we should regard this specific Kantian argument about maintaining trust and attaining peace in any particular case, attractive as it may be at some deep moral level.

That said, Additional Protocol 1 does prohibit some of the wartime measures Kant considered particularly diabolical and malicious. Article 37 of additional protocol I (and its precursor, Article 23(b) of the Hague Regulations), prohibit perfidy that results in killing, injuring or capturing an enemy.[41] This is the source of the specific prohibition on assassination (as opposed to the more general prohibition on murder and the *jus in bello* prohibition on targeting civilians) and it applies to the perfidious killing of soldiers as well as civilians, most notably by means of feigning non-combatant status.

But even with the crime of perfidious killing—in which case we may accept Kant's logic as the rule—it is difficult to view the resulting norm as an absolute moral prohibition. An example of what many might consider a possible moral exception to the rule against perfidious killing, albeit of combatants, can be found in Walzer's retelling of an account provided by a German officer in WWII, Captain Helmut Tausend, of an ambush on German soldiers as they marched through the French countryside in the years of the German occupation. His story is recorded in a scene from the documentary film *The Sorrow and the Pity*:

They passed a group of young men, French peasants, or so it seemed, digging potatoes. But these were not in fact peasants; they were members of the Resistance. As the Germans marched by, the "peasants" dropped their shovels, picked up guns hidden in the field, and opened fire. Fourteen of the soldiers were hit. Years later, their Captain was still indignant. "You call that 'partisan' resistance? I don't. Partisans for me are men who can be identified, men who wear a special armband or cap, something with which to recognize them. What happened in that potato field was murder."[42]

Murder

Kant's argument is inconclusive in determining international law, and not comprehensive in determining our moral judgment in all cases of treacherous killing. Despite Kant's powerful arguments about trust and honor along with its *post-bellum* rationale, the Law of Armed Conflict (LOAC) does not prohibit spying. While perfidious killing is legally prohibited, few would argue for an absolute moral prohibition applicable in every instance.

Waldron supplies a final argument against assassination, in keeping with his more general defense of civilian immunity.[43] Waldron worries rightly about the unraveling of the norm against homicide, particularly when politicians face challenges, such as insurgencies, to which assassination presents a tempting response.[44] He reminds us that the point of orientation in the area of deliberate killing is the prohibition on murder—absent the LOAC we are prohibited from killing anyone at all—and so any argument favoring the killing of anyone, even in wartime, carries a heavy burden of proof to justify moving us away from this default position.[45] According to Waldron, we accept the traditional principle of discrimination which permits the killing of soldiers

> not because good reasons can be identified for allowing combatants to be killed, though sometimes they can, but largely because it looks as though this is a regulative line that can be defended (just!) in the midst of an activity that is otherwise comprehensively murderous.[46]

Lacking any realistic prospect of prohibiting war altogether, he argues, we adopt the principle of discrimination largely because it has "proved roughly sustainable and administrable. . . . We cling to it not because we think the killing of combatants is OK but because we are doubtful of our ability to hold any other line."[47]

But now, Waldron worries, the arguments supporting targeted killing seem to be moving in the opposite direction, assuming as their point of departure the proposition that we are entirely justified in killing certain people in wartime (i.e., soldiers), and working their way permissively outwards from that assumption:

> It seems that the first instinct is to search for areas where killing is already "alright"—killing in self defense . . . or killing combatants in wartime . . .—

and then to see if we can concoct analogies between whatever reasons we can associate with such licenses and the new area of homicide we want to explore. In my view, *that is how a norm against murder unravels*.[48]

Understanding the moral background as the prohibition on murder along with the precariousness of sustaining limitations on killing in war should make us extremely cautious, Waldron argues, about attempts to introduce permissive changes into the LOAC.[49] Killing is never "alright," only unavoidably tolerated in wartime, and it is therefore morally erroneous, and often opportunistic and inherently abusive, to proceed to unravel the taboo against killing by reasoning that "We are allowed to kill some people by principles we already have; surely, by the same reasoning, there must be other people we are also allowed to kill."[50]

Waldron's argument poses a significant challenge to any defense of assassination policies, most certainly including the targeting of scientists, because any plausible argument for expanding liability beyond the category of combatants has to proceed precisely in this way. This is not to say that this challenge cannot be met, or that the justification of *in bello* discrimination is primarily its usefulness in narrowing the cycle of violence and its relative enforceability in the heat of conflict. Granted that the point of orientation is the general prohibition on murder, most non-pacifists nonetheless assert that some wartime killings are justified, and not merely inevitably tolerated.[51]

Recall Walzer's explanation of how soldiers lose their natural immunity in war: "That right is lost by those who bear arms 'effectively' because they pose a danger to other people. It is retained by those who don't bear arms at all."[52] And though this criterion of liability to attack is not unanimously accepted, most just war theorists believe there are good identifiable reasons for allowing at least some combatants to be killed in war. Figuring out these reasons is the first step toward the type of argument that Waldron cautions against, because he believes it leads irresponsibly to an unraveling of our existing restrictions on killing in war, though he admits that philosophers who make these arguments do so mostly in good faith.[53]

Walzer's further comments on the principle of distinction supply the most prominent illustration of the unraveling Waldron envisions. After explaining how posing a threat can deprive a person of his or her natural immunity from attack, Walzer writes:

> We begin with the distinction between soldiers engaged in combat and soldiers at rest; then we shift to the distinction between soldiers as a class and civilians; and then we concede this or that group of civilians as the processes of economic mobilization establish its direct contribution to the business of fighting.[54]

In the case of targeted killing specifically, however, it is crucial to note that it is usually adopted as a means of actually narrowing the cycle of violence rather than extending it. Targeted killing kills fewer people, whether directly or collaterally, than conventional warfare does. Philosophical arguments for targeted killing admittedly expand the class of individuals who are liable to attack beyond the category of uniformed combatants, but the actual number of people killed in targeting operations is deliberately limited. Targeting is usually adopted as a substitute for large-scale military operations, or as an alternative to pursuing a more costly tactic, in terms of human life, in the course of an ongoing conflict. The very essence of pinpointed attacks is the achievement of necessary military goals with a minimum of casualties, both directly and collaterally. Any argument that regards all wartime killing—of combatants as well as civilians—as an encroachment on the taboo against homicide ought to accord considerable merit to a tactic that drastically reduces the number of fatalities amidst both classes of individuals.

It remains questionable whether civilian scientists can ever be legitimate targets of attack, even if their targeting is the most economical means toward achieving military advantage. One final task in advancing our moral reasoning in the contemporary cases of nuclear scientists is to consider the class of civilians who manufacture arms in light of the liabilities and protections accorded them in international law as well as by various theories of the just war.

Munitions workers

An atomic scientist is legally a civilian who, at worst, can be described as taking an indirect part in hostilities. Like any munitions worker, his facility is vulnerable to harm during wartime and may be destroyed if it is providing military capability: "Civilians cannot enjoy protection from attack when they enter military objectives (e.g., by working in a military base or in a munitions factory)."[55] But the off-duty munitions worker is protected from harm.[56]

Thomas Nagel and Michael Walzer have argued that combatant status may be partially extended to munitions workers. Both suggest that the threatening nature which (on their traditional accounts of just war theory) justifies the wartime vulnerability of combatants extends to on-duty munitions workers as well, rendering them liable to attack. Nagel writes that:

> . . . the threat presented by an army and its members does not consist merely in the fact that they are men, but in the fact that they are armed and are using their arms in the pursuit of certain objectives. Contributions to their arms and logistics are contributions to this threat; contributions to their mere existence as men are not.[57]

Similarly, Walzer explains the vulnerability of munitions workers as a partial extension of combatant status to some who are "at least nominally civilians" but who produce the equipment that soldiers require specifically in order to fight.[58] On this understanding, munitions workers are partially assimilated to the class of combatants due to the threat they pose to their enemy, while other civilians, including those who contribute less directly to the war effort, remain immune from attack.[59]

From the perspective of the Law of International Armed Conflict, on the other hand, munitions workers are not assimilated to the class of combatants at all, not even part-time. Their civilian contribution does not constitute "direct participation" in hostilities; hence they are not legitimate wartime targets. Causing the deaths of munitions workers is permissible only as foreseeable collateral harm to civilians, assumed to be proportionate in relation to the targeting of their facility as a legitimate military objective.[60] Yoram Dinstein explains that:

> A civilian working in a munitions factory does not cease to be a civilian—and does not lose his general mantle of protection—although he is patently running a risk while he is present on the premises of what constitutes a military objective.[61]

"That presence does not permanently contaminate the laborers, turning them *ipso facto* into 'quasi-combatants'."[62]

Either way, however, both the law and the traditional account of just war theory agree that while at work munitions workers are partly vulnerable, either directly or collaterally, but that: "Upon leaving the factories, civilian laborers shed the risk of being subject to attack. The attacker is forbidden to follow the workforce home and hit civilians there."[63]

Neither the legal nor the moralized account of munitions workers is acceptable to revisionist just war theorists, who question the underlying principle of distinction between combatants and civilians, and the moralized notion that it serves to separate threatening personnel from those who are doing no harm. Apart from anything else, McMahan argues, "It is, however, a notorious problem in just war theory that there are many people who pose a threat in war who would not be considered combatants by anyone."[64] The orthodox explanation of the legal requirement of distinction is problematic because not all combatants in fact pose a threat, while some civilians pose grave threats.

More specifically, McMahan supplies an extremely pertinent and timely example of the issue at hand:

> Elderly professors of physics working for the Manhattan project in laboratories at Los Alamos and the University of Chicago posed a far greater threat to the Japanese than any ordinary American soldier, but no one would say that they were combatants. Nor would any defendant of the moralized notion of a combatant be willing to extend combatant status to a computer science professor whose research during a time of war will soon have many applications including improvements in weapons technologies that will be used against her country's enemies.[65]

By contributing to munitions production one does not forfeit civilian status, even though such contributions may be considerably more threatening to the enemy than serving as a plain soldier at the front. For McMahan, this, among other examples, points to the deficiency in the traditional just war theory notion that posing a threat to others is the correct criterion of liability to attack in war.

Citing Walzer and Nagel as the prominent proponents of the idea that posing a threat establishes combatant status, McMahan continues,

> Various writers in the just war tradition have sought to narrow the gap between the moralized notion of combatant status and the ordinary concept of a combatant by conceding that a limited class of people outside the military count as combatants, while denying that combatant status extends any further among civilians.[66]

But, McMahan argues, they have not gone far enough:

> . . . even this gloss on the moralized notion of combatant status does not solve the problem. For the work that a computer scientist is doing quietly in her campus office may well produce some medical technology that a wounded soldier needs to live, but it will also provide military hardware that other soldiers will find enormously useful in fighting. Although she is not legally a combatant, it seems that she must be a combatant in the moralized sense and thus must be a legitimate target of attack according to the reigning theory of the just war—despite the fact that few if any of that theory's proponents would accept that this is really an implication of their view.[67]

Scientists are legally civilians.[68] According to McMahan, neither Walzer nor Nagel would be willing to extend his moralized notion of "combatants" far enough away from the law in order to include "off-duty" scientists, such as professors on campus, thus essentially leaving the gravest military threats immune from attack. At the same time, they sanction the wholesale killing of all combatants in wartime, however minor the degree of their contribution to the war effort and regardless of the justice of their cause. This, according to McMahan, cannot be morally right, though here again he concedes that maintaining the traditional distinction between combatants and civilians offers considerable consequential advantages in terms of narrowing the cycle of violence, and ought to be legally preserved for that reason.[69]

On deep moral reflection, however, once again in this connection McMahan questions the traditional assertion that posing a threat is the correct criterion for acquiring combatant status. If this were the case, McMahan argues, a computer science professor working to produce new military hardware at her university office would qualify for combatant status by virtue of the threat she poses, and consequently constitute a legitimate target of attack.[70] Walzer and Nagel, he suggests, are involved in an inconsistency when they deny this.

Overall, as we have seen throughout, the core content of McMahan's individualist account of just war theory is his alternative criterion for liability to attack in wartime: moral responsibility for an objectively unjustified or wrongful threat, rather than merely posing a threat.[71] This would presumably include some scientists developing prohibited weapons as legitimate targets. It might license the killing of various physicists and computer scientists, if this proves necessary and proportionate in order to avert an unjust threat.

McMahan also believes that it is the responsibility of any individual, (even young conscripted soldiers, and certainly a well-educated mature adult), to establish the moral nature of the projects in which he is involved, and to refuse to participate in those that prove to be unjust. When people ignore this responsibility to inquire into the justice of their nation's conflicts and subsequently to refuse to participate in injustice, they are thereby, in McMahan's terms, morally liable to harm.[72]

McMahan's morality of war paves the way toward legitimizing wartime assaults on specific civilians, including some professors of physics and computer scientists.[73] On this account, nuclear scientists who contribute to an unjust threat render themselves liable to attack; killing them in order to avert the threat is therefore permissible, subject to necessity and proportionality. McMahan's examples are intended to suggest that revisionist just war theory does better than the orthodox approach in explaining our moral intuitions in the case of scientists and others. On this issue as well, however, his revisionist approach is not without its problems, and some of the general critiques of this theory may carry over into the specific case.

McMahan assumes that establishing whether a threat is just or unjust is a matter of discernable fact, accessible to the scientists in his examples as well as to ourselves. Beyond the obvious difficulty in establishing objective justice (did the physics professors at Los Alamos pose an unjust threat to the Japanese?), the degree of moral responsibility attributable to civilians is also problematic, most notably for present purposes in the case of professors. Professors do not instigate hostilities, command them or carry them out. When professors contribute to a nuclear program they may form part of a threat which could, arguably, render them liable to attack under a traditional criterion of liability. Establishing their moral responsibility for an unjust threat, however, is a more complicated and controversial task. A scientist may intend to contribute only to his nation's nuclear energy program, rather than to the creation of nuclear weapons. Within a totalitarian regime, he may have little say on what he is required to do. Even in a democracy, there is usually little opportunity of employment for nuclear scientists outside government projects.

McMahan concedes that individuals (such as conscripts or coerced scientists) who succumb to overwhelming pressure from a totalitarian regime often possess a full moral excuse for participating in injustice. He maintains, nonetheless, that individuals who contribute to an unjust threat, even under duress, such as scientists who build genocidal weapons for totalitarian regimes, lack justification (as opposed to possible excuses) for their wrongful action, and are therefore liable to attack.[74] A scientist in a totalitarian regime might have refused to study nuclear physics to begin with. If compelled to do so, or mislead into believing he would work only on civilian nuclear power, the scientist could accept martyrdom instead of building genocidal weapons.

Reservations notwithstanding, McMahan's alternative morality of war has gained prominence within contemporary just war theory and offers an important perspective on the issue in hand. By continuing to participate in injustice, whatever the excuse, the scientist renders himself liable to defensive attack by those defending themselves against the threat he has contributed to creating. In cases in which a state openly threatens its adversaries with nuclear aggression McMahan would insist on its scientists' responsibility to be knowledgeable about, or at least suspicious of, their country's intentions.[75] If they continue to contribute directly to the production of nuclear arms for an aggressive regime they would, on McMahan's account of just war theory, certainly be liable to attack regardless of their whereabouts, if their removal is both necessary and proportionate in countering the threat.

As McMahan himself recognizes, however, there is no principled barrier to reaching this conclusion regarding the liability of nuclear scientists from a traditional perspective as well. Walzer comments on the nature of necessity, regarding civilians who directly contribute to the business of fighting (such as seamen on merchant ships or ships carrying military supplies) that:

> Once direct contribution has been established, only "military necessity" can determine whether the civilians involved are attacked or not. They ought not to be attacked if their activities can be stopped, or their products seized or destroyed, in some other way without significant risk . . . But whenever seizure without shooting ceases to be possible, the obligation ceases also and the right lapses.[76]

On this traditional account, scientists developing nuclear armaments may be construed as direct contributors to the business of war. As Nagel points out, contributions to arms and logistics are contributions to the threat.[77] In Walzer's terms, they produce the equipment that soldiers require specifically in order to fight. Once this direct contribution is established, military necessity may dictate that they be attacked if there is no other way of seizing or destroying their products.[78] If Walzer is correct in arguing that the nature of wartime necessity may be such as to authorize the seizure or destruction of military products by attacking the civilians who produce or transport them, then the targeting of scientists might be viewed as similarly necessary for destroying their military know-how or expertise—such as their intellectual capacity to develop a program to enrich uranium.

There remains an important legal difference between Walzer's example and the assassination of scientists. The crew on ships carrying military supplies is subject to collateral harm when this is incidentally necessary for seizing their goods. There is no way to sink a merchant ship without endangering the crew, but the members of the crew are themselves collateral to the military value of the target. By contrast, the direct targeting of scientists, even in order to destroy their inseparable expertise, cannot conceivably be construed as collateral. Killing the scientist may be a secondary intention in relation to destroying his professional skills or rendering them unusable, but this killing is nonetheless an intended effect.

As opposed to the LOAC, however, Walzer and Nagel's respective discussions of direct contribution do not regard the killing of arms transporters or munitions workers as civilian collateral damage. Instead, both partially extend combatant status to direct contributors, rendering them liable to intentional attack.[79] As McMahan points out, they concede that a limited class of people outside the military count as combatants.[80] In fact, Walzer and Nagel's account of munitions workers as partial combatants—taken to its natural conclusion—could license even the killing of off-duty munitions workers, as McMahan rightly observes.[81]

Arguing against the view that "civilians working in munitions factories assume the status of so-called 'quasi-combatants'," Dinstein points out that if they did, it would be difficult to understand why they may not be attacked before having reached the factory, or after leaving it.[82] While combatants are not liable to attack when they are on vacation—when out of uniform and in their homes—they may be targeted on their way to the base or while off duty and at rest within it. If munitions workers are partly assimilated into the class of combatants, as Walzer and Nagel assert, then it is indeed unclear that this would not license their targeting in their cars to and from work, or wherever they are engaged in the business of war, at least in exceptional circumstances of necessity. McMahan correctly observes that traditional just war theory, which applies distinction on the basis of threat and partly extends to munitions workers, ought logically also to extend to nuclear scientists.[83]

Furthermore, the threat posed by nuclear scientists is far greater than the harmful nature of civilian workers in a bullet factory, both in terms of magnitude of the created threat and in terms of the extent of the workers' contribution to it. Moreover, while munitions workers cease to be threatening when they leave the factory, and soldiers on leave pose no threat to the enemy, this is far from the case with nuclear scientists. Nuclear scientists carry their knowledge with them in their minds, and their products may be reproduced wherever they go. In the age of personal computers it is sometimes difficult to distinguish the on-duty from the off-duty munitions worker (when is the scientist at her computer working on the A-bomb as opposed to playing Tetris?). It has become virtually impossible to separate the workplace from the worker or the product from its producer. If even the simplest of munitions workers are partially assimilated to the class of combatants, as Walzer and Nagel suggest, there is then no barrier to targeting nuclear scientists directly, if and when this is commanded by military necessity.

Partly extending combatant status to the class of munitions workers would generate a morally neutral permission to kill scientists contributing to a credible threat, regardless of the justness or injustice of their nation's cause for war. McMahan's account, by contrast, supports only a non-neutral principle that might permit the assassination of a scientist working for an unscrupulous regime, but not the assassination of scientists working for a just regime. Walzer and Nagel's logic would extend symmetrically to the killing of all scientists who produce weapons for their governments, including our own, provided they pose a threat to their adversaries and that there is no reasonable alternative for hampering that threat.

Traditional neutrality with regard to *jus ad bellum* does not, however, entail moral symmetry between individuals who pose a threat and those who do not. Following Walzer's example of civilian ships carrying military supplies, the license to kill arms transporters or manufacturers applies only to those who contribute directly to a threat (whether just or unjust) and whose removal is dictated by military necessity as a last resort option. With regard to the production of nuclear weapons specifically, such a rule would not apply equally to nuclear scientists working for benign democracies and those manufacturing nuclear weapons for threatening regimes. In keeping with the reigning theory of the just war, nations who threaten their adversaries with nuclear weapons may render their scientists vulnerable to attack by virtue of their contribution to that threat, if removing them is necessary to countering it. This might well apply to scientists working for regimes that threaten to carry out genocidal attacks.

To summarize, both contemporary leading accounts of just war theory offer interesting insights into recent assassinations of nuclear scientists, insights that serve to explain any mixed intuitions in contemporary cases. Civilian immunity notwithstanding, orthodox just war theory, as well as McMahan's individualist morality of war, suggests that scientists who directly participate in the business of war may be liable to attack in exceptional circumstances in which their removal is dictated by military necessity. In an age in which high-ranking munitions workers, such as nuclear scientists, may be inseparable from their military knowledge or its products, it is arguable that killing them can, in rare cases, be dictated by the urgent military necessity of destroying their intellectual property, or expertise. Though admittedly controversial, this suggestion places the killing of scientists on a par with Walzer's more traditional examples of civilians who directly contribute to the business of fighting, such as munitions workers or the crew of merchant ships carrying military supplies.

Concluding remarks

The direct targeting of civilians is illegal, and for good reason. Whatever the degree of threat they pose, civilians are defenseless persons rightly protected by the laws of war. Killing defenseless individuals is morally repugnant and reminiscent of terrorism, though it is not always tantamount to it. Assassins, Walzer tells us, ought to be marked off for the better from those who terrorize by killing at random, regardless of whether or not we support their cause.[84] Gaining moral superiority over terrorists is, however, a small victory for assassins and the nations that dispatch them. Most assassins remain despicable murderers. Any exceptions require overwhelming justification in terms of the liability of the victim and the urgent necessity of their removal, in order to outweigh the breach of the relevant moral and legal taboos. That said, however, producing atomic weapons for a threatening regime—directly contributing to a potentially genocidal nuclear project—would probably serve to overcome these restraints, on any account of the morality of war.

From a purely consequential perspective, assassination is the lesser of two evils when a few acts of killing can substitute for large scale war. Whether or not recent assassinations aim to substitute war against Iran, or whether they aim to complement preemptive war by removing the agents who could subsequently rebuild Iran's nuclear program in its aftermath, remains to be seen. The potential success of either of these projects—retarding Iran's nuclear project without resorting to war, or enhancing any future military achievements by removing its scientists in advance—also remain an open question that cannot be settled in the realm of philosophy or law.

Assassination is more easily justified in terms of human rights when the status of the victim is assimilated, at least in part, to the class of combatants. This type of move is admittedly problematic, as Waldron points out, in terms of loosening the taboo against homicide.[85] Nevertheless, just assassinations are at least possible. No one, I think, would deny that there have been some just assassins in the course of recorded history. Justifying the assassination of Iranian nuclear scientists specifically would require settling a wide range of surrounding practical issues that remain largely unknown and controversial, such as the identity and precise motive of the perpetrators, the gravity of any Iranian threat and the projected expediency of assassination in removing or retarding such a threat. In principle, however, these recent cases are potentially justifiable on either accounts of the just war tradition.

In spite of the rule against targeting civilians, both of the central theories of the morality of war contain resources for sanctioning attacks on key scientists in highly constrained circumstances of necessity, such as contending with an existential threat. On either account, establishing liability to attack would constitute a justification for killing rather than an excuse. No residual guilt remains to tarnish the hands of those who order and carry out these killings. Specific categories of people (on the Walzer–Nagel account), or particularly blameworthy individuals (on McMahan's account), who are "at least nominally civilians,"[86] may lose their immunity from military attack so that we do them no wrong by harming them. Killing them would not be murder.

While these deaths are clearly intentional rather than incidental, they are secondary to the military necessity of destroying their victims' military expertise or know-how; as such they may be morally justified, particularly when deemed essential to averting or retarding a military threat of existential proportions.

Such justifications, however, if and when they are possible, constitute exceptions that prove the rule, rather than supplanting it. In order to overcome both the legal and moral rule against targeting civilians and the consequential drawbacks of relaxing it, the threat must be grave and credible, and the prospect of impeding it by assassination must be realistic. The scientist's contribution to the materialization of the threat must be crucial, and there must be no realistic possibility of a diplomatic solution.[87] Nuclear projects developed by scientists who are indispensable to them and that place catastrophic threats in the hands of regimes that are impervious to diplomatic pressure are not hypothetical scenarios, but they are not very common either. Pointing to rare exceptions of urgent necessity, in which targeting scientists might be morally justifiable, establishes no incongruity between morality and the law. As with assassination more generally, all the good moral arguments for the rule prohibiting it apply. The laws prohibiting murder, the wartime targeting of civilians and perfidious killing remain the best legal norms from any moral perspective.

Notes

1. Protocol Additional to the Geneva Conventions of August 12, 1949, and relating to the Protection of Victims of International Armed Conflicts (Protocol I), June 8, 1977, Article 37. www.icrc.org/ihl.nsf/full/470?opendocument. See also Michael L. Gross, "Assassination: Killing in the Shadow of Self-Defense," in Irwin J. (ed.), *War and Virtual War: The Challenges of Communities* (Amsterdam: Rodopi, 2004), 99–116, at 100.
2. Protocol I, ibid, Art. 37(c).
3. Jeremy Waldron, "Can Targeted Killing Work as a Neutral Principle?," *New York University Public Law and Legal Theory Working Papers* (2011), 1–14. Available at: http://papers.ssrn.com/sol3/papers.cfm?abstract_id=1788226. Jeremy Waldron, "Justifying Targeted Killing with a Neutral Principle," in Claire Finkelstein, Jens David Ohlin, and Andrew Altman (eds), *Targeted Killings—Law and Morality in an Asymmetrical World* (Oxford: Oxford University Press, 2012), Chapter 4, 112–131.
4. Protocol 1 added to the Geneva Conventions, 1977, Chapter II: Civilians and Civilian Population: Article 51(3). The criteria for direct participation are extremely controversial. See ICRC, "Interpretive Guidance on the Notion of Direct Participation in Hostilities under International Humanitarian Law," 90 (872) *International Review of the Red Cross* (2008), 991–1047, 997. Available at: www.icrc.org/eng/resources/documents/article/review/review-872-p991.htm. The interpretation of "direct participation" has been a serious issue of contention with regard to Israel and the United States' policy on targeted killing. See e.g.: Kristen Eichensehr, "On Target? The Israeli Supreme Court and the Expansion of Targeted Killing," 116 (8) *The Yale Law Journal* (2007), 1873–1881.
5. For analysis of concrete cases of assassination—past and present—and of the practical pros and cons of covert assassination policies, see William Tobey, "Nuclear Scientists as Assassination Targets," 68 (1) *Bulletin of the Atomic Scientists* (Sage Publications, 2012), 61–69.
6. Jeff McMahan, "The Ethics of Killing in War," 114 (4) *Ethics* (2004), 693–733. Jeff McMahan, *Killing in War* (Oxford: Oxford University Press, 2009).
7. Such adjustments are considered by Michael Gross, *Moral Dilemmas of Modern War* (New York: Cambridge University Press, 2009).
8. Michael Walzer, "Political Action: The Problem of Dirty Hands," 2 (2) *Philosophy and Public Affairs* (1973), 160–180, 167, reprinted in Sanford Levinson (ed.), *Torture—A Collection* (Oxford and New-York: Oxford University Press, 2004), 61–76, at 64–65.
9. See: Michael Walzer, *Just and Unjust Wars* (New York: Basic Books, 1977), 199–200.
10. As Michael Gross explains: "targeted killing properly understood as named killing rather than perfidious assassination offers a solution necessitated by the lack of uniforms among combatants." *Moral Dilemmas of Modern War*, 121.
11. See e.g. Amos Guiora, "Targeted Killing as Active Self-Defense," 36 *Case Western Research Journal Int'l Law* (2004), 31934, esp. 327–330.
12. HCJ 769/02 [December 11, 2005], Par.28. Available at: http://elyon1.court.gov.il/Files_ENG/02/690/007/a34/02007690.a34.pdf.
13. Ibid, Para. 31. See also Para 27–31 for Justice Barak's characterization of "civilians who are unlawful combatants."
14. Tobey, "Nuclear Scientists as Assassination Targets," 65, lists deniability as an advantage (viewed from the perspective of the attacking nation) of targeting scientists with covert action.
15. Walzer, *Just and Unjust Wars*, 199.

16. Walzer, ibid., 199–200.
17. This objective is clearly stated in the preamble to The Hague Convention: Laws and Customs of War on Land (Hague IV) October 18, 1907. http://net.lib.byu.edu/~rdh7/wwi/hague/hague5.html
18. See the discussion of civilian immunity in Chapter 2.
19. Walzer, *Just and Unjust Wars*, 199.
20. Walzer, ibid., 197, 203.
21. On Heisenberg and other cases since, see: Tobey, "Nuclear Scientists as Assassination Targets," 62–64.
22. Walzer, *Just and Unjust Wars*, 199. As Paul Gilbert comments, "Assassination is, however, far from the worst offence against the prohibition on attacking civilians that we witness in new wars." Paul Gilbert, *New Terror, New Wars* (Edinburgh: Edinburgh University Press, 2003), 94.
23. Walzer, ibid.
24. Walzer, ibid., 198–199.
25. Walzer, ibid., 199–200.
26. Walzer, ibid., 200–201: "The threatening character of the soldier's activities is a matter of fact; the unjust or oppressive character of the official's activity is a matter of political judgment. For this reason the political code has never attained the same status as the war convention. . . . In the eyes of those of us whose judgment of oppression and injustice differ from their own, political assassins are simply murderers, exactly like the killers of ordinary citizens."
27. Jeremy Waldron, "Can Targeted Killing Work as a Neutral Principle?," 1–9. Waldron, "Justifying Targeted Killing with a Neutral Principle," in *Targeted Killings—Law and Morality in an Asymmetrical World*, 112–131, 112–120, esp. 112–113, 117–120.
28. In February 2012 an explosion hit an Israeli diplomatic car near the Israeli embassy in New Delhi, injuring the wife of an Israeli diplomat stationed in India. In Georgia, an explosive device was found in a Tbilisi embassy employee's car and was neutralized safely.
29. Waldron, "Can Targeted Killing Work as a Neutral Principle?," 1. Waldron, "Justifying Targeted Killing with a Neutral Principle," in *Targeted Killings*, 112.
30. I am grateful to Michael Gross for this example and the accompanying analogy.
31. Michael L. Gross, "Fighting by Other Means in the Mid-East: A Critical Analysis of Israel's Assassination Policy," 51 *Political Studies* (2003), 350–368, at 356–358. Michael Gross, "Assassination: Killing in the Shadow of Self-Defense," 99–116, at 100–101.
32. Gross, *Moral Dilemmas of Modern War*, 119.
33. Immanuel Kant, *The Metaphysics of Morals* (6:347), cited in Waldron, "Can Targeted Killing Work as a Neutral Principle?" Section 7, p. 10. Waldron, "Justifying Targeted Killing with a Neutral Principle", 124–125.
34. Waldron, "Can Targeted Killing Work as a Neutral Principle?," ibid, 10; Waldron, "Justifying Targeted Killing with a Neutral Principle," 125 with reference to Immanuel Kant, "Perpetual Peace" (8:346).
35. Waldron, "Can Targeted Killing Work as a Neutral Principle?," ibid, 10–11; Waldron, "Justifying Targeted Killing with a Neutral Principle," 125.
36. Immanuel Kant, "Towards Perpetual Peace," in Pauline Kleingeld (ed.), *Toward Perpetual Peace and other Writings on Politics, Peace, and History, Immanuel Kant*, trans. David L. Colclasure (New Haven & London: Yale University Press, 2006), (8:346), 70. Immanuel Kant, *The Metaphysics of Morals* (1797) in Kleingeld (ed.), *Toward Perpetual Peace and other Writings on Politics, Peace, and History* (6:347), 143.
37. Kant, "Towards Perpetual Peace" (8:346), in Kleingeld (ed.), ibid, 71.
38. Immanuel Kant, *The Metaphysics of Morals* (6:347), in Kleingeld (ed.), ibid, 143.
39. Yoram Dinstein, *The Conduct of Hostilities Under the Law of International Armed Conflict* (Cambridge: Cambridge University Press, 2004), 208–211: International law and practice effectively regard spies as irregular combatants, leaving them virtually unprotected, thought they are guaranteed a trial prior to punishment. Their "unlawful" identity, however, is not in itself an offense under international law. Like assassins, spies lack any war rights

of soldiers and are rightly subject to prosecution and punishment, imprisonment or execution as murderers, "but only on the basis of the national criminal legislation of the belligerent state against whose interests he acted" (p. 211). See also: George Fletcher, *Romantics at War—Glory and Guilt in the Age of Terrorism* (Princeton, NJ: Princeton University Press, 2002), 106, 110.

40. Tobey, "Nuclear Scientists as Assassination Targets", at 66–67, discusses the negative effects of assassination on mutual trust and the prospect of negotiating peaceful solutions in the Iranian case, while at the same time recognizing the inconclusive nature of this consideration. Killing Iranian scientists raises levels of hostility and mistrust, and hardens Teheran's position. Nevertheless, "it is not clear that a negotiated solution to the nuclear crisis is or ever was possible" (p. 67).

41. Protocol 1 Additional to the Geneva Conventions, Article 37. www.icrc.org/ihl.nsf/full/470?opendocument. The Hague Regulations (IV): Laws and Customs of War on Land and its October 18, 1907, 1907, Section II Chapter I, Art. 23 (b). Article 23(a) prohibits the use of poison. www.icrc.org/ihl.nsf/WebART/195-200033?OpenDocument. See also Dinstein, *The Conduct of Hostilities*, 2001; and: Gross, "Assassination: Killing in the Shadow of Self-Defense," 100.

42. Walzer, *Just and Unjust Wars*, 176. Walzer recognizes the partisans' act of perfidy as clearly illegal, regarding their execution by Germans as legitimate. Nonetheless, he refrains from morally condemning the partisans' perfidious killing. He sums up his view of the situation on p. 178 as follows: "resistance is legitimate and the punishment of resistance is legitimate as well."

43. Waldron, "Can Targeted Killing Work as a Neutral Principle?," 13–14; Waldron, "Justifying Targeted Killing with a Neutral Principle," 126–130. On civilian immunity, see: Jeremy Waldron, "Civilians, Terrorism and Deadly Serious Conventions," in Jeremy Waldron, *Torture, Terror and Tradeoffs—Philosophy for the White House* (Oxford: Oxford University Press, 2010), Chapter 4, pp. 80–110.

44. Waldron, "Can Targeted Killing Work as a Neutral Principle?" ibid, 13–14 Waldron, "Justifying Targeted Killing with a Neutral Principle," 128–130.

45. Waldron, ibid, 11–14; Waldron, "Justifying Targeted Killing with a Neutral Principle," 126-8. See also Waldron, "Civilians, Terrorism and Deadly Serious Conventions," 109. Michael Walzer makes a similar point back in *Just and Unjust Wars*, 144–145: "the theoretical problem is not to explain how immunity is gained, but how it is lost. We are all immune to start with; our right not to be attacked is a feature of normal human relationships."

46. Waldron, "Justifying Targeted Killing with a Neutral Principle," 127; Waldron, "Can Targeted Killing Work as a Neutral Principle?," 11.

47. Waldron, "Justifying Targeted Killing with a Neutral Principle," 127; Waldron, Waldron, "Can Targeted Killing Work as a Neutral Principle?," 12, see also 14.

48. Waldron, "Can Targeted Killing Work as a Neutral Principle?," 14; See also Waldron, "Justifying Targeted Killing with a Neutral Principle," 128.

49. Waldron, "Can Targeted Killing Work as a Neutral Principle?," 12; Waldron, "Justifying Targeted Killing with a Neutral Principle," 127–128.

50. Waldron, "Can Targeted Killing Work as a Neutral Principle?," 14; see also Waldron, "Justifying Targeted Killing with a Neutral Principle," 128.

51. In "Justifying Targeted Killing with a Neutral Principle," 127, Waldron accepts that sometimes good reasons can be identified for allowing combatants to be killed.

52. Walzer, *Just and Unjust Wars*, 144–145.

53. Waldron, "Can Targeted Killing Work as a Neutral Principle," 12–14. Waldron, "Justifying Targeted Killing with a Neutral Principle," 128–130.

54. Walzer, *Just and Unjust Wars*, 146.

55. Dinstein, *The Conduct of Hostilities*, 129.

56. In principle, even the on-duty munitions worker is protected from disproportionate harm, although if we assume his facility is a significant military target, his death will usually count as legitimate and proportional collateral harm.

57. Thomas Nagel, "War and Massacre," 1 (2) *Philosophy and Public Affairs* (1972), 123–144, 140.
58. Walzer, *Just and Unjust Wars*, 145–146.
59. This distinction is widely, but not unanimously, accepted within just war theory. For a prominent critique, see Cecile Fabre, "Guns, Food, and Liability to Attack in War," 120 *Ethics* (2009), 36–63.
60. See International Committee of the Red Cross (ICRC), "Interpretive Guidance on the Notion of Direct Participation in Hostilities under International Humanitarian Law," *International Review of the Red Cross* 90 (no. 872) (2008), 991–1047, at 995, 1009–1010. According to this series of reports on direct participation commissioned by the ICRC, civilian employees are protected from direct attack, though their presence in a military facility exposes them to a greater risk of incidental death, even if they do not take a direct part in hostilities. The guidelines concerning criteria that constitute direct participation remain somewhat vague and controversial (pp. 995–996, 1012–1019). Nevertheless, the document clearly states that general contributions to the war effort: "e.g. design, production and shipment of weapons and military equipment . . ." do not constitute acts of "direct participation" (pp. 1020–1022).
61. Dinstein, *The Conduct of Hostilities*, 152. See also 124.
62. Dinstein, Ibid., 124.
63. Dinstein, ibid., 124.
64. Jeff McMahan, *Killing in War*, 12.
65. McMahan, ibid., 12.
66. McMahan, ibid., 13.
67. McMahan, ibid. See also 205.
68. Moreover, their civilian contribution is not usually understood by legal experts to qualify as "direct participation." The ICRC report lists scientific research and design, as well as production and transport of weapons as examples of merely indirect participation "unless carried out as an integral part of a specific military operation designed to directly cause the required threshold of harm" ("Interpretive Guidance on the Notion of Direct Participation in Hostilities under International Humanitarian Law," 90 (872) *International Review of the Red Cross* (2008), 991–1047 p. 1022). Furthermore, when discussing preparatory measures, the report states that "preparatory measures aiming to establish the general capacity to carry out unspecified hostile acts do not" qualify as direct participation (p. 1032). The document's examples of preparations which would *not* entail loss of protection include weapons productions (p. 1032).
69. Jeff McMahan, "The Morality of War and the Law of War," in D. Rodin and H. Shue (eds.), *Just and Unjust Warriors: The Moral and Legal Status of Soldiers* (Oxford: Oxford University Press, 2008), 19–43, at 27–30. McMahan, *Killing in War*, 234–235.
70. McMahan, *Killing in War*, 13, 205.
71. McMahan, "The Morality of War and the Law of War," 21–22. McMahan, *Killing in War*, 38.
72. Jeff McMahan, "The Ethics of Killing in War," 114 (4) *Ethics* (2004), 693–733, 702–708, 722–5; Jeff McMahan, "Just Cause for War," 19 (3) *Ethics & International Affairs* (December 2005), 1–21. McMahan, *Killing in War*, 182–188.
73. McMahan, *Killing in War*, Chapter 5, esp. 205.
74. For duress and ignorance as an excuse, rather than justification, for participating in injustice, see McMahan, *Killing in War*, 110–121.
75. On individual responsibility, see: McMahan, "The Ethics of Killing in War," 702–708 and 722–5; Jeff McMahan, "Just Cause for War" (2005) 19 (1) *Ethics & International Affairs*. McMahan, *Killing in War*, 182–188.
76. Walzer, *Just and Unjust Wars*, 146.
77. Nagel, "War and Massacre," 140.
78. Walzer, *Just and Unjust Wars*, 145–146.
79. Ibid, 145.
80. McMahan, ibid., 13.

81. McMahan, *Killing in War*, 13.
82. Dinstein, *The Conduct of Hostilities*, 124.
83. See: McMahan, *Killing in War*, 13; Nagel, "War and Massacre," 140; Walzer, *Just and Unjust Wars*, 145–146.
84. Walzer, *Just and Unjust Wars*, 199.
85. Waldron, "Can Targeted Killing Work as a Neutral Principle?" esp. 13–14 Waldron, "Justifying Targeted Killing with a Neutral Principle," esp. 128–130.
86. Walzer, *Just and Unjust Wars*, 145–146.
87. I draw here on William Tobey's description of the conditions under which nations consider resorting to assassination of nuclear scientists. See Tobey, "Nuclear Scientists as Assassination Targets," 67–68.

8

CONCLUSIONS

Revisionism revisited

My aim in this book has been to defend traditional just war theory as the chief ethical doctrine that ought to guide our actions during armed conflict. Like everyone else, I began with Walzer's *Just and Unjust Wars* as "the bible" of just war theory.[1] The rest is commentary.

The basic rules of this tradition have become practically common knowledge in most cultures, and are reflected almost verbatim in our international laws of war. The rudiments are widely familiar to citizens of liberal democracies and beyond, and among many soldiers and civilians who have never heard of Michael Walzer or attended a university class: soldiers are equally licensed to kill in wartime, and are all legitimate wartime targets, whereas non-combatants (notably civilians and prisoners) are neither liable to direct attack, nor are they entitled to fight with impunity. Military action must be proportionate, in relation to its objectives. All this holds firm regardless of the causes and aims of war, its justness or urgency.

Much important work has been done in the past few decades by philosophers who question the moral validity of these "orthodox" understandings. The first Chapters offered a defense of these well-established principles, as against the revisionist, "neo-classic," or "individualist" accounts that have emerged in recent years. While this book attempts to re-affirm the conventional rules, it also recognizes the perceptiveness and contribution of the revisionist approach, as well as the important work contributed by the many scholars who embrace it.

Theoretically, revisionism raises several welcome and illuminating points of criticism that are both important and virtually unarguable, particularly as wars become even more deadly and devastating. War is a terrible business, which can only be justified as defense against aggression, either of compatriots (faced with armed attack, and perhaps also in its anticipation) or else on behalf of a third party in need of rescue. Revisionists question the logic of separating justice of cause from the rules of conduct in war. No war can be just on both sides. Some wars are entirely futile; while in others no more than one side can reasonably be described as defending itself against aggression. Consequently, most killing in war is unjust, either on both sides (when the war is pointless) or at least on the part of the aggressors. Nevertheless, we curiously free all participants from legal repercussions for maiming and killing in war, just so long as they fight and kill by the rule book.

By and large, we also regard all soldiers as morally blameless for killing their adversaries in battle, and harbor no long-lasting hard feelings towards them, as though they were fighting some tournament and did it all in good sport. Revisionist just war theorists find this objectionable. Nothing illustrates this slightly obscene sporting attitude towards warfare more vividly than the notorious WWI tales of British and German soldiers emerging from their trenches on Christmas day 1914, greeting each other, chatting, joking, playing football, even exchanging gifts, before resuming fire at nightfall.

Revisionists view such myths of civilized warfare and male comradery with disdain, even repugnance, and they certainly have a point. They ask us to discourage teenagers from impulsively running off into battle without sufficient philosophical reflection on the justness of cause for which they will fight and kill. Viewing them all as honorable adversaries—whether playing football or killing each other— regardless of cause and with no need for justification, guarantees even the most blatantly aggressive states a sufficient number of warriors to prosecute unjust wars.[2] National recruitment encourages unreflective fighting, and conscription requires as much, attributing blame and demanding justification only from those who refuse to enlist.

Nevertheless, Chapter 1 argued that soldiers cannot be expected to determine justice of cause; they cannot be proved personally guilty of injustice or wrongdoing to any significant degree and are entitled to a presumption of innocence, morally as well as legally. Ultimately, the symmetry thesis holds because young soldiers' predicament and moral choices, both leading up to war and throughout it, closely mirror each other on all sides of the battlefield.[3] That is part of the tragedy of war, and we ought not to add to it by blaming its primary victims.

Individualists regard these universal wartime circumstances as excuses (millions and millions of individual excuses), mitigations of guilt, rather than as collective justification for participating in injustice. Soldiers fighting for the Axis powers in WWII (or any soldier during WWI) apparently could have known, and therefore should have known, that they were making the wrong choice. Why regard them as morally equal to the soldiers on the defensive side who were resisting Nazi aggression?

Walzer's response to McMahan is that:

> The soldiers . . . were doing the done thing, what everybody else was doing, what their parents and friends, teachers and pastors, and the leaders of their country, insisted was the right thing to do—and so in fact we didn't compel them to explain themselves, one by one. Once again, we collectivized their legal and moral status.[4]

In fact, these soldiers were doing precisely what our boys do when we go to war. Moreover, given the circumstances of adolescents in wartime, most soldiers make the best moral choice that they can. And so it has made good sense (moral sense) throughout the ages, to regard them all as equally blameless, rather than guilty with an explanation. When their war is unjust, and their choice turns out to have been manifestly wrong, we blame the grown-ups who sent them out to kill and be killed.

Revisionist-individualists may accept some of this as a matter of good practice, but they are quick to point out that it deviates dramatically from the normal way we ascribe individual responsibility in peacetime. They insist that at the deep moral level only defensive killing is ever morally justifiable in the name of good cause, while the agents of aggression, in war as in peacetime, are morally blameworthy, at least to some degree. Viewed from the philosopher's armchair, with a god's-eye perspective, I doubt anyone would disagree. Morality, however, is more commonly understood as an action guiding enterprise, intended to direct the behavior of men, not gods, and supplying an overarching answer to questions of what is to be done, right and wrong. If the deep moral level remains inaccessible to most human agents in the relevant situation, what is its significance to directing conduct in war?

Revisionist moral theories of war do not translate directly into practical ethics, let alone legal prescriptions. Revisionism does not speak in one voice on any of the implications of their theory to practice, and in this sense it does not yet form a cohesive and coherent doctrine to be reckoned with.

Few revisionists attempt complex positions on the relationship between morality and the law. Adil Haque helpfully offers an instrumentalist account of the laws of war, suggesting that the optimal laws of war will be those that best help soldiers conform to the (revisionist/individualist) morality of war.[5] Other individualists, most notably McMahan himself, rightly urge potential combatants to have a good think about justice before going off to kill people in battle. All are however short on guidance for soldiers who predictably determine their cause is just and proceed to fight for king and country,[6] as well as on more specific advice for those who phrase the international laws and military handbooks by which these soldiers are to fight.

Revisionism mostly ignores, or down plays, the tension between their deep morality of war and practical ethics. Consequently, it is no wonder that some deep disagreements between the two theories may in practice end up yielding similar laws of war. Perhaps this is the difference between ideal and non-ideal moral theory. If so, how would a revisionist non-ideal theory differ from Walzer's *Just and Unjust Wars*, and what relevance would remain for the ideal (deep moral) level of such a non-ideal practice? What does a revisionist *shallow* morality of war look like, as distinct from just war theory, or our laws of armed conflict, as well as their own deeper morality of war?[7]

On this last point, revisionism is often defended by its adherents as constituting a different of project, or preforming an entirely different task, than the "orthodox" just war theory. The revisionist morality of war is not necessarily intended directly to guide soldiers in action. It is a philosophically reflective, non-action guiding, version of morality aimed at uncovering the true fundamental moral principles that govern conduct in war. Recommending this as a worthwhile project, Haque describes it as an attempt to "isolate and analyze the deep or fundamental moral considerations that must be applied to the context of war," regardless of various pragmatic and epistemic considerations in an attempt to gain "a clear view of the moral considerations that may remain constant."[8] Another way Haque puts this is in terms of fact-relative versus evidence-relative reasoning: traditionalists assume the rules of war (moral and legal) "exist solely to guide conduct in light of the evidence. However, the deep morality of war exists also to govern conduct in light of the facts."[9]

> The laws of war provide soldiers with a decision procedure that explains how soldiers ought to deliberate while the deep morality of war provides us all with a standard of rightness that explains what makes acts in war right or wrong.[10]

As a result, the discourse between traditional just war theorists and revisionist moral philosophers often degenerates into a dialogue of the deaf, with traditionalists describing military ethics and legal standards, while revisionists philosophize about deep moral truths. To the extent that my first chapter runs into this dead end, it also makes the following point patently clear: if this individualist theory is to remain important, it must explain and specify exactly what it has to offer to combatants in the way of practical moral guidance, as well as to our international laws of war.

Theorizing about war

In theory, revisionists unanimously reject the independence-symmetry thesis, which attributes equal rights and liabilities to all soldiers, based on the mutual threat they post to one another regardless of cause. As per McMahan,

> The correct criterion of liability to attack in these cases is not posing a threat, nor even posing an unjust threat, but moral responsibility for an unjust threat.[11]

Unjust soldiers have no right to kill just soldiers. What about non-combatants? Ostensibly, McMahan's criterion of liability suggests that some civilians and prisoners responsible for posing an unjust threat may be liable to direct targeting in war. Revisionists may shy away from applying this moral conclusion in practice because of the consequential benefits of an overall rule against targeting civilians. As we saw in Chapter 2, McMahan himself limits this deep moral license to rare instances in which attacking unjust civilians or prisoners would be seriously conducive to removing their unjust threat. Moreover, at least for the time being, he does not recommend translating even this narrow license to kill non-combatants into legal permissions, or recommend subjecting civilians and prisoners to punitive harm.[12] Even David Rodin who recommends a closer alignment of the law with considerations of morality regarding the liability of combatants,[13] entirely rejects any license to kill unjust civilians; arguing instead that revisionist *jus in bello* asymmetry is only half right: prohibiting the attack on just combatants but upholding the equal immunity of non-combatants.[14]

Chapter 2 suggested that traditional non-combatant immunity is based on an age-old and cross-cultural deep moral commitment towards defenseless human beings, which stands quite apart from any responsibility they may (and often do) share for instigating or supporting an unjust war. Chapter 3 suggested that this foundational commitment to non-combatants may requires maintaining the independence of *jus ad bellum* from *jus in Bello*. Considering civil war as an actual case of combatant asymmetry indicates that relinquishing the independence-symmetry thesis in international armed conflicts might make matters much worse for civilians.

The legal regime governing non-international armed conflict is the closest example we have in reality for combatant inequality, though it admittedly does not represent an objective moral determination on just cause, as revisionists envision. Nonetheless, in civil wars, one side (the rebels) are forewarned about the criminality of their participation and their individual legal culpability for it, even if they abide by *jus in bello*. Rebels are denied POW rights if captured and are susceptible to criminal charges *post bellum*, if they lose, whether they target civilians or combatants. Such criminalization and advance warning seem to have done nothing to reduce participation in civil conflict, which remains the most common form of warfare since WWII.

Moreover, civil wars are typified by participants' disregard for *jus in bello* immunities, with catastrophic results for civilians and prisoners. While there are various explanations for reduced compliance within civil conflict, one obvious reason is lack of incentive on the part of the revolutionaries, while their adversaries regard them as criminals and pursue them at all costs. This serves as a high indicator that doing away with combatant equality, "the independence-symmetry thesis," in the international arena, may not be such a good idea, particularly for the wellbeing of defenseless civilians and prisoners. Any level of morality, I argued, must consider the implications of its moral prescriptions for the lives of countless non-combatants caught up in war, many of whom will also be morally innocent even on the revisionist account of responsibility. It may well be impossible in practice, possibly incoherent in theory, to maintain a revisionist regime of just war theory that is only half right. The laws of war work in consort with each other, so that relinquishing one facet (independence-combatant symmetry) may have an entirely debilitating effect on its most central aspect, namely civilian immunity.

Notwithstanding, revisionists raise another strong theoretical point against *jus in bello* neutrality when they consider the rule about proportionality in war. Chapter 4 presented the concept of wartime proportionality in all its variety. This standard, alongside charges of disproportionality, may apply to a war in its entirety, or refer to the means of its prosecution, and may be employed either in the legal and/or the moral sense. Traditionally and legally, *jus in bello* proportionality adds a further layer of protection to civilian immunity, beyond the prohibition on directly attacking civilians and civilian objects. Proportionality requires that military objectives be attained at the lowest possible cost to genuine civilians, so as to avoid not only unnecessary, but also excessive, incidental civilian casualties on either side.

Revisionists argue that we cannot make any intricate calculations about the justifiable level of wartime destruction without reference to the cause for which the war is being fought on either side. In keeping with their overall account that ties just cause to the rules of engagement, revisionists insist that any harms inflicted in the course of pursuing injustice, whether on combatants of civilians, are totally impermissible, unjustifiable, and therefore necessarily disproportionate.[15] Moreover, revisionism suggests that the extent of harm that can be justified as proportionate even in the course of a just war must be judged in relation to the overall importance and urgency of attaining the war's just ends, rather than merely with reference to concrete military objectives.[16]

It is both impossible, and at the same time unnecessary, to refute these revisionist observations. Insofar as revisionism objectively evaluates the morality of and in war from a purely philosophical perspective, these deep-level points are uncontroversial. No contemporary just war theorist that I know of denies that aggressive killing is morally unjustified, or that moral judgements about the ills of war must ultimately refer in some way to the war's moral (not merely military) merits. To this extent again, philosophical disagreements on proportionality are somewhat artificial. In principle, traditionalists will readily concede that useless killing for a bad purpose cannot be morally proportionate, while revisionists mostly concede the consequential benefits of maintaining a neutral rule of proportionality (independent of *jus ad bellum*) within the laws of armed conflict.[17]

Some practical issues

That said, what can a revised, individualist-neoclassic, *ethics* of war have to say to combatants and their armies about wartime proportionality?[18] Since the rules of war are primarily standards for self-application, any restrictions on unjust aggressors will effectively apply to no-one at all. No party in war applies moral standards under the assumption that they are unjustly and unjustifiably prosecuting an immoral war. On the other hand, and in keeping with my argument on civilian immunity, both parties share the moral obligation to pay due care to defenseless non-combatants, irrespective of anything else.

In practical terms, paying due care to civilians in wartime will involve weighing the military value of each target as against the harm to their surroundings and taking relevant precautions, such as those concerning the location and precise timing of attack, selecting appropriate methods and weapons. This is not a very determinate or restrictive limitation on war-making, but it is significant. For one thing, attaining a military objective at the minimal cost to civilians may also require placing heavier, even riskier, burdens on soldiers, requiring them to engage more closely with the enemy so as to avoid indiscriminate killing from a safe distance.

Contemporary battlegrounds, often orchestrated by terrorists, are particularly hazardous to civilians. Just war theorists from both camps will often require soldiers to shoulder some of the burdens that their war inevitably inflicts on enemy civilians, though their accounts differ in their reasoning for this requirement as well as its extent. For traditional just war theory defended throughout, this obligation is an unavoidable derivative of the civilians-combatant distinction, and the deep moral commitment to unarmed non-combatants, as such.[19]

Following Walzer and David Luban on this point suggests that the level of risk imposed on soldiers is not easily determinable with any precision, and ought not to be exaggerated. An army's legitimate mission should not be hampered, while the lives and safety of its soldiers also demand due care, particularly from their commanding officers. Sadly, combatting terrorism in the midst of civilians, much like resolving hostage crises, will likely result in severe damage and loss of life. Armies must combat terrorism in principle, as well as in practice, by doing their best to prevent civilian casualties while at the same time defeating an enemy who targets our civilians, hides among their own and places them in the front lines. This is no easy task, and possibly mission impossible even for the most benevolent soldiers and well-meaning armies. At the end of the day, a high casualty count when reluctantly fighting terrorists amidst civilians is no indication, in itself, that the army did not try hard enough.

Chapter 5 looks beyond the requirement of proportionality in military attacks and considers the moral implications of this standard for softer military tactics, specifically economic measures. Legally, the wartime requirement of proportionality applies narrowly only to armed attacks. The standard of proportionality, in both just war theory and international law, restricts collateral damage to non-combatants. Such limitations, moral as well as legal, are not readily applicable to economic measures whose primary targets are often civilians. The central sections of Chapter 5 focused on the puzzles and anomalies posed by economic warfare to just war theory's keystone commitment to civilian immunity. More concretely, this chapter applied traditional, "Walzerian" just war theory to the practical contemporary issues concerning Israel's restrictions on and around the Gaza Strip. Revisionism, for its part, has yet to take as clear a stand on sieges and blockades, as well as on other non-kinetic tactics short of war. It would indeed be interesting to see the individualist theory developed in these new directions as well.

Combatting threats that loom in the distance, but have not as yet materialized, pose another challenge to contemporary just war theory in all its variety, as well as to legal scholars. Here, both traditional and revisionists just war theorists have had a say; both camps recognize not only the dangers of sanctioning anticipatory attacks as a rule, but also the possible utility and moral legitimacy of particular preemptive strikes, under certain conditions.

To repeat, while legal scholars regard the existence of an imminent threat as a necessary component of self-defense, Walzer's classic justification of preemptive military action requires: "A manifest intent to injure, a degree of active preparation that makes that intent a positive danger, and a general situation in which waiting, or doing anything other than fighting, greatly magnifies the risk."[20]

As with maintaining the legal equality of combatants and civilian immunity, revisionist may share conclusions reached by traditional scholars, but they do so for different reasons, and reasons matter. In the case of anticipation, the key issue for revisionists will be whether the individual targets of preemption are morally liable to attack, based on their responsibility for creating or posing an unjust threat to their adversaries. On this logic, preemption may be justifiable to revisionists where its potential targets are consciously active in creating an aggressive threat, and when removing them, or their equipment, may seriously hinder their unjust threat from maturing.

Beyond theory, I suggested that under conditions of last resort and reasonable chance of success, a preemptive Israeli attack on Iran may be justifiable by both sets of criteria, at least at some point down the line. Even legally, I argued, interpretations of "imminent threat" in probabilistic, rather than purely temporal, terms, could eventually license a preemptive Israeli strike on Iran's nuclear facilities.

Targeting individual civilians away from these facilities is a horse of a different color. Deliberately killing civilians is illegal, and rightly so. Beyond plain murder, peacetime assassinations violate state sovereignty. Even in wartime, it often involves perfidy, and is always a violation of civilian immunity and an assault on defenseless persons. All this is more than enough reason to uphold a stringent moral prohibition on targeting civilians and an absolute legal ban on assassination. When civilians are randomly murdered, we call this terrorism, and condemn it without exception, regardless of cause and circumstances. No justification can be offered.[21]

An absolute moral prohibition on assassination, allowing for no exceptions, is more difficult to sustain.[22] Plausible exceptions arise where particular civilians contribute directly to the business of fighting and/or bear responsibility for the emergence of an unjust threat, depending on which version of the morality of war one subscribes to. Even in such cases, I suggested, the threat to be averted must be unusually grave, perhaps of holocaust dimensions, and military necessity must be established. No such rare exception ought to be reflected in our laws of war or peace, or acknowledged as the deep morality of war. Extreme cases that may arouse sympathy are poor bases for general rules. Justifications should not to be concocted and new unraveling norms ought not to be introduced. In exceptional emergencies in which targeting key-civilians may be justifiable, even warranted, as the lesser of evils, hypocrisy and denial are probably the best tributes to the law and moral norms.

Concluding remarks

Having spent much of this book defending traditional just war theory, its final two chapters rely partly on both traditional and revisionist accounts. Can we embrace traditional just war theory and nonetheless hold on to some elements of revisionist morality of war?

Considering the two theories of just war throughout this book emphasized their basic differences, but also sheds light on their points of convergence. Revisionism is fundamentally an "individualist" morality of war: it appeals to the way we usually assign moral responsibility in peacetime, and applies these individualized judgements to the circumstances of war, insisting that justice remains constant regardless of the drastic difference between war and peace. Traditionalists deny this, arguing, in Walzer's words, that war is in its essence a coercively collectivizing, tyrannical, and universally oppressive, enterprise, that overrides individuality, and makes the kind of attention that we would like to pay to each person's moral standing utterly impossible: "Just war theory is adapted to the moral reality of war, which means that 'justice' in the theory lives, so to speak, under a cloud."[23]

Walzer clearly laments these features of war and the second rate brand of justice that it has to offer. "Orthodox" just war theorists are no militarists; they are also individualists, who ordinarily assign moral responsibility on a well-scrutinized individual basis. They merely deny the applicability of their everyday moral prescriptions to the unfortunate reality of war. On a practical level, many revisionists agree. It should therefore come as no surprise to find considerable convergence between the two theories in those rare instances in which war lends itself to individualized moral judgements.

The comparison between revisionists and traditionalists in the last two chapters also helps to explain any mixed intuitions we are left with at the end of the day regarding our theoretical allegiances. Revisionism, or individualism, is at its best when war (or pre-war conflict) can be broken up into singular attacks or individualized targets. Traditionalists focus on levels of threat and contribution to the business of fighting. In unusual cases in which threatening targets are pre-selected individuals, and/or isolated facilities, it is possible, and therefore desirable, to revert in part to our normal moral commitments and add specific questions about individual responsibility and liability to attack. This should make sense to everyone, not only revisionists.

Notes

1. Michael Walzer, *Just and Unjust Wars* (New York: Basic Books, 1977).
2. Jeff McMahan, *Killing in War* (Oxford: Oxford University Press, 2009), 3, 6–7.
3. C.A.J. (Tony) Coady, "The Status of Combatants," David Rodin and Henry Shue (eds.) *Just and Unjust Warriors: The Moral and Legal Status of Soldiers* (Oxford: Oxford University Press, 2008), Chapter 8, 153–175, 164–165.
4. Michael Walzer, "Response to McMahan's Paper," 34 (1) *Philosophia* (2006), 43–45, 44.
5. E.g. most recently, Adil Ahmad Haque, "Law and Morality at War," 8 (1) *Criminal Law and Philosophy* (2014), 79–97. See also, Adil Ahmad Haque, *Law and Morality at War* (Oxford: Oxford Legal Philosophy, Oxford University Press, 2017).
6. Henry Shue, "Do We Need a 'Morality of War'?," in Rodin and Shue (eds.) *Just and Unjust Warriors* (Oxford University Press, 2008) 87–111, esp. 105, 107–109.
7. Cf: Shue, "Do We Need a 'Morality of War'?," ibid, 87–111.
8. Haque, "Law and Morality at War," 8 (1) *Criminal Law and Philosophy*, 82.
9. Haque, ibid.
10. Ibid, 82–83.
11. Jeff McMahan, "The Morality of War and the Law of War," in Rodin and Shue, *Just and Unjust Warriors: The Moral and Legal Status of Soldiers* (Oxford: Oxford University Press, 2008), 19–43, 21–22. See also, McMahan, *Killing in War*, 35.

12. McMahan, "The Morality of War and the Law of War," 22; McMahan, *Killing in War*, e.g. 108–109, 221–235; Jeff McMahan, "Torture, Morality and Law," *Case Western Reserve Journal of International Law*, 37 2/3 Law Module (2006), 241–248, 248.
13. David Rodin, "The Moral Inequality of Soldiers: Why *jus in bello* Asymmetry is Half Right" 44–68, in Rodin and Shue (eds.) *Just and Unjust Warriors: The Moral and Legal Status of Soldiers* (Oxford: Oxford University Press, 2008), Chapter 3: 44–68, 63–64.
14. Rodin, The Moral Inequality of Soldiers", ibid, 45: ". . . soldiers who fight in an unjust war have no right to use force against just combatants and should be held responsible for unjust killing *post bellum*, but just combatants do not possess additional *in bello* privileges. In particular, they do not have the right to target non-combatants.
15. Jeff McMahan, "The Ethics of Killing in War" 114 *Ethics* (2004), 693–733, at sec. V, 708–718. McMahan, *Killing in War*, 18–32, esp. 24–32; Jeff McMahan, "The Just Distribution of Harm between Combatants and Noncombatants," 38 (4) *Philosophy and Public Affairs* (2010), 342–79, esp. 350–558, 351, 358.
16. Thomas Hurka, "Proportionality in the Morality of War," 33 (1) *Philosophy & Public Affairs* (2005), 34–66, 44–45.
17. McMahan, *Killing in War*, 30–31; Hurka, 45. See also Steven P. Lee, *Ethics and War An Introduction* (New York: Cambridge University Press, 2012), 214–215.
18. CF: Shue, "Do We Need a 'Morality of War'?," esp. 108–109.
19. Michael Walzer and Avishai Margalit: "Israel: Civilians & Combatants," 56 (8) *The New York Review of Books*, May 14, 2009, 2. See also the follow-up on this exchange in: Asa Kasher and Major General Amos Yadlin, with a reply by Margalit and Walzer, "Israel & the Rules of War: An Exchange," *New York Review of Books*, June 11, 2009. www.nybooks.com/articles/archives/2009/jun/11/israel-the-rules-of-war-an-exchange/
20. Walzer, *Just and Unjust Wars*, 81.
21. Walzer, *Just and Unjust Wars*, Chapter 12: "Terrorism," 197–206, 197, 203.
22. Ibid.
23. Walzer, "Response to McMahan's Paper," 43.

BIBLIOGRAPHY

Aristotle (1981) *The Politics* (revised edition), London: Penguin Classics.

Avineri, Shlomo and Shternhell Zeev (2009) "Israel: Civilians and Combatants: An Exchange, Reply by Avishai Margalit and Michael Walzer", *The New York Review of Books* 56 (August 13, 2009).

Barak, Aharon (2007) "Proportional Effect: the Israeli Experience", *University of Toronto Law Journal* 57 (2): pp. 369–382.

Benbaji, Yitzhak (2007) "The Responsibility of Soldiers and the Ethics of Killing in War" *The Philosophical Quarterly* 57 (229) (October 2007): pp. 558–572.

Benbaji, Yitzhak (2008) "A Defense of the Traditional War Convention", *Ethics* 118 (3) (April 2008): pp. 464–495.

Benbaji, Yitzhak (2009) "The War Convention and the Moral Division of Labor", *The Philosophical Quarterly* 59 (237) (October 2009): pp. 593–617.

Benbaji, Yitzhak and Sussmann, Naomi (eds.) (2014) *Reading Walzer*, London & New York: Routledge.

Benvenisti, Eyal (2009) "The Law on the Unilateral Termination of Occupation", in A. Zimmermann and T. Geigerich (eds.) *Verofentlichungen des Walter-Schucking-Instituts fur Internationalis Recht an der Universitat Keil.* Available at: http://papers.ssrn.com/sol3/papers.cfm?abstract_id=1254523

Berman, Paul (2003) *Terror and Liberalism*, New York & London: Norton.

Brahimi, Alia (2010) *Jihad and Just War in the War on Terror*, Oxford: Oxford University Press.

Buchanan, Allen and Keohane, Robert O. (2004) "The Preventive Use of Force: A Cosmopolitan Institutional Proposal", *Ethics and International Affairs* 18: pp. 1–22.

Buchanan, Allen (2006) "Institutionalizing the Just War", *Philosophy and Public Affairs* 34: pp. 2–38.

Buchanan, Allen (2013) "The Ethics of Revolution and Its Implications for the Ethics of Intervention", *Philosophy and Public Affairs* 41 (4): pp. 291–323.

Bugnion, François (2003) "*Jus ad Bellum, Jus in Bello* and Non-International Armed Conflicts", in *The Year Book of International Humanitarian Law*, Vol. VI, T.M.C Asser Press: pp. 167–198.

Byers, Michael (2003) "Preemptive Self-Defense, Hegemony, Equality and Strategies of Legal Change", *The Journal of Political Philosophy* 11: pp. 171–190.

Cassese, Antonio (2008) *The Human Dimension of International Law*, Oxford, NY: Oxford University Press.

Coady, C.A.J (Tony) (2008) "The Status of Combatants", in David Rodin and Henry Shue (eds.) *Just and Unjust Warriors*, Oxford University Press: pp. 153–175.

Coates, Anthony (2008) "Is the Independent Application of *jus in bello* the Way to Limit War?" in David Rodin and Henry Shue (eds.) *Just and Unjust Warriors*, Oxford University Press: pp. 176–192.

Crawford, Neta (2007) "The False Promise of Preventive War", in Henry Shue and David Rodin (eds.) *Preemption—Military Action and Moral Justification*, Oxford University Press: Chapter 4, pp. 89–125.

Dapo, Akande (2010) "Legal Issues Raised by Israel's Blockade of Gaza", *EJIL Analysis* Available at: www.ejiltalk.org/legal-issues-raised-by-israels-blockade-of-gaza/

Dapo, Akande (2012) "Classification of Armed Conflict: Relevant Legal Concept" in Elizabeth Wilmshurst (ed.) *International Law and the Classification of Conflicts*, Oxford University Press.

Dershowitz, Alan (2009) "Israel's Policy is Perfectly Proportionate", in the Wall Street Journal (January 2009): p. 2. Available at: http://online.wsj.com/article/SB12308592562174 7981.html

Dinstein, Yoram (1988) *War, Aggression and Self Defense*, Cambridge: Grotius Publications.

Dinstein, Yoram (2004) *The Conduct of Hostilities Under the Law of International Armed Conflict*, Cambridge: Cambridge University Press.

Eichensehr, Kristen (2007) "On Target? The Israeli Supreme Court and the Expansion of Targeted Killing", *The Yale Law Journal* 116 (8): pp. 1873–1881.

Fabre, Cecile (2007) "Mandatory Rescue Killing", *Journal of Political Philosophy* 15 (4): pp. 363–384.

Fabre, Cecile (2009) "Guns, Food, and Liability to Attack in War", *Ethics* 120: pp. 36–63.

Fabre, Cecile (2012) *Cosmopolitan War*, Oxford: Oxford University Press.

Fearon, James D. and Laitin, David D. (2003), "Ethnicity, Insurgency, and Civil War", *American Political Science Review* 97 (1): pp. 75–90.

Fearon, James D. and Laitin, David D. (2007) "Civil War Termination", *Annual Meetings of the American Political Science Association*. Chicago, IL. Available at: www.stanford.edu/~jfearon/papers/termination.pdf. Accessed March 7, 2013.

Fearon, James D. (2004) "Why Do Some Civil Wars Last So Much Longer Than Others?" *Journal of Peace Research* 41 (3): pp. 271–301.

Finlay, Christopher J. (2009) "Legitimacy and Non-State Actors", *Journal of Political Philosophy* 18: pp. 287–312.

Finlay, Christopher J. (2015) *Terrorism and the Right to Resist—A Theory of Just Revolutionary War*, Cambridge: Cambridge University press.

Fisher, David (2001) *Morality and War: Can War be Just in the Twenty-First Century?*, Oxford: Oxford University Press.

Fletcher, George (1998) *Basic Concepts of Criminal Law*, Oxford: Oxford University Press.

Fletcher, George P. (2002) *Romantics at War—Glory and Guilt in the Age of Terrorism*, Princeton: Princeton University Press.

Fletcher, George P. and Ohlin, Jens David (2008) *Defending Humanity—When Force is Justified and Why*, Oxford: Oxford University Press.

Forge, John (2009) "Proportionality, Just War Theory and Weapons Innovation", *Science & Engineering Ethics* 15: pp. 25–38.

Gardam, Judith (1993) "Proportionality and Force in International Law", *American Journal of International Law* 87: pp. 391–413.

Gardam, Judith (2004) *Necessity, Proportionality, and the Use of Force by States*, Cambridge: Cambridge University Press.

Gardam, Judith (2005) "A Role for Proportionality in the War on Terror", *Nordic Journal of International Law* 74: pp. 3–25.

Gilbert, Paul (2003) *New Terror, New Wars*, Edinburgh University Press.

Green, Leslie C. (2008) *The Contemporary Law of Armed Conflict* (third edition), Manchester University Press.

Grey, Christine (2008) *International Law and the Use of Force* (third edition), Oxford: Oxford University Press.

Gross, Michael L. (2003) "Fighting by Other Means in the Mid-East: A Critical Analysis of Israel's Assassination Policy", *Political Studies* 51: pp. 350–368.

Gross, Michael L. (2004) "Assassination: Killing in the Shadow of Self-Defense", in Irwin J. (ed.) *War and Virtual War: The Challenges of Communities*, Amsterdam: Rodopi: pp. 99–116.

Gross, Michael L. (2010) *Moral Dilemmas of Modern War*, New York: Cambridge University Press.

Gross, Michael L. and Meisels, Tamar (2013) "Just War Theory and the 2008–2009 Gaza Invasion" (A Response to Jerome Slater) *International Security* 38 (1) (Summer 2013): pp. 164–167.

Gross, Michael L. (2015) *The Ethics of Insurgency—A Critical Guide to Just Guerrilla Warfare*, New York: Oxford University Press.

Guiora, Amos (2004) "Targeted Killing as Active Self-Defense", *Case Western Research Journal Int'l Law* 36: pp. 319–334.

Halbertal, Moshe (November 2009) "The Goldstone Illusion—What the U.N. report gets wrong about Gaza—and War", *The New Republic.* Available at: www.tnr.com/article/world/the-goldstone-illusion?page=0,3

Hobbes, Thomas (1991) *Leviathan*, in R. Tuck (ed.), Cambridge: Cambridge University Press.

Haque, Adil Ahmad (2014) "Law and Morality at War", *Criminal Law and Philosophy* 8 (1): pp. 79–97.

Haque, Adil Ahmad (2017) *Law and Morality at War*, Oxford: Oxford Legal Philosophy, Oxford University Press.

Hoeffler, Anke (2012) "On the causes of Civil War" in *The Oxford Handbook of Economics of Peace and Conflict*, Oxford Handbooks: pp. 179–204.

Hurka, Thomas (2005) "Proportionality in the Morality of War", *Philosophy & Public Affairs* 33 (1): pp. 34–66.

Hurka, Thomas (2008) "Proportionality and Necessity" in Larry May (ed.) *Essays in Political Philosophy*, Cambridge: Cambridge University Press: pp. 127–144. Available at: www.chass.utoronto.ca/~thurka/docs/propandnec.pdf

Kalyvas, Stathis N. (2006) *The Logic of Violence in Civil War*, Cambridge: Cambridge University Press.

Kalyvas, Stathis N. (2009) "Civil War", in Carles Boix and Susan C. Stokes (eds.) *The Oxford Handbook of Comparative Politics*, Oxford University Press: Chapter 18, pp. 416–435.

Kalyvas, Stathis N. (2011), "The Changing Character of Civil Wars", in Hew Strachan and Sibylle Scheipers (eds.) *The Changing Character of War*, Oxford University Press.

Kant, Immanuel (2006) "Toward Perpetual Peace and other Writings on Politics, Peace, and History", Pauline Kleingeld (ed.), David L. Colclasure (trans.), New Haven & London: Yale University Press.

Kasher, Asa and Yadlin, Amos (Winter-Spring 2005) "Assassination and Preventive Killing", *SAIS Review* 25 (1): pp. 47–57.

Kasher, Asa (Summer 2009) "Operation Cast Lead and the Ethics of Just War", *AZURE* 37: pp. 43–75. www.azure.org.il/article.php?id=502&page=all

Kasher, Asa, and Yadlin, Amos (2009) "Israel & the Rules of War: An Exchange", New York Review of Books (June 11, 2009). www.nybooks.com/articles/archives/2009/jun/11/israel-the-rules-of-war-an-exchange/

Kaufman, Whitley (2005) "What's Wrong with Preventive War? The Moral and Legal Basis for the Preventive Use of Force", Ethics and International Affairs 19: pp. 23–28.

Kutz, Christopher (2008) "Fearful Symmetry", in David Rodin and Henry Shue (eds.), Just and Unjust Warriors: The Moral and Legal Status of Soldiers, New York: Oxford University Press: pp. 69–86.

Lacina, Bethany (2006) "Explaining the Severity of Civil Wars", Journal of Conflict Resolution 50 (2): pp. 276–289.

Lazar, Seth (2010) "Necessity, Vulnerability, and Noncombatant Immunity", unpublished manuscript, cited with permission from the author.

Lazar, Seth (2015) Sparing Civilians, Oxford: Oxford University Press.

Lazar, Seth, (forthcoming) "Just War Theory: Revisionists Versus Traditionalists", Annual Review of Political Science (2017, forthcoming): 20.4–4.18.

Lee, Steven P. (2012) Ethics and War An Introduction, New York: Cambridge University Press.

Levinson, Sanford (2004) Torture—A Collection, New York: Oxford University Press.

Lichtenberg, Judith (2008) "How to Judge Soldiers Whose Cause is Unjust", in David Rodin and Henry Shue (eds.), Just and Unjust Warriors: The Moral and Legal Status of Soldiers, New York: Oxford University Press: pp. 112–130.

Locke, John (1960) Two Treatises of Government. Peter Laslett (ed.), Cambridge University Press.

Luban, David (2004) "Preventive War", Philosophy and Public Affairs 32: pp. 207–248.

Luban, David (2007) "Preventive War and Human Rights" in Henry Shue and David Rodin (eds.) Preemption—Military Action and Moral Justification, Oxford University Press: Chapter 7, pp. 171–201.

Luban, David (2014) "Risk Taking and Force Protection", in Reading Walzer, Yitzhak Benbaji and Naomi Sussman (eds.) London & New York: Routledge: Chapter 13, pp. 277–301.

Mari, Mustapha (2007) "The Israeli Disengagement from the Gaza Strip: An End of the Occupation?" in Tim McCormack (ed.) Yearbook of International Humanitarian Law 8: pp. 356–268.

McMahan, Jeff and Mckin, Robert (1993) "The Just War and the Gulf War", Canadian Journal of Philosophy 23: pp. 501–541.

McMahan, Jeff (2004) "The Ethics of Killing in War", Ethics 114 (4) (July): pp. 693–733.

McMahan, Jeff (2005) "Just Cause For War", Ethics & International Affairs 19 (3): pp. 1–21.

McMahan, Jeff (2006a) "Torture, Morality and Law", Case Western Reserve Journal of International Law 37 (2/3 Law Module): pp. 241–248.

McMahan, Jeff (2006b) "Killing in War: A Reply to Walzer", Philosophia 34: pp. 47–51.

McMahan, Jeff (2006c) "Preventive War and the Killing of the Innocent", in Richard Sorabji and David Rodin (eds.) The Ethics of War: Shared problems in Different Traditions, Aldershot UK: Ashgate: Chapter 9, pp. 169–190.

McMahan, Jeff (2008) "The Morality of War and the Law of War", in David Rodin and Henry Shue (eds.) Just and Unjust Warriors: The Moral and Legal Status of Soldiers, Oxford: Oxford University Press: pp. 19–43.

McMahan, Jeff (2009) Killing in War, Oxford: Oxford University Press.

McMahan, Jeff (2010) "The Just Distribution of Harm Between Combatants and Noncombatants", Philosophy and Public Affairs 38 (4): pp. 342–379.

McMahan, Jeff (2012) "Rethinking the Just War", The New York Times (November 11, 2012).

Moyn, Samuel (2013) "John Locke on Intervention, Uncertainty, and Insurgency", in Stefano Recchia and Jennifer M. Welsh (eds.) Just and Unjust Military Intervention – European Thinkers from Victoria to Mill (Cambridge: Cambridge University Press, 2013), Chapter 5, 113–131.

Nagel, Thomas (1972) "War and Massacre", *Philosophy and Public Affairs* 1: pp. 123–143.

O'Donovan, Oliver (2003) *The Just War Revisited*, Cambridge University Press.

Posner, Eric A. and Sykes, Alan O. (2004) "Optimal War and Jus Ad Bellum", University of Chicago Law and Economics Working Paper Series, Olin Working Paper no. 211; U. of Chicago Public Law Working Paper no. 63: pp. 1–41. Available at: http://papers.ssrn.com/sol3/papers.cfm?abstract_id=546104. Last accessed June 8, 2014.

Reichberg, Gregory M. (2008) "Just War and Regular War: Competing Paradigms", in David Rodin and Henry Shue (eds.) *Just and Unjust Warriors: The Moral and Legal Status of Soldiers*, Oxford University Press: pp. 193–213.

Roberts, Adam (2008) "The Principle of Equal Application of the Laws of War", in David Rodin and Henry Shue (eds.) *Just and Unjust Warriors: The Moral and Legal Status of Soldiers*, Oxford University Press: pp. 226–254.

Rodin, David (2003) *War and Self-Defense*, Oxford: Oxford University Press.

Rodin, David (2006) "The Ethics of Asymmetric War", in David Rodin and Richard Sorabji (eds.) *The Ethics of War: Shared Problems in Different Traditions*, London: Ashgate.

Rodin, David (2007) "The Problem with Prevention", in Henry Shue and David Rodin (eds.) *Preemption—Military Action and Moral Justification*, Oxford University Press: Chapter 6, 143–170.

Rodin, David and Shue, Henry (eds.) (2008) *Just and Unjust Warriors: The Moral and Legal Status of Soldiers*, Oxford University Press.

Rodin, David (2008) "The Moral Inequality of Soldiers: Why jus in bello Asymmetry is Half Right", in David Rodin and Henry Shue (eds.) *Just and Unjust Warriors: The Moral and Legal Status of Soldiers*, Oxford University Press: pp. 44–68.

Rodin, David (2008) "Two Emerging Issues of Jus Post Bellum: War Termination and the Liability of Soldiers for Crimes of Aggression" in Carsten Stahn and Jann K. Kleffner (eds.) *Jus Post Bellum—Towards a Law of Transition From Conflict to Peace*, The Hague: Asser Press: Chapter 3, pp. 53–76.

Rousseau, Jean Jacque (1993) *The Social Contract and Discourses*, London and Vermont: Everyman.

Sambanis, Nicolas (2001) "Do Ethnic and Nonethnic Civil Wars have the Same Causes? A Theoretical and Empirical Inquiry (part 1)", *Journal of Conflict Resolution* 45: pp. 259–282.

Schweller, Randall L. (1992) "Domestic Structure and Preventive War—Are Democracies more Pacific?", *World Politics* 44: 235–269.

Shani, Yuval (2007) "Faraway, So Close: The Legal Status of Gaza after Israel's Disengagement", in Tim McCormack (ed.) *Yearbook of International Humanitarian Law 8*: pp. 369–383.

Shue, Henry (1978) "Torture", *Philosophy and Public Affair* 7 (2): pp. 124–143.

Shue, Henry and Rodin, David (eds.) (2007) *Preemption—Military Action and Moral Justification*, Oxford University Press.

Shue, Henry (2007) "What Would a Justified Preventive Military Attack Look like?", in Henry Shue and David Rodin (eds.) *Preemption—Military Action and Moral Justification*, Oxford University Press: Chapter 9, pp. 222–246.

Shue, Henry (2008) "Do We Need a 'Morality of War'?", in David Rodin and Henry Shue (eds.) *Just and Unjust Warriors*, Oxford University Press: pp. 87–111.

Shtull-Trauring, A. (2010) "It Might Have Been Wise to Look the Other Way", *Haaretz* (June 13, 2010) (interview with Micheal Walzer). Available at: www.haaretz.com/print-edition/features/it-might-have-been-wise-to-look-the-other-way-1.295795

Sinnot-Armstrong, Walter (2007) "Preventive War—What is it Good For?", in Henry Shue and David Rodin (eds.) *Preemption—Military Action and Moral Justification*, Oxford University Press: Chapter 8, 202–221.

Small, Melvin and Singer, J. David (1982) *Resort to Arms: International and Civil War, 1816–1980*, Beverly Hills, CA: Sage.

Solana, Javier (2003) "A Secure Europe in a Better World—European Security Strategy", Document adopted by the heads of States and Government at the European Council in Brussels December 12, 2003. Available at: www.iss.europa.eu/uploads/media/solanae.pdf

Statman, Daniel (2003) "Targeted Killing", *Theoretical Inquiries in Law* 5: pp. 179–198.

Suarez, Francisco (1944) "On War", in J.B. Scott (ed.) *Selections from Three Works of Francisco Suarez (1621)*, Oxford: Clarendon Press.

Tobey, William (2012) "Nuclear Scientists as Assassination Targets", *Bulletin of the Atomic Scientists* 68 (1), Sage Publications: pp. 61–69.

Uniacke, Suzanne (2007) "On Getting One's Retaliation in First", in Henry Shue and David Rodin (eds.) *Preemption—Military Action and Moral Justification*, Oxford University Press: Chapter 3, 69–88.

Vattel, Emer de (1995) *The Law of Nations or Principles of Natural Law Applied to the Conduct and Affairs of Nations and Sovereigns*, translated by Charles G. Fenwick (Washington D.C., Carnegie Institute, 1916), new edition: William S. Hein, Buffalo, N.Y. 1995; first edition: London 1758).

Vitoria, Francisco de (1991) "On the Law of War", in Anthony Pagden and Jeremy Lawrence (eds.) *F. de Vitoria Political Writings*, Cambridge University Press.

Waldron, Jeremy (2010) *Torture, Terror and Tradeoffs—Philosophy for the White House*, Oxford University Press.

Waldron, Jeremy (2011) "Can Targeted Killing Work as a Neutral Principle?", New York University Public Law and Legal Theory Working Papers: pp. 1–14. Available at: http://papers.ssrn.com/sol3/papers.cfm?abstract_id=1788226

Waldron, Jeremy (2012) "Justifying Targeted Killing with a Neutral Principle", in Claire Finkelstein, Jens David Ohlin, and Andrew Altman (eds.) *Targeted Killings—Law and Morality in an Asymmetrical World*, Oxford University: Chapter 4, pp. 112–131.

Walzer, Michael (1973) "Political Action: The Problem of Dirty Hands", *Philosophy and Public Affairs* 2(2): pp. 160–180 and in Sanford Levinson (ed.) (2004), *Torture—A Collection*, Oxford University Press: pp. 61–76.

Walzer, Michael (1977) *Just and Unjust Wars—A Moral Argument with Historical Illustrations* (third edition), New York: Basic Books.

Walzer, Michael (2006) "Response to McMahan's Paper", *Philosophia* 34: pp. 43–45.

Walzer, Michael (2006) "How Aggressive Should Israel Be?", *The New Republic* (July 2006).

Walzer, Michael (2009) "On Proportionality", *Dissent* (January 8, 2009). Available at: www.dissentmagazine.org/online.php?id=191

Walzer, Michael (2013) "Coda: Can the Good Guys Win?" *The European Journal of International Law* 24 (1): pp. 433–444.

Walzer Michael and Margalit, Avishai (2009) "Israel: Civilians & Combatants", *The New York Review of Books* 56 (8) (May 14, 2009).

Yoo, John (2004) "Using Force", *University of Chicago Law Review* 71: pp. 1–61. Available at: http://papers.ssrn.com/sol3/papers.cfm?abstract_id=530022. Last accessed June 8, 2014.

Zupan, Dan (2008) "A Presumption of the Moral Equality of Combatants", in David Rodin and Henry Shue (eds.) *Just and Unjust Warriors*, Oxford University Press: pp. 214–225.

Further sources

BBC News, Middle East: "Iran's Rouhani calls Israel 'old wound' on Islamic world", August 2, 2013. www.bbc.com/news/world-middle-east-23548906. Accessed June 8, 2014.

Borger, Julian and Booths, Robert (2009) "Britain walks out of conference as Ahmadinejad calls Israel 'racist'", *The Guardian* (April 20, 2009). www.guardian.co.uk/world/2009/apr/20/un-conference-boycott-ahmadinejad. Accessed June 8, 2014.

Bronner, Ethan (2006) "Just How Far Did They Go, Those Words Against Israel?" *The New York Times* (June 11, 2006). Available at: www.nytimes.com/2006/06/11/weekin review/11bronner.html?_r=1 Accessed June 8, 2014.

Charter of the United Nations, Chapter VII. Available at: www.un.org/en/documents/charter/chapter7.shtml

Geneva Convention IV (1949) "Relative to the Protection of Civilian Persons in Time of War."

Harnden, Toby (2009) "The New York Times Explains Away Mahmud Ahmadinejad's threat to destroy Israel", *The Telegraph* (May 15, 2009). Available at: http://blogs.tele graph.co.uk/news/tobyharnden/9804928/New_York_Times_explains_away_Mahmud _Ahmadinejads_threat_to_destroy_Israel/. Accessed June 8, 2014.

HCJ 9132/07, interim decision (November 29, 2007). Available at: www.gisha.org/UserFiles/File/Legal%20Documents%20/fuel%20and%20electricity_oct_07/english_docs/English%20Translation%20of%20HCJ9132%20decision%20_2_.pdf

HCJ 9132/07 (January 30, 2008). Available at: www.mfa.gov.il/NR/rdonlyres/938CCD2E-89C7-4E77-B071-56772DFF79CC/0/HCJGazaelectricity.pdf

HCJ 6659/06 Anonymous V. The State of Israel (Judgment June 11, 2008). Available at: www.asil.org/ilib080717.cfm#j4

HCJ 769/02 (December 11, 2005), Par.28. Available at: http://elyon1.court.gov.il/Files_ENG/02/690/007/a34/02007690.a34.pdf

ICRC (2008) "Interpretive Guidance on the Notion of Direct Participation in Hostilities under International Humanitarian Law", *International Review of the Red Cross* 90 (872): 991–1047. Available at: www.icrc.org/eng/resources/documents/article/review/review-872-p991.htm

Lazar, Seth (2010) "Necessity, Vulnerability, and Noncombatant Immunity", unpublished manuscript, cited with permission from the author.

Protocol I—Additional to the Geneva Conventions (1977). Available at: www.icrc.org/ihl. nsf/7c4d08d9b287a42141256739003e636b/f6c8b9fee14a77fdc125641e0052b079

Regulations Concerning the Laws and Customs of War on Land. The Hague, October 18, 1907. Available at: http://net.lib.byu.edu/~rdh7/wwi/hague/hague5.html

Rome Statute of the International Criminal Court. Available at: http://untreaty.un.org/cod/icc/statute/romefra.htm

Roosevelt, Franklin Delano (1933) First Inaugural Address. Available at: www.bartleby.com/124/pres49.html. Accessed June 8, 2014.

Shtull-Trauring, Asaf (2010) "It Might Have Been Wise to Look the Other Way", *Haaretz*, June 13, 2010 (interview with Michael Walzer). Available at: www.haaretz.com/print-edition/features/it-might-have-been-wise-to-look-the-other-way-1.295795.

The Los Angeles Times (April 20, 2008). Available at: www.latimes.com/news/nationworld/world/la-fggaza20apr20,1,1887049.story?track=rss

The National Security Strategy of the United States of America (September 2002). Available at: http://georgewbushwhitehouse.archives.gov/nsc/nss/2002/

UN General Assembly, 2005 World Summit Outcome, A/60/L1, paragraphs 138–140. Available at: www.un.org/en/preventgenocide/adviser/responsibility.shtml

UN Security Council Resolution 1737 (2006) (December 23, 2006). Available at: www. america.gov/st/texttrans-english/2010/December/20101210123546su0.3019482.html#. Accessed June 8, 2014.

INDEX